Mechanism Design
with Creo Elements/Pro 5.0
(Pro/ENGINEER Wildfire 5.0)

Kuang-Hua Chang, Ph.D.
School of Aerospace and Mechanical Engineering
The University of Oklahoma
Norman, OK

ISBN: 978-1-58503-650-9

PUBLICATIONS

Schroff Development Corporation

www.SDCpublications.com

Schroff Development Corporation
P.O. Box 1334
Mission KS 66222
(913) 262-2664
www.SDCpublications.com

Publisher: Stephen Schroff

About Creo Elements/Pro 5.0 and Pro/ENGINEER Wildfire 5.0:

At the time of publication, Parametric Technology Corporation (PTC) has recently rebranded their Pro/ENGINEER product line to Creo Elements/Pro. The Creo Elements/Pro software is the same as Pro/ENGINEER Wildfire 5.0, and for this edition the two names are considered interchangeable.

Copyright © 2011 by Kuang-Hua Chang.

All rights reserved. This document may not be copied, photocopied, reproduced, transmitted, or translated in any form or for any purpose without the express written consent of the publisher Schroff Development Corporation.

IT IS A VIOLATION OF UNITED STATES COPYRIGHT LAWS TO MAKE COPIES IN ANY FORM OR MEDIA OF THE CONTENTS OF THIS BOOK FOR EITHER COMMERCIAL OR EDUCATIONAL PURPOSES WITHOUT EXPRESS WRITTEN PERMISSION.

Examination Copies:

Books received as examination copies are for review purposes only and may not be made available for student use. Resale of examination copies is prohibited.

Electronic Files:

Any electronic files associated with this book are licensed to the original user only. These files may not be transferred to any other party.

Preface

This book is prepared to help you become familiar with *Mechanism Design*, a module of the *Creo Elements/Pro* (formerly *Pro/ENGINEER*) software family, which supports modeling and analysis (or simulation) of mechanisms in a virtual (computer) environment. Capabilities in *Mechanism Design* allow users to simulate and visualize mechanism performance. Using *Mechanism Design* early in the product development stage could prevent costly redesign due to design defects found in the physical testing phase; therefore, contributing to a more cost effective, reliable, and efficient product development process.

This book covers major concepts and frequently used commands required to advance readers from a novice to an intermediate level in using *Mechanism Design*. Basic concepts discussed in this book include motion model creation, such as body and joint definitions; analysis type selection, such as static analysis, kinematics and dynamics; and results visualization. These concepts are introduced using simple, yet realistic examples.

Verifying the results obtained from the computer simulation is extremely important. One of the unique features about this book is the incorporation of theoretical discussions for kinematic and dynamic analyses in conjunction with the simulation results obtained using *Mechanism Design*. The purpose of the theoretical discussions lies in simply supporting the verification of simulation results, rather than providing an in-depth discussion on the subjects of kinematics and dynamics. *Mechanism Design* is not foolproof. It requires a certain level of experience and expertise to master the software. Before arriving at that level, it will be very helpful for you to verify the simulation results whenever possible. Verifying the simulation results will increase your confidence in using the software and prevent you from being fooled (hopefully, only occasionally) by any erroneous simulations produced by the software. Example model files have been prepared for you to go through the lessons. In addition, *Excel* spreadsheets that support the theoretical verifications of selected examples are also available. You may download all model files and *Excel* spreadsheets by going to this book's web page on the *Schroff Development Corporation* website:

http://www.SDCpublications.com/

In addition to the files prepared for each lessons, completely assembled models with simulation results are provided for your references. You may want to start each lesson by reviewing the introduction section and opening the assembled model in *Mechanism Design* to see the motion simulation, in hopes of gaining more understanding about the example problems.

This book is written following the project-based learning approach and is intentionally kept simple to help you learn *Mechanism Design*. Therefore, this book may not contain every single detail about *Mechanism Design*. For a complete reference of *Mechanism Design*, you may use on-line help in *Mechanism Design*, or visit the web site of *Parametric Technology Corporation* at:

http://www.ptc.com/

This book should serve self-learners well. If such describes you, you are expected to have the basic *Physics* and *Mathematics* background, preferably a Bachelor's degree in science or engineering. In addition, this book assumes that you are familiar with the basic concept and operation of *Pro/ENGINEER* part and assembly modes. A self-learner should be able to complete all lessons in this book in about 50 hours. An investment of 50 hours should advance you from a novice to an intermediate level user.

This book also serves class instruction well. It would likely be used as a supplemental textbook for courses like Mechanism Design, Rigid Body Dynamics, Computer-Aided Design, or Computer-Aided

Engineering. This book should cover 6 to 8 weeks of class instruction, depending on how the courses are taught and the technical background of the students. Some of the exercise problems given at the end of the lessons may take significant effort for students to complete. The author strongly encourages instructors and/or teaching assistants to go through those exercises before assigning them to students.

KHC
Norman, Oklahoma
December 28, 2010

Acknowledgements

I would like to thank my family for the patience and support they have given to me in completing this book, especially, my wife Sheng-Mei for her unconditional giving and encouragement. Thanks are due to my children, Charles and Annie, for their understanding, caring, and appreciation. Especially, I appreciate their patience in reviewing the whole book and correcting a few sentences for me.

Acknowledgment is due to Mr. Stephen Schroff at Schroff Development Corporation for his encouragement and help. Without his encouragement, this book would still be in its primitive stage.

Thanks are also due to the undergraduate students at the University of Oklahoma (OU) for their help in testing the examples included in this book. They made numerous suggestions that improved clarity of presentation and found numerous errors that would have otherwise crept into the book. Their contributions to this book are greatly appreciated.

I am grateful to my current and former students, Thomas Cates, Petr Sramek, Tyler Bunting, and Trey Wheeler, for their excellent efforts in creating examples for the application lessons; especially, *Lessons 9* and *10*. Both the assistive device and the racecar projects were extremely successful and highly recognized.

Finally, I would like to thank to our Creator, who has given me the strength and intelligence to accomplish this book.

About the Author

Dr. Kuang-Hua Chang is a *Williams Companies Foundation Presidential Professor* at the University of Oklahoma (OU), Norman, OK. He received his diploma in Mechanical Engineering from the National Taipei Institute of Technology, Taiwan, in 1980; and a M.S. and Ph.D. in Mechanical Engineering from the University of Iowa in 1987 and 1990, respectively. Since then, he has joined the Center for Computer-Aided Design (CCAD) at Iowa as a Research Scientist and CAE Technical Manager. In 1996, he joined Northern Illinois University as an Assistant Professor. In 1997, he joined OU. He teaches mechanical design and manufacturing, in addition to conducting research in computer-aided modeling and simulation for design and manufacturing of mechanical systems as well as bioengineering applications. His research work has been published in more than 100 articles in international journals and conference proceedings.

His work has been published in 3 books and more than 100 articles in international journals and conference proceedings. He has also served as technical consultants to US industry and foreign companies, including LG-Electronics, Seagate Technology, etc. Dr. Chang received numerous awards for his teaching and research in the past few years, including the presidential professorship in 2005 for "meeting the highest standards of excellence in scholarship and teaching," OU Regents Award for Superior Accomplishment in Research and Creative Activity in 2004, and OU Regents Award for Superior Teaching in 2010. In 2006, he was awarded a Ralph R. Teetor Educational Award by SAE *in recognition of significant contributions to teaching, research and student development*. Dr. Chang was honored by the OKC Mayor's Committee on Disability Concerns with the 2009 Don Davis Award, *the highest honor granted in public recognition of extraordinarily meritorious service which has substantially advanced opportunities for people with disabilities by removing social, attitudinal & environmental barriers in the greater Oklahoma City area.*

About the Cover Page

The picture shown on the cover page is the solid model of a Formula SAE (Society of Automotive Engineers) style racecar designed and built by engineering students at the University of Oklahoma (OU) during 2005-2006. The racecar model was built in *Pro/ENGINEER* with about 1400 parts and assemblies. Even though this was a team effort, most parts and assemblies were created and managed by then-Senior Mechanical Engineering student, Mr. Dave Oubre (Super Dave). His dedication in creating such a detailed and accurate racecar solid model is admirable. His effort is highly appreciated.

Each year engineering students throughout the world design and build formula-style racecars and participate in the annual Formula SAE competitions (students.sae.org/competitions/formulaseries). The result is a great experience for young engineers in a meaningful engineering project as well as the opportunity to work in a dedicated team effort. The OU team has been very competitive in the Formula SAE competitions. The team won numerous awards throughout the years, and finished 12th and 8th overall at the Formula SAE and Formula SAE West competitions, respectively, in 2006. Their 2005 racecar design also won the prestigious 2005 PTC Award in the Education, Colleges, and Universities category. The worldwide competition is sponsored by Parametric Technology Corporation.

A quarter of the racecar suspension has been employed as the final application example to be discussed in *Lesson 10* of this book. You will find more technical details of the racecar suspension in that lesson.

Table of Contents

Preface i

Acknowledgments ii

About the Author iii

About the Cover Page iii

Table of Contents iv

Lesson 1: Introduction to *Mechanism Design*

    1.1   Overview of the Lesson 1-1
    1.2   What is *Mechanism Design*? 1-1
    1.3   Mechanism and Motion Analysis 1-3
    1.4   *Mechanism Design* Capabilities 1-5
    1.5   Open Lesson 1 Model 1-12
    1.6   Motion Examples 1-13

Lesson 2: The Ball Throwing Example

    2.1   Overview of the Lesson 2-1
    2.2   The Ball Throwing Example 2-1
    2.3   Using *Mechanism Design* 2-3
    2.4   Result Verifications 2-13
    Exercises 2-15

Lesson 3: A Spring Mass System

    3.1   Overview of the Lesson 3-1
    3.2   The Spring-Mass System 3-1
    3.3   Using *Mechanism Design* 3-3
    3.4   Result Verifications 3-10
    Exercises 3-14

Lesson 4: A Simple Pendulum

    4.1   Overview of the Lesson 4-1
    4.2   The Simple Pendulum Example 4-1
    4.3   Using *Mechanism Design* 4-3
    4.4   Result Verifications 4-9
    Exercises 4-13

Lesson 5: A Slider-Crank Mechanism—Static and Motion Analyses

    5.1   Overview of the Lesson 5-1
    5.2   The Slider-Crank Example.. 5-1
    5.3   Using *Mechanism Design* 5-4
    5.4   Result Verifications.. 5-16
    Exercises 5-20

Lesson 6: A Compound Spur Gear Train

    6.1   Overview of the Lesson 6-1
    6.2   The Gear Train Example.. 6-2
    6.3   Using *Mechanism Design* 6-4
    Exercises 6-14

Lesson 7: Planetary Gear Train Systems

    7.1   Overview of the Lesson 7-1
    7.2   The Planetary Gear Train Examples 7-2
    7.3   Using *Mechanism Design* 7-5
    Exercises 7-16

Lesson 8: Cam and Follower

    8.1   Overview of the Lesson 8-1
    8.2   The Cam and Follower Example.. 8-1
    8.3   Using *Mechanism Design* 8-4
    Exercises 8-13

Lesson 9: Assistive Device for Wheelchair Soccer Game

    9.1   Overview of the Lesson 9-1
    9.2   The Assistive Device.. 9-1
    9.3   Using *Mechanism Design* 9-3
    9.4   Result Discussion... 9-10

Lesson 10: Kinematic Analysis for Racecar Suspension

    10.1   Overview of the Lesson 10-1
    10.2   The Quarter Suspension 10-2
    10.3   Using *Mechanism Design* 10-5

Appendix A: Defining Joints A-1

Appendix B: Defining Measures B-1

Appendix C: The Default Unit System C-1

Appendix D: The Magnitude Settings D-1

Lesson 1: Introduction to *Mechanism Design*

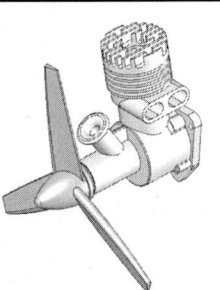

1.1 Overview of the Lesson

The purpose of this lesson is to provide you with a brief overview of *Mechanism Design*. *Mechanism Design* is a virtual prototyping tool that supports mechanism analysis and design. Instead of building and testing physical prototypes of the mechanism, you may use *Mechanism Design* to evaluate and refine the mechanism before finalizing the design and entering the functional prototyping stage. *Mechanism Design* will help you analyze and eventually design better engineering products. More specifically, the software enables you to size motors and actuators, determine power consumption, layout linkages, develop cams, understand gear trains, size springs and dampers, and determine interference between parts, which would usually require tests of physical prototypes. With such information, you will gain insight on how the mechanism works and why it behaves in certain ways. You will be able to modify the design and often achieve better design alternatives using the more convenient and less expensive virtual prototypes. In the long run, using virtual prototyping tools, such as *Mechanism Design*, will help you become a more experienced and competent design engineer.

In this lesson, we will start with a brief introduction to *Mechanism Design* and the various types of physical problems that *Mechanism Design* is capable of solving. We will then discuss capabilities offered by *Mechanism Design* for creating motion models, conducting motion analyses, and viewing motion analysis results. In the final section, we will mention examples employed in this book and topics to learn from these examples.

Note that materials presented in this lesson will be kept brief. More details on various aspects of mechanism design and analysis using *Mechanism Design* will be given in later lessons.

1.2 What is *Mechanism Design*?

Mechanism Design is a computer software tool that supports engineers in analyzing and designing mechanisms. *Mechanism Design* is a module of the *Pro/ENGINEER* product family developed by *Parametric Technology Corporation*. This software supports users in creating virtual mechanisms that answer general questions in product design such as those described next. An internal combustion engine shown in Figures 1-1 and 1-2 will be used to illustrate some typical questions.

1. Will the components of the mechanism collide in operation? For example, will the connecting rod collide with the inner surface of the piston or the inner surface of the engine case during operation?

2. Will the components in the mechanism you design move according to your intent? For example, will the piston stay entirely in the piston sleeve? Will the system lock up when the firing force aligns vertically with the connecting rod?

3. How much torque or force does it take to drive the mechanism? For example, what will be the minimum firing load to move the piston? Note that in this case, proper friction forces must be added to simulate the resistance of the mechanism before a realistic firing force can be calculated.

4. How fast will the components move; e.g., the longitudinal motion of the piston?

5. What is the reaction force or torque generated at a connection (also called *joint* or *constraint*) between components (or bodies) during motion? For example, what is the reaction force at the joint between the connecting rod and the piston pin? This reaction force is critical since the structural integrity of the piston pin and the connecting rod must be ensured; i.e., they must be strong and durable enough to sustain the load in operation.

The modeling and analysis capabilities in *Mechanism Design* will help you answer these common questions accurately and realistically, as long as the motion model is properly defined.

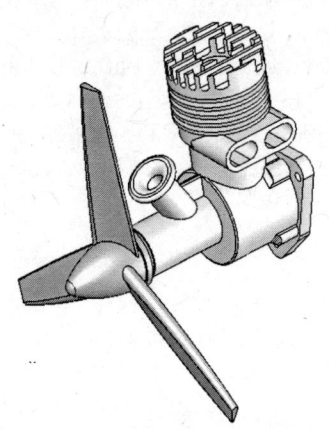

Figure 1-1 An Internal Combustion Engine (Unexploded View)

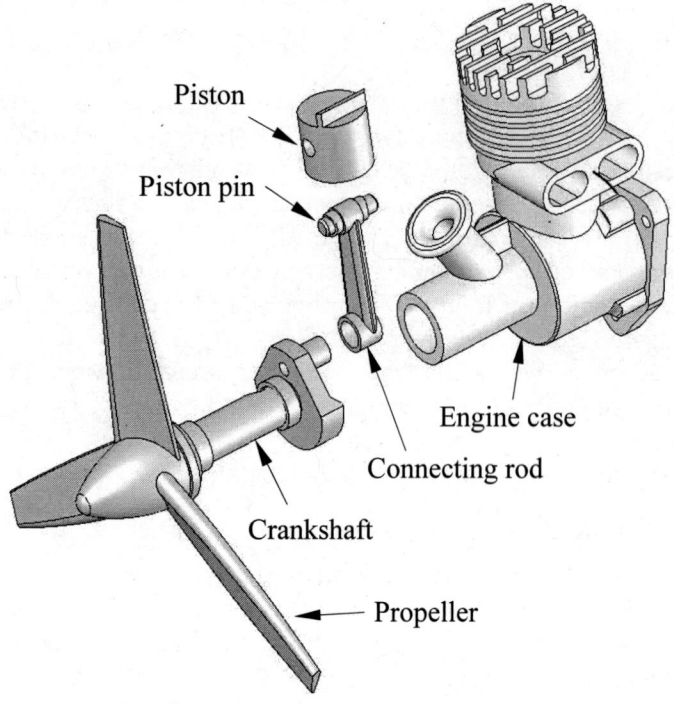

Figure 1-2 Internal Combustion Engine (Exploded View)

The capabilities available in *Mechanism Design* also help you search for better design alternatives. A better design alternative is very much problem-dependent. It is critical that a design problem be clearly defined by the designer up front before searching for better design alternatives. For the engine example, a better design alternative can be a design that reveals:

1. A smaller reaction force applied to the connecting rod, and
2. No collisions or interference between components.

In order to vary component sizes for exploring better design alternatives, the parts and assembly must be adequately parameterized to capture design intents. At the parts level, design parameterization implies creating solid features and relating dimensions properly. At the assembly level, design parameterization involves defining assembly mates and relating dimensions across parts. When a solid model is fully parameterized, a change in dimension value can be propagated to all parts affected automatically. Parts affected must be rebuilt successfully, and at the same time, they will have to maintain proper position and orientation with respect to one another without violating any assembly mates or revealing part penetration or excessive gaps. For example, in this engine example, a change in the bore diameter of the engine case will alter not only the geometry of the case itself, but all other parts affected, such as the piston, piston sleeve, and even the crankshaft, as illustrated in Figure 1-3. Moreover, they all have to be rebuilt properly and the entire assembly must stay intact through assembly mates.

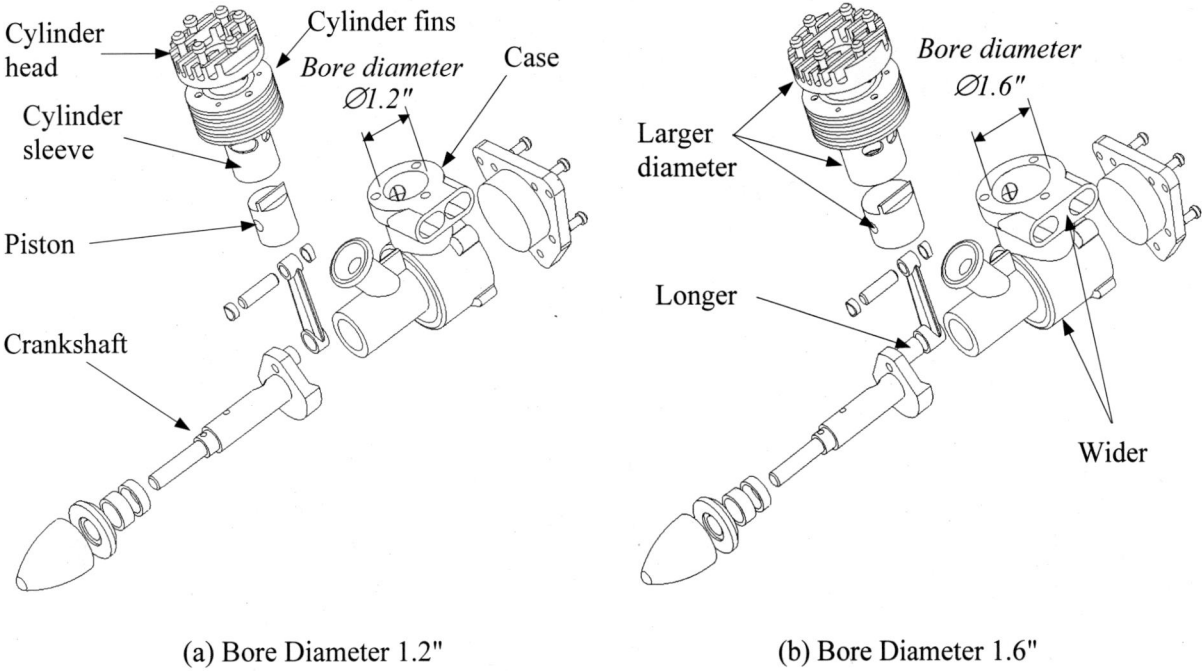

(a) Bore Diameter 1.2"   (b) Bore Diameter 1.6"

Figure 1-3 Internal Combustion Engine—Exploded View

1.3 Mechanism and Motion Analysis

A mechanism is a mechanical device that transfers motion and/or force from a source to an output. It can be an abstraction (simplified model) of a mechanical system. A linkage consists of links (or bodies), which are connected by connections (or joints), such as a pin joint, to form open or closed chains (or loops, see Figure 1-4). Such kinematic chains, with at least one link fixed, become mechanisms. In this book, all links are assumed rigid. In general, a mechanism can be represented by its corresponding schematic drawing for analysis and design purposes. For example, a slider-crank mechanism represents the engine motion, as shown in Figure 1-5, which is a closed loop mechanism.

In general, there are two types of motion problems that you will solve in order to answer general questions regarding mechanism analysis and design: kinematics and dynamics.

Kinematics is the study of motion without regard for the forces that cause the motion. A kinematic mechanism must be driven by a servo motor (or driver) so that the position, velocity, and acceleration of each link of the mechanism can be analyzed at any given time. Typically, a kinematic analysis must be conducted before dynamic behavior of the mechanism can be simulated properly.

Dynamics is the study of motion in response to externally applied loads. The dynamic behavior of a mechanism is governed by Newton's laws of motion. The simplest dynamic problem is the particle dynamics covered in Sophomore Dynamics – for example, a spring-mass-damper system shown in Figure 1-6. In this case, motion of the mass is governed by the following equation derived from Newton's second law,

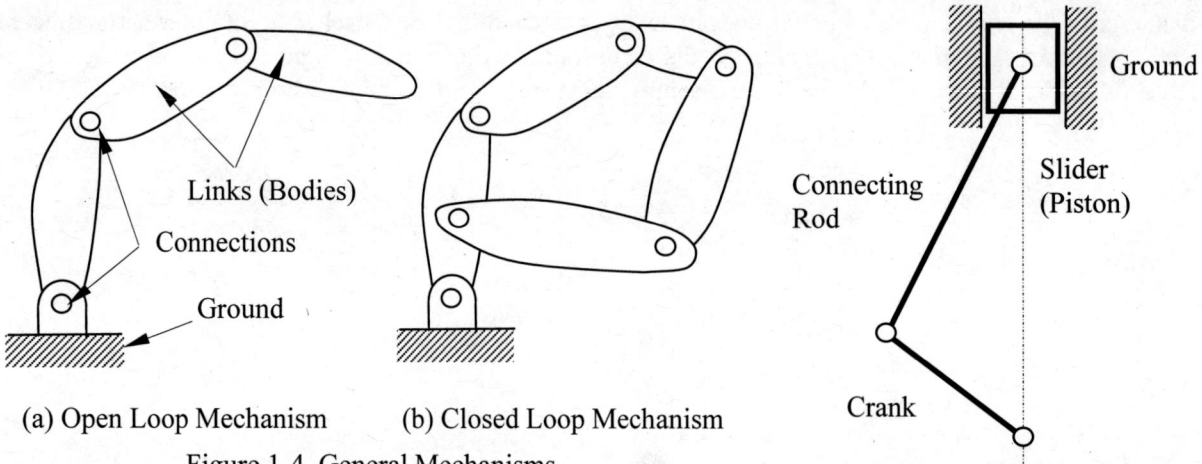

(a) Open Loop Mechanism   (b) Closed Loop Mechanism

Figure 1-4 General Mechanisms

Figure 1-5 Schematic View of the Engine Motion Model

$$\sum F = p(t) - kx - c\dot{x} = m\ddot{x} \tag{1.1}$$

where (·) appearing on top of the physical quantity represents time derivative of the quantity, m is the total mass of the block, k is the spring constant, and c is the damping coefficient.

For a rigid body, mass properties (such as the total mass, center of mass, moment of inertia, etc.) are taken into account for dynamic analysis. For example, motion of a pendulum shown in Figure 1-7 is governed by the following equation of motion,

$$\sum M = -mg\ell \sin\theta = J\ddot{\theta} = m\ell^2 \ddot{\theta} \tag{1.2}$$

where M is the external moment (or torque), J is the polar moment of inertia of the pendulum, m is the pendulum mass, g is the gravitational acceleration, and $\ddot{\theta}$ is the angular acceleration of the pendulum.

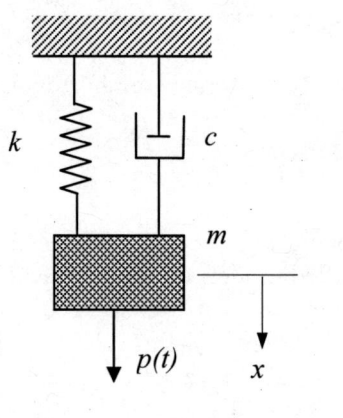

Figure 1-6 The Spring-Mass-Damper System

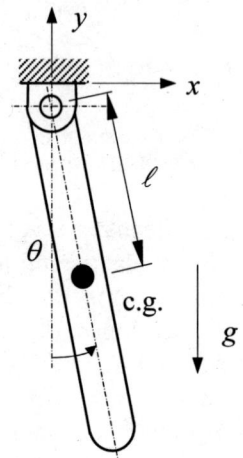

Figure 1-7 A Simple Pendulum

Dynamics of a rigid body system, such as those illustrated in Figure 1-4, is a lot more complicated than the single body problems. Usually, a system of differential and algebraic equations governs the motion and the dynamic behavior of the system. Newton's law must be obeyed by every single body in the system at all times. The motion of the system will be determined by the loads acting on the bodies or joint axes (e.g., a torque driving the system). Reaction loads at the joint connections hold the bodies together.

Note that in *Mechanism Design*, you may create a kinematic analysis model; for example, using a servo motor to drive the mechanism before carrying out a dynamic analysis. In this case, position, velocity, and acceleration results may be similar to those of kinematic analysis; however, the inertia of the bodies will be taken into account for dynamic analysis; therefore, reaction forces will be calculated between bodies.

1.4 *Mechanism Design* Capabilities

Overall Process

The overall process of using *Mechanism Design* for analyzing a mechanism consists of three main steps: model creation, analysis, and result visualization, as illustrated in Figure 1-8. Key entities that constitute a motion model include a ground body that is always fixed, bodies that are movable, connections (or joints) that connect bodies, servo motors (drivers) that drive the mechanism for kinematic analysis, loads, and the initial conditions. More details about these entities will be discussed later in this lesson.

The analysis capabilities in *Mechanism Design* include position (initial assembly), static (equilibrium configuration), motion (kinematic and dynamic), and force balance (to retain the system in a prescribed configuration).

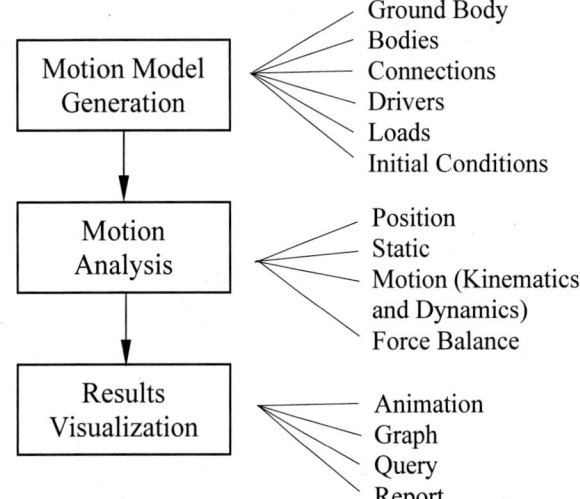

Figure 1-8 General Process of Using *Mechanism Design*

For example, the position analysis brings bodies closer within a prescribed tolerance at each connection to create an initial assembled configuration of the mechanism. More details about the analysis capabilities in *Mechanism Design* will be discussed later in this lesson.

The analysis results can be visualized in various forms. You may animate motion of the mechanism, or generate graphs for more specific information, such as the reaction force of a joint in the time domain. You may also query results at specific locations for a given time. Furthermore, you may ask for a report on results that you specified, such as the acceleration of a moving body in the time domain.

Operation Mode

Mechanism Design is embedded into *Pro/ENGINEER*. It is indeed an integrated module of *Pro/ENGINEER*, and transition from *Pro/ENGINEER* to *Mechanism Design* is seamless. All the solid models, placement constraints, etc. defined in *Pro/ENGINEER* are automatically carried over into *Mechanism Design*. *Mechanism Design* can be accessed through menus and windows inside *Pro/ENGINEER*. The same assembly is used in both *Pro/ENGINEER* and *Mechanism Design*.

Body geometry is essential for mass property computations in motion analysis. In *Mechanism Design,* all mass properties are ready for use. In addition, the detailed part geometry for interference checking is also available.

User Interface

User interface of the *Mechanism Design* is identical to that of *Pro/ENGINEER*, as shown in Figure 1-9. *Pro/ENGINEER* users should find it is straightforward to maneuver in *Mechanism Design*.

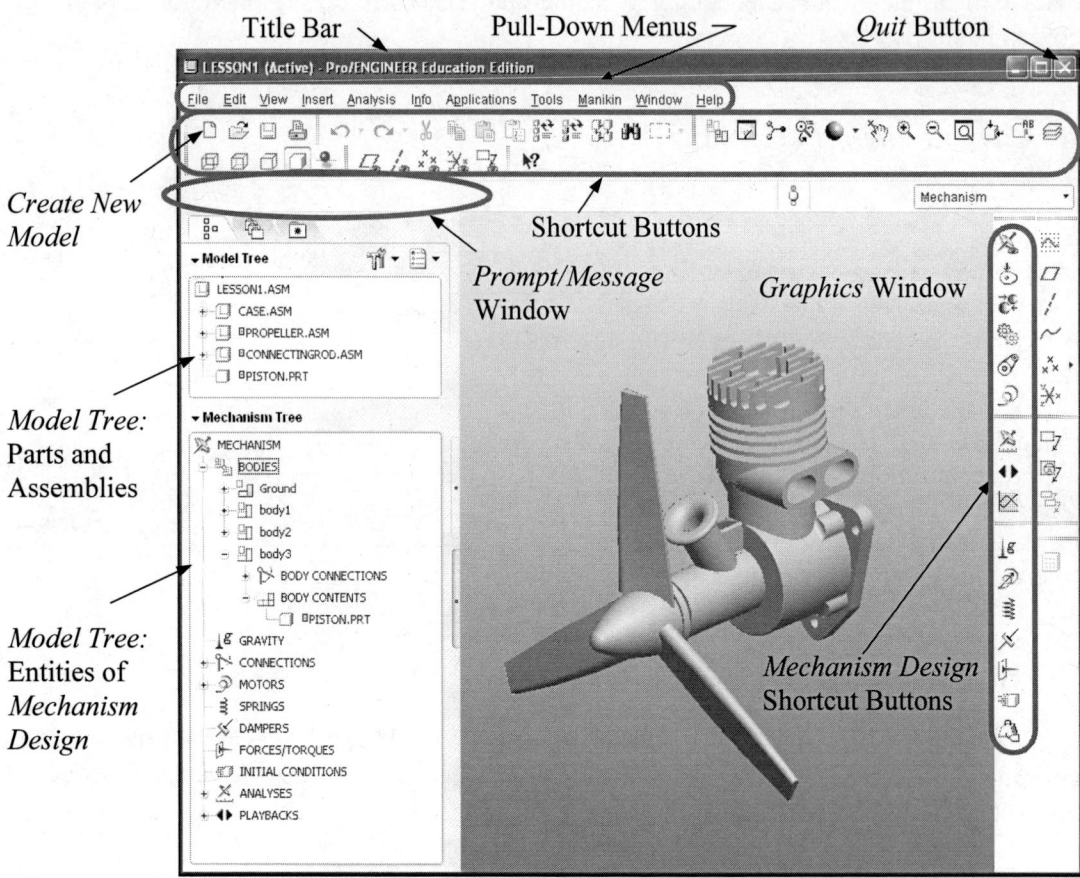

Figure 1-9 User Interface of *Mechanism Design*

As shown in Figure 1-9, the user interface window of *Mechanism Design* consists of pull-down menus, shortcut buttons, prompt/message window, scroll-down menu, graphics window, and model tree window.,

The *Graphics* window displays the motion model with which you are working. The pull-down menus and the shortcut buttons at the top of the screen provide typical *Pro/ENGINEER* functions. The *Mechanism Design* shortcut buttons to the right provide all the functions required to create and modify motion models, create and run analyses, and visualize results. When you click the menu options, the *Prompt/Message* window shows brief messages describing the menu commands. It also shows system messages following command execution. The shortcut buttons in *Mechanism Design* and their functions are summarized in Table 1-1.

Defining Motion (or Mechanism Design) Entities

The basic entities of a motion (or simulation) model created in *Mechanical Design* consist of ground, bodies, connections, initial conditions, drivers, and loads. Each of the basic entities will be briefly introduced. More details can be found in later lessons.

Table 1-1 The Shortcut Buttons in *Mechanism Design*

Button Symbol	Name	Function
	Display Entities	Turn icon visibility on or off in your assembly.
	Cam-Follower Connection Definition	Create a new cam-follower.
	Gear Pairs	Create a new gear pair.
	Servo Motors	Define a servo motor (driver).
	Analysis Definition	Define and run an analysis.
	Playbacks	Play back the results of your analysis run. You can also save or export the results or restore previously saved results.
	Measure Results	Create measures, and select measures and result sets to display. You can also graph the results or save them to a table.
	Gravity	Define gravity.
	Force Motors	Define a new force motor.
	Springs	Define a new spring.
	Dampers	Define a new damper.
	Forces/Torques	Define a force or a torque.
	Initial Condition Definition	Specify initial position snapshots, and define the velocity initial conditions for a point, motion axis or body.
	Mass Properties	Specify mass properties for a part or specify density for an assembly.

Ground Body

A ground (or ground body) represents a fixed location in space. The root assembly is always fixed; therefore, becoming the ground body (or part of the ground body). Also, the datum coordinate system of the root assembly is assigned as the *WCS* (World Coordinate System) by default. All datum features and parts fixed to the root assembly are part of the ground body.

Bodies

A body represents a single rigid component (or link) that moves relative to the other body (or bodies in some cases). A body may consist of several *Pro/ENGINEER* parts fully constrained using placement constraints. A body must contain a local coordinate system (*LCS*), body points (created as datum points), and mass properties. Note that body points are created for defining connections, force applications, etc.

A spatial body consists of three translational and three rotational degrees of freedom (dof's). That is, a rigid body can translate and rotate along the *X*-, *Y*-, and *Z*-axes of a coordinate system. Rotation of a rigid body is measured by referring the orientation of its *LCS* to *WCS*, which is fixed to the ground body.

In *Mechanism Design*, the *LCS* is assigned automatically, usually, to the default datum coordinate system of the body (either part or assembly), and the mass properties are calculated using part geometry and material properties referring to the *LCS*. Datum axes and points are essential in creating the motion model since they are employed for defining connections and the location of external load application.

Connections

A connection in *Mechanism Design* can be a joint, cam, or gear that connects two bodies. Typical joints include a pin, slider, bearing, cylinder, etc. The connection will constrain the relative motion between bodies. Each independent movement permitted by a connection is called a degree of freedom (dof). The degrees of freedom that a connection allows can be translation and rotation along three perpendicular axes, as shown in Figure 1-10.

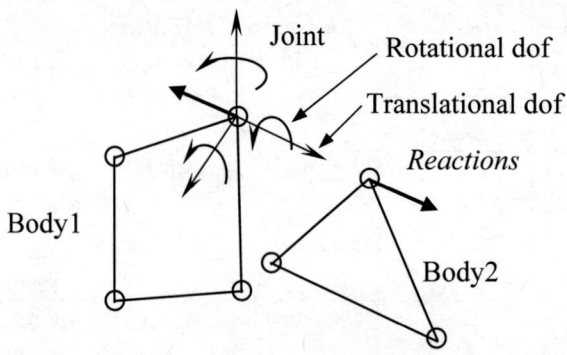

Figure 1-10 A Typical Joint in *Mechanism Design*

Note that joints are created by employing regular assembly placement constraints, such as align, mate, etc. However, instead of completely fixing all the movements, certain dof's (translations and/or rotations) are left to allow designated movement. For example, a ball joint is created simply by aligning two datum points in their respective bodies, allowing all three rotational dof's.

The connections produce equal and opposite reactions (forces and/or torques) on the bodies connected. The symbol of a given joint tells the translational and/or rotational dof that the joint allows in regard to movement. Understanding the basic four symbols shown in Figure 1-11 will enable you to read any existing joints in motion models. More details about joint types available in *Mechanism Design* will be discussed in later lessons. A complete list of joints available in *Mechanism Design* can be found in Appendix A.

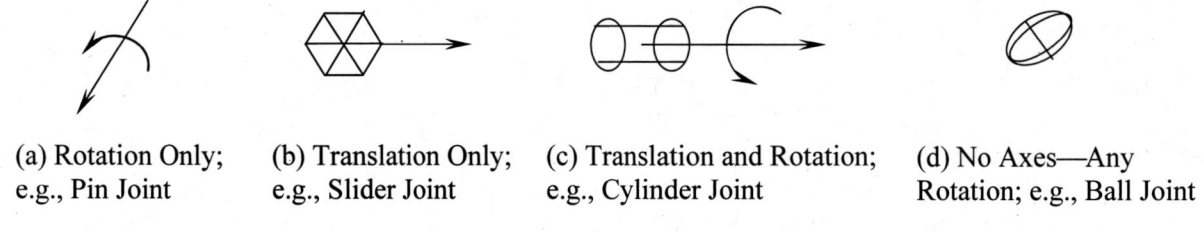

(a) Rotation Only; e.g., Pin Joint

(b) Translation Only; e.g., Slider Joint

(c) Translation and Rotation; e.g., Cylinder Joint

(d) No Axes—Any Rotation; e.g., Ball Joint

Figure 1-11 Basic Joint Symbols

Degrees of Freedom

As mentioned earlier, an unconstrained body in space has six degrees of freedom, three translational and three rotational. When joints are added to connect bodies, constraints are imposed to restrict the relative motion between them

For example, a pin joint allows one rotational motion between bodies. As defined in the engine example shown in Figure 1-12, joint *Pin1* restricts movement on five dof's so that only one rotational motion is allowed between the propeller assembly and the ground body (*case.asm*). Since the engine case is a ground body, the propeller assembly will rotate along the axis of the pin joint, as illustrated in the symbol shown in Figure 1-12. Therefore, there is only one degree of freedom left for the propeller assembly. For a given motion model, you can determine its number of degrees of freedom using the Gruebler's count.

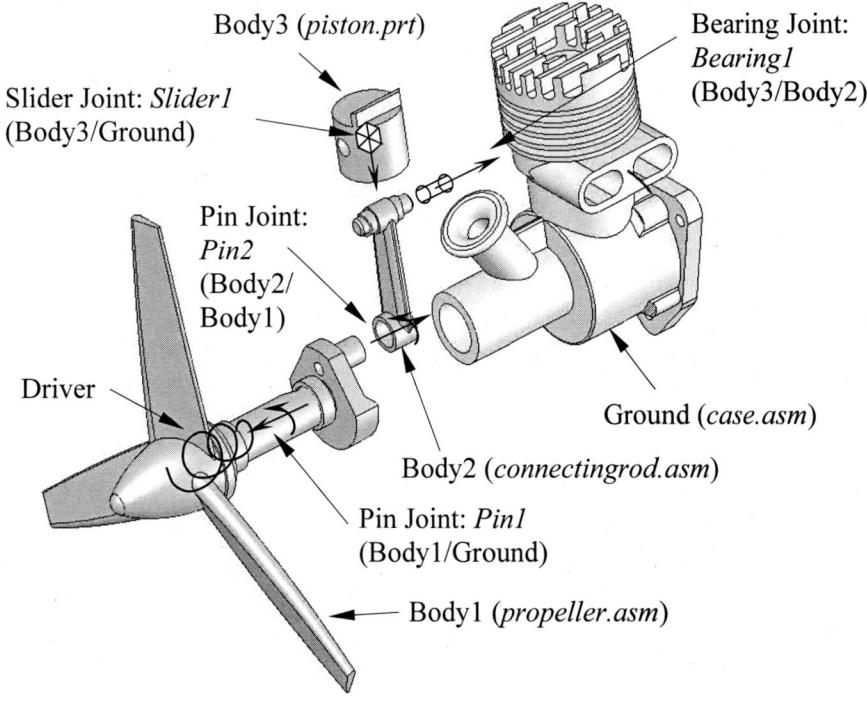

Figure 1-12 A Typical Motion Model in Exploded View

Mechanical Design uses the following equation to calculate the Gruebler's count:

$$D = 6M - N - O \tag{1.3}$$

where D is the Gruebler's count representing the overall free degrees of freedom of the mechanism, M is the number of bodies excluding the ground body, N is the number of dof's restricted by all joints, and O is the number of motion drivers defined in the system.

In general, a valid motion model should have a Gruebler's count *0*. However, in creating motion models, some joints remove redundant dof's. For example, two hinges, modeled using two pin joints, support a door. The second pin joint adds five redundant dof's. The Gruebler's count becomes:

$$D = 6 \times 1 - 2 \times 5 = -4$$

For kinematic analysis, the Gruebler's count must be equal to or less than *0*. The solver recognizes and deactivates redundant constraints during analysis. For a kinematic analysis, if you create a model and try to animate it with a Gruebler's count greater than *0*, the animation will not run and an error message will appear.

The single-piston engine shown in Figure 1-12 consists of three bodies (excluding the ground body), two pin joints, one slider joint, and one bearing joint. A pin or slider joint removes five degrees of freedom, and a bearing joint removes two dof's. In addition, a motion driver is added to the rotational dof of the joint *Pin1*. Therefore, according to Eq. 1.3, the Gruebler's count for the engine example is

$D = 6 \times 3 - (3 \times 5 + 1 \times 2) - 1 \times 1 = 0$

If the Gruebler's count is less than zero, the solver will automatically remove redundancies. In this engine example, if the bearing joint between the connecting rod and the crank shaft is replaced by a pin joint, the Gruebler's count becomes

$D = 6 \times 3 - 4 \times 5 - 1 \times 1 = -3$

To get the Gruebler's count to zero, it is often possible to replace joints that remove a large number of constraints with joints that remove a smaller number of constraints and still restrict the mechanism motion in the same way. *Mechanism Design* detects the redundancies and ignores redundant dof's in all analyses. In dynamic analysis, the redundancies lead to an outcome with a possibility of incorrect reaction results, yet the motion is correct. For complete and accurate reaction forces, it is critical that you eliminate redundancies from your mechanism. The challenge is to find the joints that will impose non-redundant constraints and still allow for the intended motion. Examples included in this book should give you some ideas in choosing proper joints.

Loads

Loads are used to drive a mechanism. Physically, loads are produced by motors, springs, dampers, gravity, tires, etc. A load entity in *Mechanism Design* can be a force or torque. The force and torque are represented by an arrow and double-arrow symbols, respectively, as shown in Figures 1-13 and 1-14. Note that a load can be applied to a body, a point in a body, or between two points in different bodies.

Figure 1-13 The Force Symbol   Figure 1-14 The Torque Symbol

Drivers or Servo Motors

Drivers or servo motors are used to impose a particular motion on a mechanism. Servo motors cause a specific type of motion to occur between two bodies in a single degree of freedom. Servo motors specify position, velocity, or acceleration as a function of time, and can control either translational or rotational motion. The driver symbol is shown in Figure 1-15.

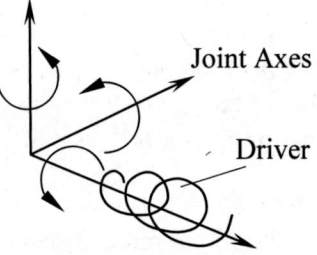

Figure 1-15 The Driver (Servo motor) Symbol

Note that a driver must be defined along a movable axis of the joint you select. Otherwise, no motion will occur. When properly defined, drivers will account for the remaining dof's of the mechanism calculated using Eq. 1.3.

An example of a typical motion model created using *Mechanism Design* is shown in Figure 1-12. In this engine example, twenty six *Pro/ENGINEER* parts are grouped into four bodies. In addition, four joints plus a driver are defined for a kinematic analysis.

Types of Mechanism Analyses

There are four analysis options supported in *Mechanism Design*: position, static, motion (kinematic, and dynamic), and force balance.

The position (or assembly analysis) that brings the mechanism together, as illustrated in Figure 1-16, is performed before any other type of analysis. The assembly analysis determines an initial configuration of the mechanism based on the body geometry, joints, and initial conditions of bodies. The points, axes, or planes chosen for defining joints will be brought within a small prescribed tolerance.

Static analysis is used to find the rest position (equilibrium condition) of a mechanism, in which none of the bodies are moving. Static analysis is related to mechanical advantage—for example, how much load can be resisted by a driving motor. A simple example of the static analysis is shown in Figure 1-17.

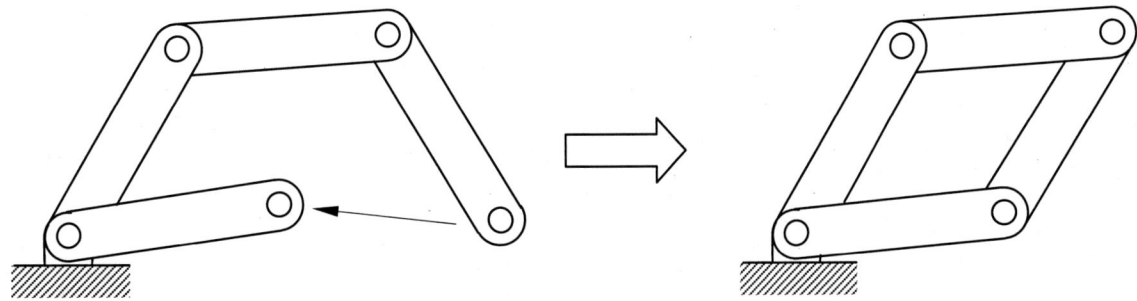

Figure 1-16 Position (Assembly) Analysis

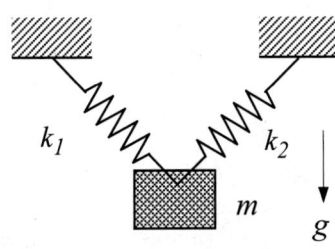

Figure 1-17 Static Analysis

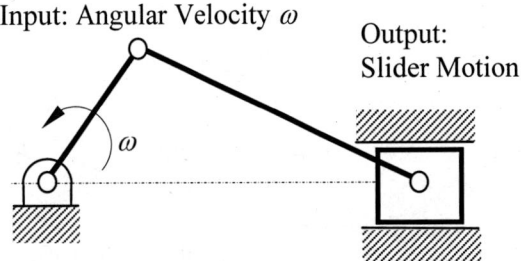

Figure 1-18 Kinematic Analysis

The motion analysis option supports both kinematic and dynamic analyses. As discussed earlier, kinematics is the study of motion without regard for the forces that cause the motion. A mechanism can be driven by a servo motor for a kinematic analysis, where the position, velocity, and acceleration of each link of the mechanism can be analyzed at any given time. For example, a servo motor drives a mechanism at a constant angular velocity in Figure 1-18.

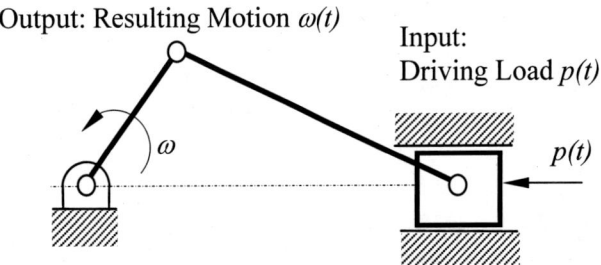

Figure 1-19 Dynamic Analysis

Dynamic analysis is used to study the mechanism motion in response to loads, as illustrated in Figure 1-19. This is the most complicated and common, but usually more time-consuming analysis.

Force balance calculates the required force and torque to retain the system in a certain configuration.

Viewing Results

In *Mechanism Design*, results of the motion analysis can be realized using animations, graphs, reports, and queries. Animations show the configuration of the mechanism in consecutive time frames. Animations will give you a global view on how the mechanism behaves, as shown in Figure 1-20.

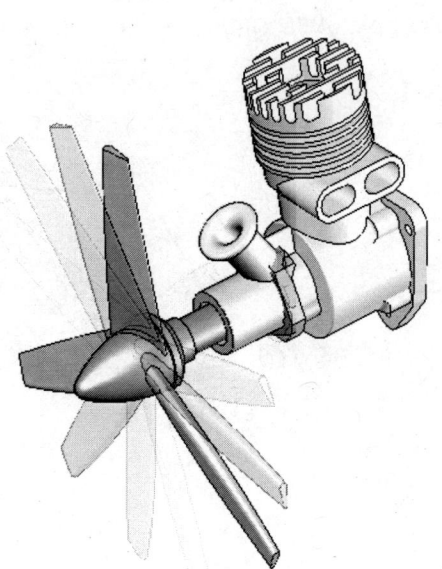

Figure 1-20 Motion AnimationFigure 1-21 Result Graph (Sample)

You may choose a joint or a point to generate result graphs, for example, the graph in Figure 1-21 shows the angular position of a simple pendulum example (please see *Lesson 4* for more details). These graphs give you a quantitative understanding on the behavior of the mechanism. You may also pick a point on the graph to query the results of your interest at a specific time frame. In addition, you may ask *Mechanism Design* for a report that includes a complete set of results output in the form of numerical data.

In addition to the capabilities discussed above, *Mechanism Design* allows you to check interference between bodies during motion (please refer to *Lesson 5*). Furthermore, the reaction forces calculated can be used to support structural analysis using, for example, *Pro/MECHANICA Structure*, a p-version finite element analysis module of *Pro/ENGINEER*.

1.5 Open Lesson 1 Model

A motion model for the single piston engine model shown in Figure 1-1 has been created for you. Download the files from www.schroff1.com, unzip them, and locate the engine model under *Lesson 1*. Copy *Lesson 1* to your hard drive.

Lesson 1: Introduction to *Mechanism Design*

Start *Pro/ENGINEER*, set working directory to *Lesson 1*, and open the assembly model: *lesson1.asm*. You should see an assembled engine model similar to that of Figure 1-1.

To enter *Mechanism Design*, simply choose from the pull-down menu

Applications > Mechanism.

You should see *Mechanism Design* window layout similar to that of Figure 1-9. To replay results click the *Replay* short-cut button on the right or choose from the pull-down menu:

Analysis > Playback.

The *Playbacks* dialog box (Figure 1-22) appears. In the *Playbacks* dialog box, click the *Open* button, and select the previously saved playback file *AnalysisDefinition1.pbk* (this file is included in the *Lesson 1* folder). Click the *Play Current Result Set* button at the top left corner. The *Animate* dialog box (Figure 1-23) opens. Click the *Play* button to play the motion of the engine. You should see the motion animation similar to that of Figure 1-20.

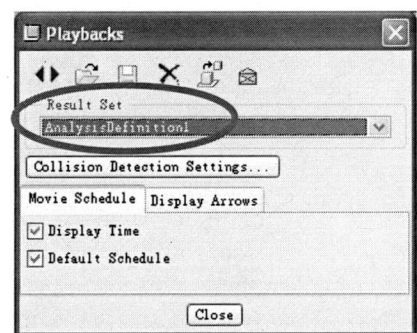

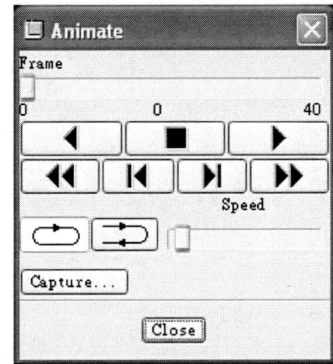

Figure 1-22 The *Playbacks* Dialog Box   Figure 2-23 The *Animate* Dialog Box

1.6 Motion Examples

Numerous motion examples will be introduced in this book to illustrate step-by-step details of modeling, analysis, and result visualization capabilities in *Mechanism Design*. We will start with a simple ball throwing example. This example will give you a quick start and a quick run-through on *Mechanism Design*. *Lessons 3* through *8* focus on modeling and analysis of basic mechanisms. In these lessons, you will learn various joint types, including pin, slider, rigid, etc.; connections, including springs, gears, cam-followers; drivers and forces; various analysis types; and measures and results. *Lessons 9* and *10* are application lessons, in which real-world mechanisms will be introduced to show you how to apply what you learn to more complicated applications. All examples and main topics to be discussed in each lesson are summarized in the Table 1-2.

Note that example files have been prepared for you to go through all the lessons. In addition to *Pro/ENGINEER* parts and assemblies, each lesson folder contains complete motion models as well as simulation result files. You may want to open the motion models and review the simulation results; e.g., play motion animations, to become more familiar with the simulations before going thought the lessons.

Table 1-2 Summary of Lessons and Motion Examples in this Book

Lesson	Title	Example	Problem Type	Things to Learn
1	Single-Piston Engine		Kinematics	1. General introduction
2	Ball Throwing Example		Particle Dynamics	1. This lesson offers a quick run-through of general modeling and analysis capabilities in *Mechanism Design*. 2. You will learn the general process of using *Mechanism Design* to construct a motion model, run analysis, and visualize the motion analysis results. 3. Simulation results are verified using analytical equations of motion.
3	Spring-Mass System		Particle Dynamics	1. This is a classical spring-mass system example you learned in Sophomore *Dynamics*. 2. You will learn how to create a mechanical spring, align the block with the slope surface, and add an external force to pull the block. 3. Simulation results are verified using analytical equations of motion.
4	A Simple Pendulum		Particle Dynamics	1. This lesson provides more in depth about creating joints in *Mechanism Design*. Pin and rigid joints will be introduced. 2. Simulation results are verified using analytical equations of motion.
5	A Slider Crank Mechanism		Multibody Kinematic and Dynamic Analyses	1. This lesson uses a slider-crank mechanism to discuss more joint types; as well as conduct position (initial assembly), kinematic, and dynamic analyses. 2. In addition to joints, you will learn to create drivers for motion analysis. 3. The interference checking capability will be discussed. 4. Simulation results are verified using analytical equations of motion.

Table 1-2 Summary of Lessons and Examples in this Book (Cont'd)

Lesson	Title	Example	Problem Type	Things to Learn
6	A Compound Spur Gear Train		Gear Train Analysis	1. This lesson focuses on simulating motion of a spur gear train. 2. You will learn how to use *Mechanism Design* to create a gear connection, analyze the gear train, and define measures for gears. 3. Simulation results are verified using analytical equations.
7	Planetary Gear Train Systems		Planetary Gear Train Analysis	1. This lesson is similar to *Lesson 6* but focuses on planetary gear trains. 2. Both single gear and multiple gears systems will be discussed. 3. Some simulation results are found incorrect using analytical equations.
8	Cam and Follower		Multibody Kinematic Analysis	1. This lesson discusses cam and followers. 2. An inlet or outlet valve system of an internal combustion engine will be created and simulated. 3. Position and velocity of the valve will be created to simulate the motion of the system as well as assess the engineering design of the system.
9	Assistive Device for Wheelchair Soccer Game		Multibody Dynamic Analysis	1. This is an application lesson. This lesson shows you how to assemble and simulate motion of an assistive device for playing wheelchair soccer game. 2. Numerous joints, spring, and force will be created for the system. 3. Measures will be defined to assess the design of the system.
10	Kinematic Analysis for Racecar Suspension		Multibody Kinematic Analysis	1. This is the second and the last application lesson of the book. A quarter of a racecar suspension will be employed for kinematic analyses. 2. A road profile will be modeled by using a cam of special profile. The cam will be connected to the tire using a cam-follower connection. 3. Various measures, including the camber angle, will be introduced to assess the design of the suspension system.

Notes:

Lesson 2: The Ball Throwing Example

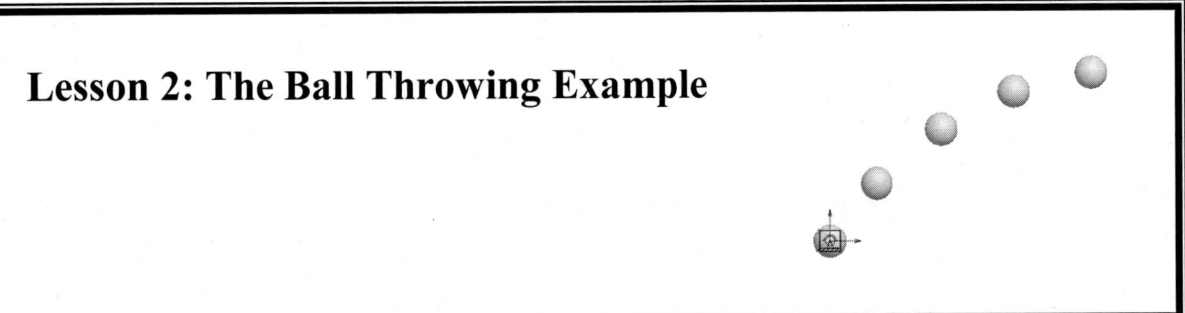

2.1 Overview of the Lesson

The purpose of this lesson is to provide a quick start for using *Pro/ENGINEER Mechanism Design*. This example simulates a ball thrown with an initial velocity. Due to gravity, the ball will travel following a parabolic trajectory, as shown in Figure 2-1. In this lesson, you will learn how to create a motion model to simulate the ball motion, run a dynamic analysis, and animate the ball motion. Dynamic analysis results of this example can be verified using particle dynamics theory that you learned Sophomore *Physics*. We will review the equation of motion, calculate the position and velocity of the ball, and compare our calculations with results obtained from *Mechanism Design*. Validating results obtained from computer simulations is extremely important. *Mechanism Design* is not foolproof. It requires a certain level of experience and expertise to master the software. Before you arrive at that level, it will be very helpful to verify the simulation results, whenever possible. Verifying the simulation results will increase your confidence in using the software and prevent you from being occasionally fooled by the erroneous simulations produced by the software. Note that very often the erroneous results are due to modeling errors.

2.2 The Ball Throwing Example

Physical Model

The physical model of the ball example is very simple. The ball is made of *STEEL* with a radius of 0.5 in. Note that the default unit system in *Pro/ENGINEER*; i.e., in-lb$_m$-sec, is assumed. The gravitational acceleration is 386 in/sec^2. Note that you may check or change the unit system by choosing from the pull-down menu

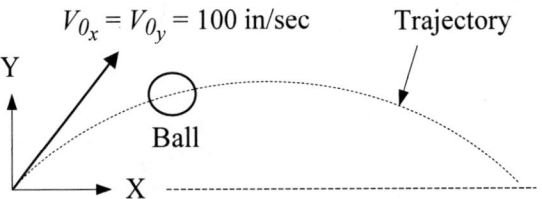

Figure 2-1 The Ball Throwing Example

File > Properties.

Details about changing the unit system can be found in later lessons; for example, *Lesson 4*.

For this lesson, the solid model of the ball has been created for you in *Pro/ENGINEER*. You can find the part file at the publisher's web site (http://www.schroff1.com/). As mentioned in *Lesson 1*, datum features are extremely important in creating motion models. *Mechanism Design* converts all datum features of the root assembly to ground body and requires users to assemble parts (or assemblies) to the ground body using proper joints. Joints are similar to the placement constraints, except that joints intentionally allow prescribed movement between bodies, which resembles physical motion of the system. *Mechanism Design* also converts the assembly datum coordinate system into the World

Coordinate System (*WCS*) for the motion model. Note that *WCS* is fixed to the ground body and serves as the ultimate reference for the definition of the motion model. Also, joints and forces are usually defined at datum features, such as points and axes. Therefore, please pay close attention to all datum features created in parts and assemblies.

Pro/ENGINEER Part and Assembly

The ball assembly consists of one single part: the ball (see Figure 2-2a). The ball part has a revolved solid feature, a datum axis (*A_1*), three datum planes (*FRONT*, *TOP*, and *RIGHT*), and a datum coordinate system (*PRT_CSYS_DEF*). Also, a datum point *PNT0* is defined at the origin of the coordinate system located at the center of the ball. We will create a new assembly and bring the ball part into the assembly.

In the root assembly, you will be given three datum planes (*ASM_RIGHT*, *ASM_TOP*, and *ASM_FRONT*), and an assembly coordinate system (*ASM_DEF_CSYS*). We will create a datum point (*APNT0*) at the origin of the assembly coordinate system (Figure 2-2b). Note that the ball will be brought into the assembly by creating a planar joint. The planar joint will be defined by aligning two datum planes: *FRONT* (ball) and *ASM_FRONT* (assembly), which are normal to the z-axis of the coordinate systems, *PRT_CSYS_DEF* and *ASM_DEF_CSYS*. As a result, the ball is free to move on the *X-Y* plane.

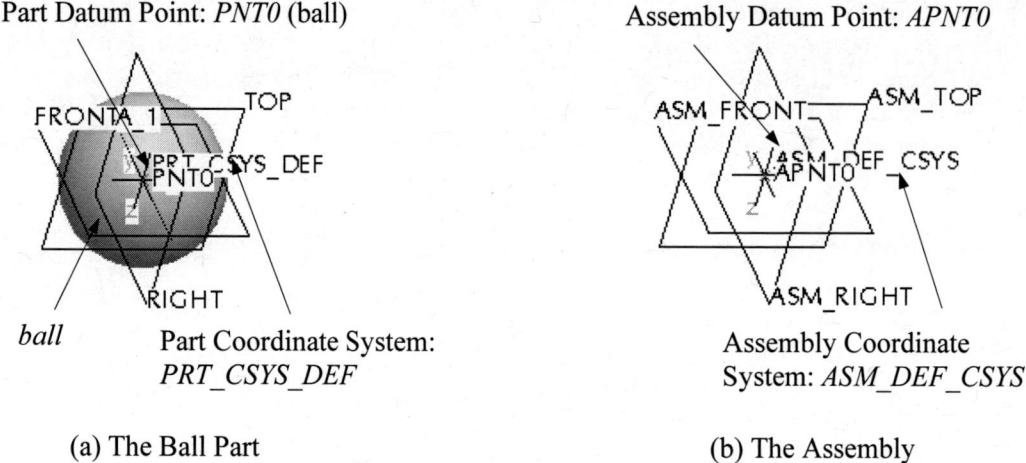

(a) The Ball Part

(b) The Assembly

Figure 2-2 The Ball Part and Assembly

As you are aware, *Pro/ENGINEER* dynamically changes the display of the model as you change the view. For example, as you spin, pan, zoom or rotate an object, you see the object changes as you move/drag the mouse. In *Pro/ENGINEER Wildfire* spin, pan, zoom and rotate are achieved by clicking the middle mouse button (*MB2*) in combination with either the *SHIFT* or *CTRL* key. You may try out these view functions following the instructions shown in Table 2-1.

Table 2-1 The View Functions Using *MB2*

Spin	*MB2*+Drag
Pan	*MB2*+*SHIFT*+Drag
Zoom	*MB2*+*CTRL*+Drag vertically
Rotate	*MB2*+*CTRL*+Drag horizontally

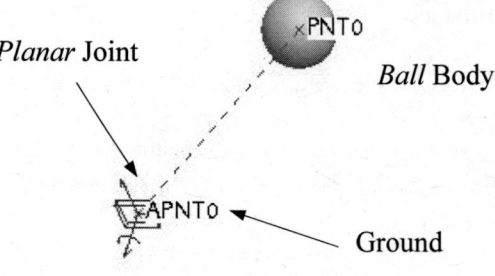

Figure 2-3 The Ball Motion Model

Lesson 2: The Ball Throwing Example

Motion Model

In this example, the ball will be the only movable body. A planar joint will be defined between the ball and the ground body (Figure 2-3). The planar joint will restrain the ball to move on the *X-Y* plane. As mentioned earlier, the ball will be thrown with an initial velocity: in this case, $V_{0_x} = V_{0_y} = 100$ in/sec. A gravitational acceleration -386 in/sec^2 will be defined in the *Y*-direction of the *WCS* (that is, the assembly coordinate system *ASM_DEF_CSYS*). The ball will reveal a parabolic trajectory due to gravity. The overall simulation will be around 0.52 seconds before the ball hits the ground. We will define measures to graph the *X*- and *Y*-positions of the ball. These measures will be defined at the datum point *PNT0*.

2.3 Using *Mechanism Design*

Creating an Assembly

Start *Pro/ENGINEER*, set the working directory, and create an assembly model: *ball_throwing.asm* (or any assembly name you prefer). You should see three assembly datum planes (*ASM_FRONT*, *ASM_TOP*, and *ASM_FRONT*) and one coordinate system (*ASM_DEF_CSYS*), as shown in Figure 2-4. We will create a datum point at the origin of the coordinate system before bringing in the ball part. To create a datum point, you may choose from the pull-down menu (Figure 2-5)

Insert > Model Datum > Point > Offset Coordinate System.

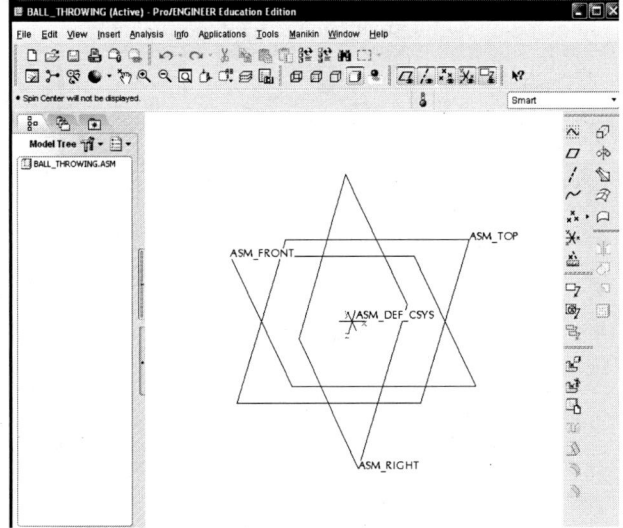

Figure 2-4 The *Pro/ENGINEER* Main Window

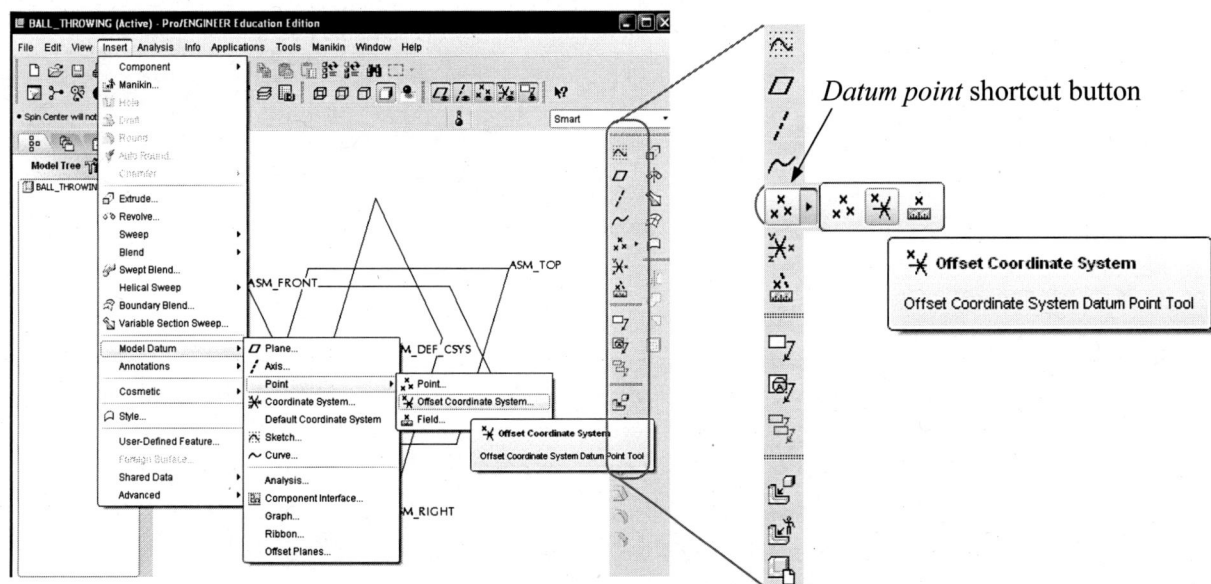

Figure 2-5 The Pull-Down Menu Option and Shortcut Buttons

The *Offset CSys Datum Point* dialog box (Figure 2-6a) appears. Note that you may also bring up this dialog box by clicking the *Datum point* shortcut button on the right (Figure 2-5) and choosing the *Offset Coordinate System Datum Point Tool* (3rd button).

We will define the datum point at the origin of the coordinate system *ASM_DEF_CSYS*. In the *Offset Csys Datum Point* dialog box (Figure 2-6a), click the *Reference* textfield. The textfield should be highlighted in yellow, indicating that it is active and is ready for you to select entities. Pick the coordinate system *ASM_DEF_CSYS* in the *Graphics* window. Then, move the pointer to the *Offset CSys Datum Point* dialog box (Figure 2-6b), and click a table cell right below the table title bar in the top row. You should see that the datum point *APNT0* is listed with a zero offset in all three axes (Figure 2-6b). Click *OK* to accept the datum point definition. Datum point *APNT0* should appear in the *Graphics* window coinciding with the coordinate system.

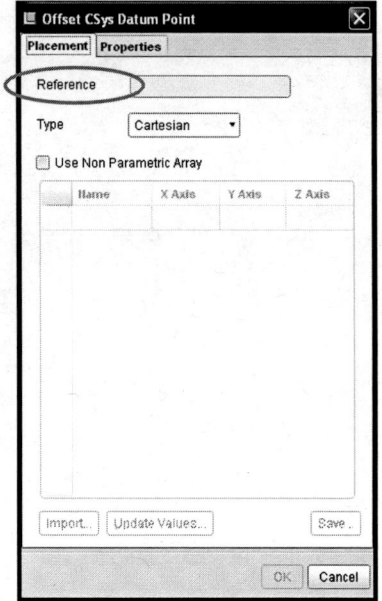 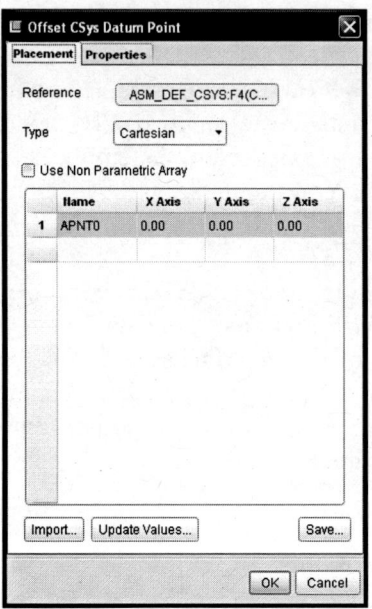

(a) Initial Window (No Selections)   (b) With Selections

Figure 2-6 The *Offset CSys Datum Point* Dialog Box

Now, we are ready to bring in the ball part. Click the *Add component* shortcut button on the right of the *Graphics* window or choose from the pull-down menu

Insert > Component > Assemble > [choose ball.prt].

The ball part will appear in the *Graphics* window (Figure 2-7). In the *Component Placement* dashboard (upper left of the *Graphics* window), choose *Planar* from the *User Defined*) list as shown in Figure 2-7.

Click datum planes *FRONT* (*ball.prt*) and *ASM_FRONT* (assembly) to define the planar joint. The planar joint symbol will appear (Figure 2-8). In addition, you should see the message at the top of the *Graphics* window: *STATUS: Connection Definition Complete*, indicating that the planar joint has been defined successfully. Click the button to the right of the *Component Placement* dashboard to accept the definition.

Lesson 2: The Ball Throwing Example

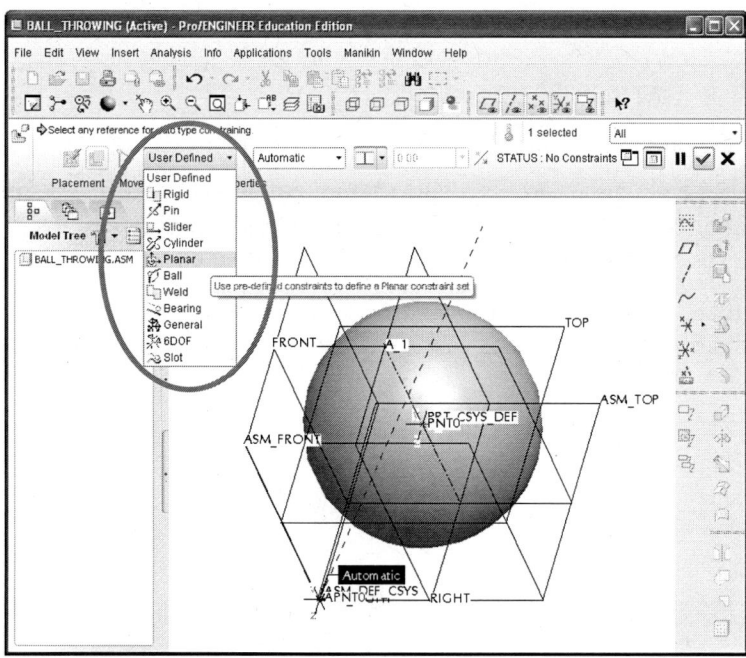

Figure 2-7 Choose *Planar* Joint from the *Component Placement* Dashboard

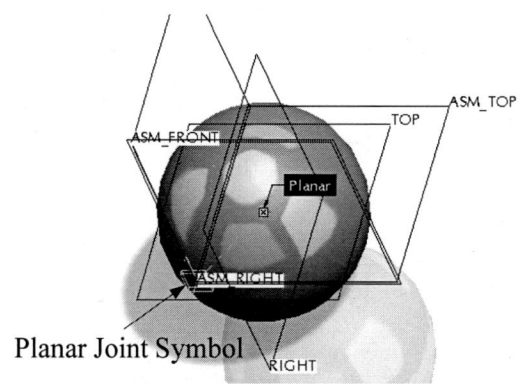

Figure 2-8 The Ball Being Assembled to the Ground Body

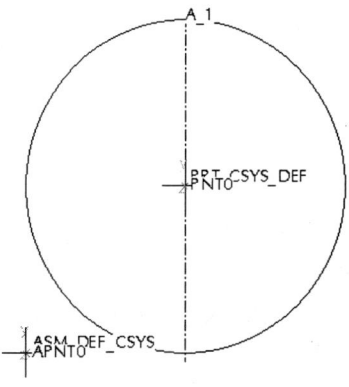

Figure 2-9 Front View (Datum Plane Display Turned Off)

Note that there are two types of options available for assembling parts in the *Component Placement* dashboard. They are *User Defined* (joint) and *Automatic* (placement). The *User Defined* type consists of commonly employed joints for defining motion models, such as the planar joint we just defined. These options offer joint definitions that are directly corresponding to connections implemented in the physical mechanism, such as rigid, pin, cylinder joints, etc. The *Automatic* constraints (or placement constraints) are regular constraints we employed for assembling parts, such as *Mate* and *Align*. Both types eliminate certain degrees of freedom between components. Some of the joints are directly equivalent to placement constraint. For example, mating two planar faces is equivalent to defining a planar joint. Some joints require a combination of placement constraints. For example, a pin joint requires an axis align and face mate placement constraints. You may use the *Convert* button at the top of the *Graphics* window to convert the placement constraints to joints or vise versa. Choose adequate joints and/or placement constraints to define your model.

Note that we would like to position the ball with its center point (*PNT0*) coincident with the assembly datum point (*APNT0*). The assembly datum point *APNT0* is fixed to the ground. In fact, all the assembly datum features belong to the ground body. This will be where the ball is positioned before any motion.

You may move the ball on the *FRONT* plane (normal to the z-axis since a planar joint is defined) by using the *Drag* option in *Pro/ENGINEER*. Before dragging the ball, you may want to set the view to be normal to the z-axis. We will choose the *FRONT* view from the saved view list. To set the view, click the *Saved View List* button at the top of the *Graphics* window and choose *FRONT*. In the *Graphics* window, you should see a view similar to that of Figure 2-9. Note that datum plane display has been turned off in Figure 2-9.

Click the *Drag Packed Components* button at the top of the *Graphics* window. The *Drag* dialog box (Figure 2-10a) should appear. Click the ball in the *Graphics* window. Without clicking the mouse again, simply move the mouse to move the ball on the *Front* plane as expected.

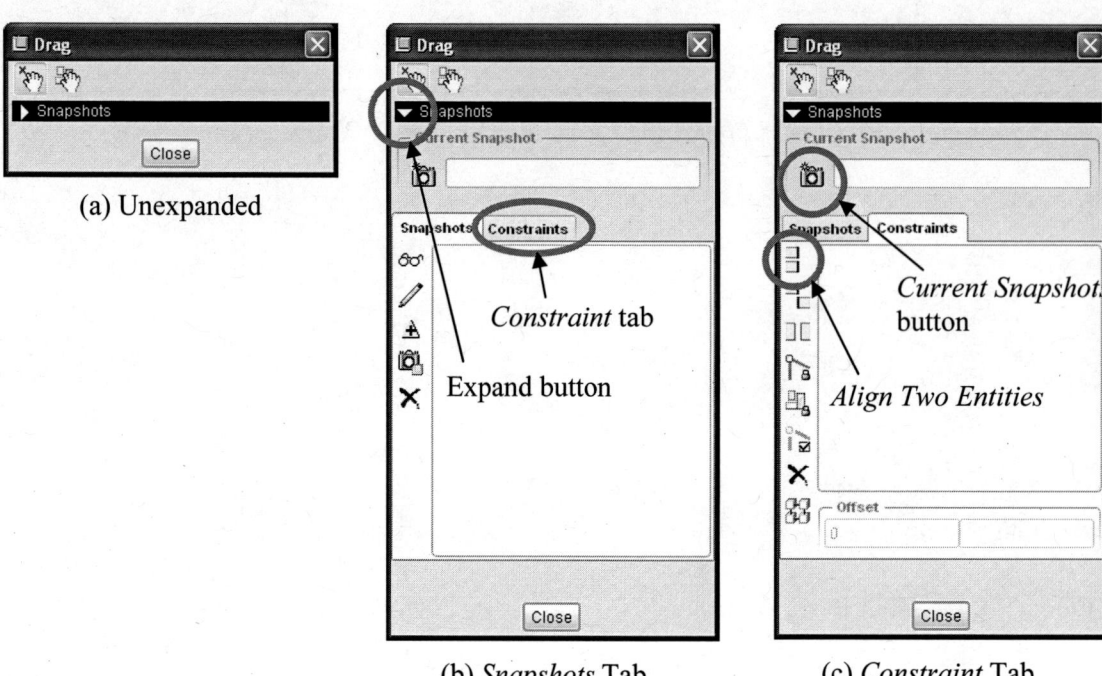

(a) Unexpanded   (b) *Snapshots* Tab   (c) *Constraint* Tab

Figure 2-10 The *Drag* Dialog Box

In the *Drag* dialog box, click the expand button (triangular shape next to the label *Snapshots*, see Figure 2-10b) to expand the window. Click the *Constraints* tab, and choose the *Align Two Entities* button (first on the left, as shown in Figure 2-10c). Choose two datum points, *PNT0* and *APNT0*. The ball should now be centered at the assembly datum point *APNT0*. Click the *Current Snapshots* button (see Figure 2-10c) to save a snapshot of the current configuration under the default name: *Snapshot1*. Note that this snapshot defines the initial position (and orientation) of the ball. Before running a motion analysis, make sure you bring this snapshot back in case the ball has been dragged away. Click *Close* to accept the snapshot.

Lesson 2: The Ball Throwing Example

Creating a Dynamic Simulation Model

We are now ready to enter *Mechanism Design* for creating a dynamic simulation model. From the pull-down menu, choose

Applications > Mechanism.

Note the change of the *Pro/ENGINEER* window (see Figure 2-11 with datum planes display turned back on, and display set in the *Standard Orientation*). First, the *Mechanism Design* shortcut buttons appear to the right, providing all the functions for creating motion models, creating and running analyses, and visualizing results. In this lesson, we will use the gravity, initial conditions, mechanism analysis, playback, and measures shortcut buttons. The second change is that the *Model Tree* window is split into two. The added lower half lists motion model entities, including bodies, connections, analysis, etc. It is convenient to review or modify existing entities by clicking the entity and pressing the right mouse button. In addition, a planar joint symbol re-appears at the center of the ball in the *Graphics* window, similar to that of Figure 2-8.

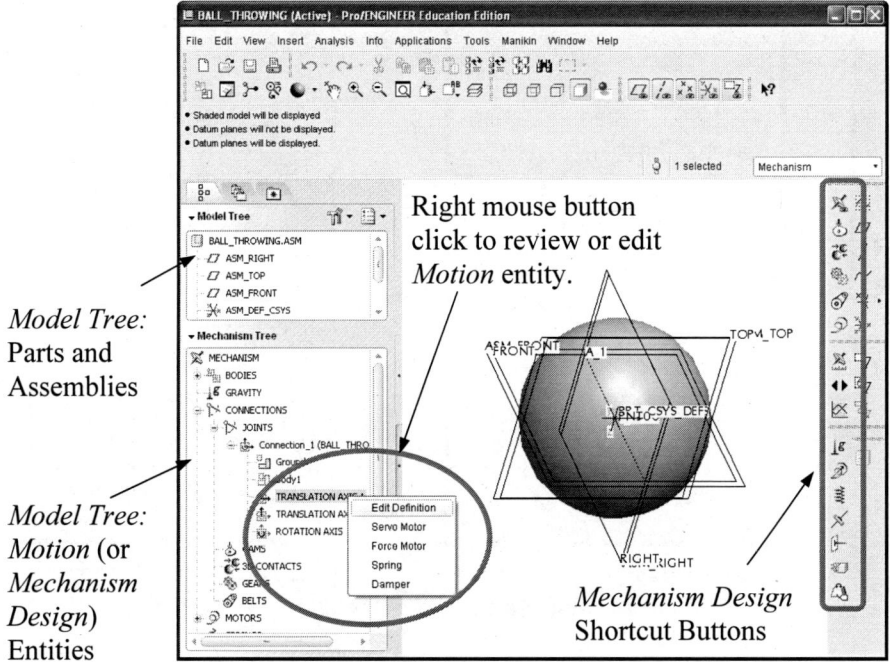 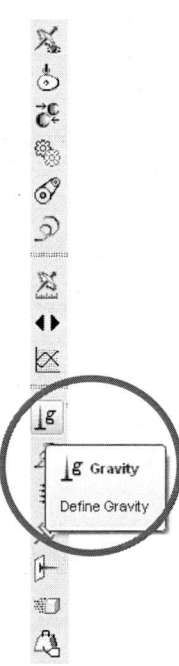

Figure 2-11 Changes in *Mechanism Design* Window

Figure 2-12 The *Gravity* Button

Next, we will define the gravitational acceleration and add an initial velocity $V_{0_x} = V_{0_y} = 100$ in/sec to the ball.

Click the *Define Gravity* shortcut button on the right (Figure 2-12) to bring up the *Gravity* dialog box (Figure 2-13). Note that the default value of acceleration (386.088) and default direction (0,–1,0) are predefined, which are what we need. No change is necessary. Simply click *OK* in the *Gravity* dialog box. You will need to activate the gravity when you define a dynamic analysis.

Click the *Initial Conditions* shortcut button on the right (next to last) or choose from the pull-down menu:

Insert > Initial Conductions.

In the *Initial Condition Definition* dialog box (Figure 2-14), click the *Define velocity of a point* button (first on the left), and then pick *PNT0* (Note: do not pick *APNT0* since the initial velocity must be defined to the ball). Use right mouse button to shuffle the overlapped entities (for example, *APNT0* and *PNT0*) in the *Graphics* window. Enter *Magnitude: 141.4* (note that the velocity magnitude is $V = \sqrt{V_{0x}^2 + V_{0y}^2}$), and *1, 1, 0* for *X, Y,* and *Z,* respectively in the *Initial Condition Definition* dialog box (see Figure 2-15). Click *OK* to accept the definition.

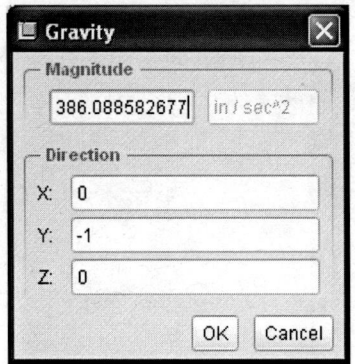

Figure 2-13 The *Gravity* Dialog Box

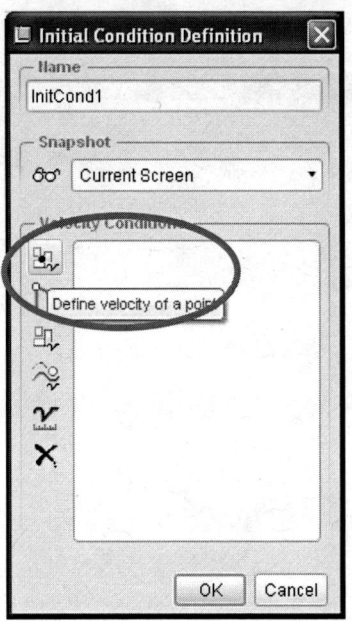

Figure 2-14 The *Initial Conduction Definition* Dialog Box

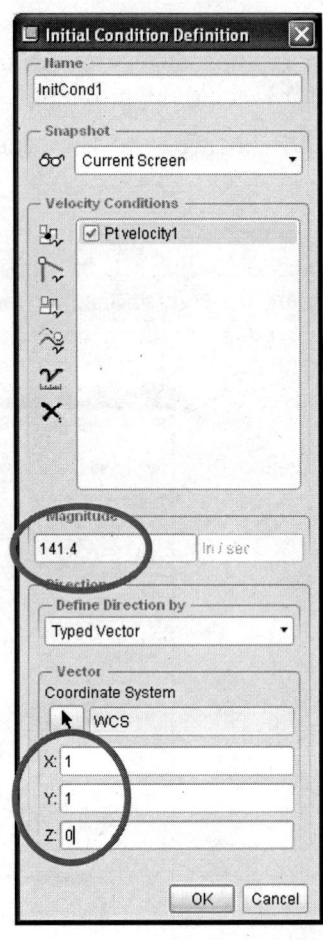

Figure 2-15 Initial Conduction Defined

Creating and Running a Dynamic Analysis

Before running a motion analysis, make sure the ball is brought back to its initial position, as defined in the snapshot (*Snapshot1*) earlier. Click the *Drag Packed Components* button at the top of the *Graphics* window. The *Drag* dialog box should appear with *Snapshot1* listed (Figure 2-16). Double click *Snapshot1* to bring back the *Snapshot1* configuration. The ball should be restored to the position and orientation defined in *Snapshot1* (if the ball has been dragged away). Click the *Close* button to close the *Drag* dialog box.

From the button list on the right, click the *Mechanism Analysis* shortcut button or choose from the pull-down menu:

Analysis > Mechanism Analysis.

Lesson 2: The Ball Throwing Example

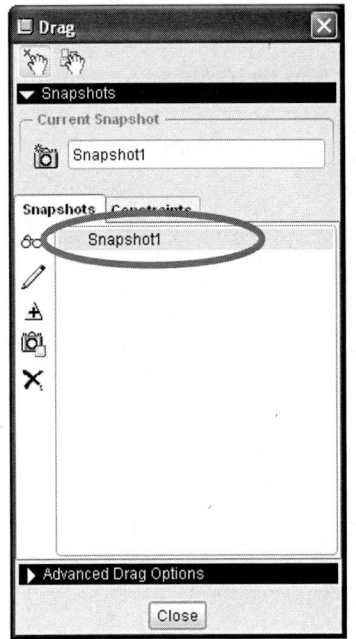

Figure 2-16 The *Drag* Dialog Box

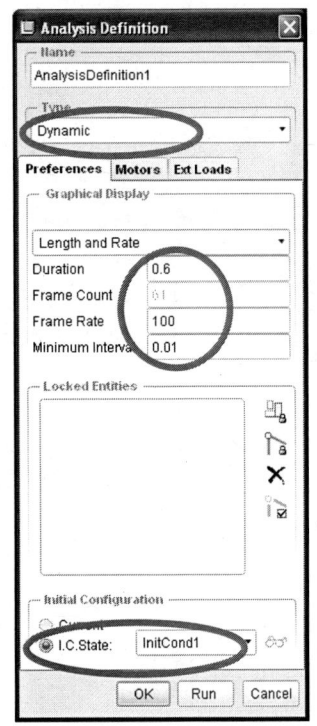

(a) *Preferences* Tab

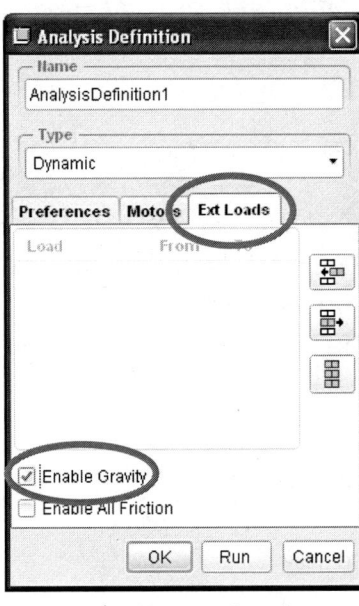

(b) *Ext. Loads* Tab

Figure 2-17 The *Analysis Definition* Dialog Box

The *Analysis Definition* dialog box (Figure 2-17a) appears.

Under *Type*, select *Dynamic*. Leave the default name, *AnalysisDefinition1*. Enter:

Duration: *0.6*
Frame Rate: *100*
Minimum Interval: *0.01*

and click the *I.C. State* radio button (*InitCond1* should be listed).

Note that the *Duration* specifies the overall simulation period. *Frame Rate* defines number of time frames and the *Minimum Interval* specifies the time interval, on which the results will be reported. Note that the *Frame Rate* and *Minimum Interval* are related; i.e., *Frame Rate = 1/Interval*.

Click the *Ext. Loads* tab, click *Enable Gravity* (Figure 2-17b), and then click *Run*.

The progress of the analysis is shown in the *Prompt/Message* window (right above the *Graphics* window), and the ball starts moving following a parabolic trajectory.

The ball will travel mostly out of the view. You may use the *Refit* button or zoom out of the *Graphics* window a few times to locate the ball. Click *OK* to close the Analysis Definition dialog box.

Note that the analysis results must be saved as a playback file in order to use them later. We will discuss how to save the results next.

Saving and Reviewing Results

To replay results click the *Replay* button ◀▶ on the right or choose from the pull-down menu:

Analysis > Playback.

The *Playbacks* dialog box (Figure 2-18) opens. In the *Playbacks* dialog box the *AnalysisDefinition1* appears in the *Result Set* field (Figure 2-18). Click the *Play Current Result Set* button ◀▶ at the top left corner. The *Animate* dialog box (Figure 2-19) appears. Click the *Play* button ▶ to play the motion of the ball. Again, you may need to refit the screen or zoom out of the *Graphics* window to see the entire trajectory (Figure 2-20). Click *Close* button to close the *Animate* dialog box.

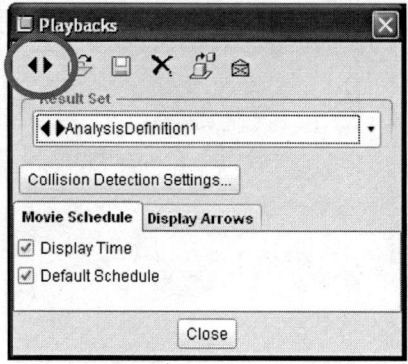

Figure 2-18 The *Playbacks* Dialog Box

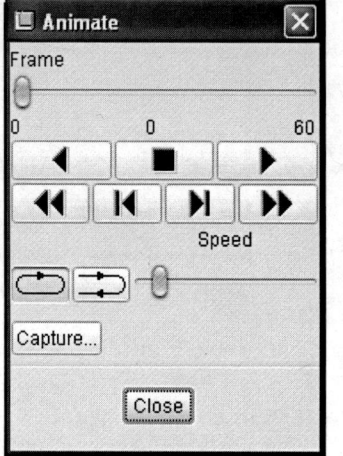

Figure 2-19 The *Animate* Dialog Box

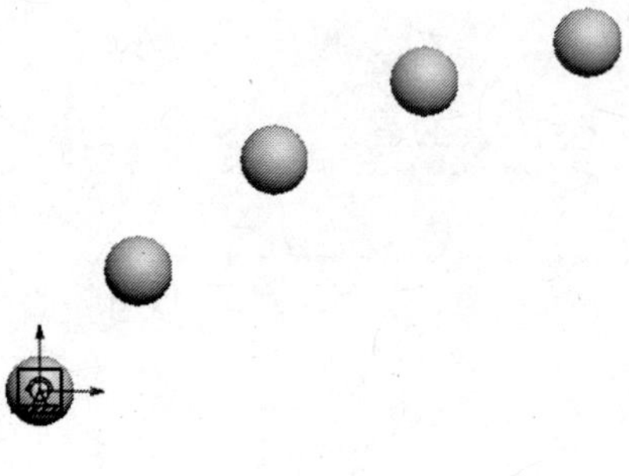

Figure 2-20 Motion Animation

In the *Playbacks* dialog box (see Figure 2-18), click the *Save* button 🖫 to save your results as a *.pbk* file. In the *Save Analysis Results* dialog box (Figure 2-21), accept the default name (*AnalysisDefinition1.pbk*) or specify another name. The default directory is the current working directory. You may also select another directory to save your file. Click *Save* to save the playback file.

You may open the *.pbk* file by clicking the *Open* button 📂 from the *Playbacks* dialog box (Figure 2-18), and selecting the previously saved playback file. Click *Close* to close the *Playbacks* dialog box.

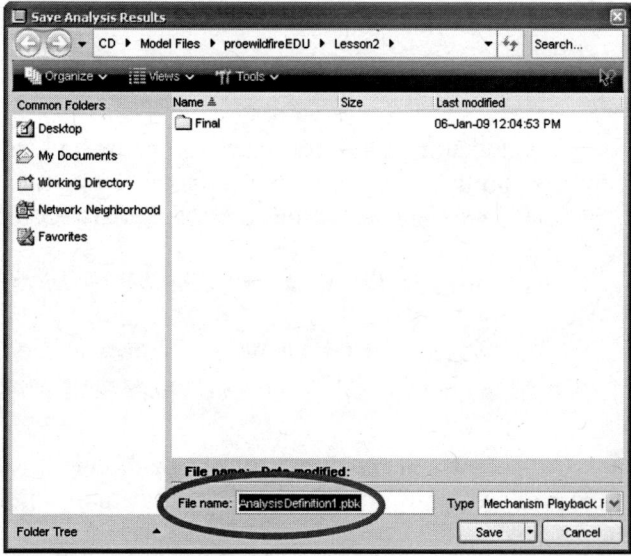

Figure 2-21 The *Save Analysis Results* Dialog Box

Lesson 2: The Ball Throwing Example 2-11

To review results in graphs, click the *Generate Measure Results of Analyses* button or choose from the pull-down menu:

Analysis > Measures.

The *Measure Results* dialog box appears (Figure 2-22). In the *Measure Results* dialog box click the *Create New Measure* button (first on the left of the *Measures* table). The *Measure Definition* dialog box opens (Figure 2-23). Enter *X_Position* for *Name*. Under *Type*, select *Position*. Click the *Select* button and pick *PNT0* in the *ball* part. Leave *WCS* as the *Coordinate System*. Choose *X-component* for the *Component*. Under *Evaluation Method*, leave *Each Time Step*. Click *OK* to accept the definition.

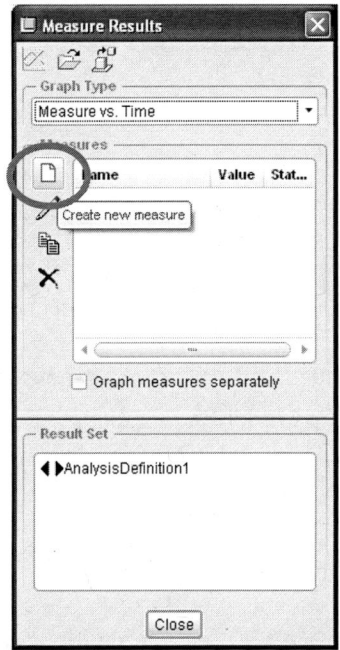

Figure 2-22 The *Measure Results* Dialog Box

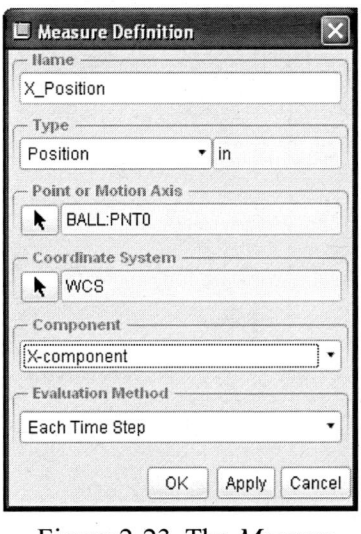

Figure 2-23 The *Measure Definition* Dialog Box

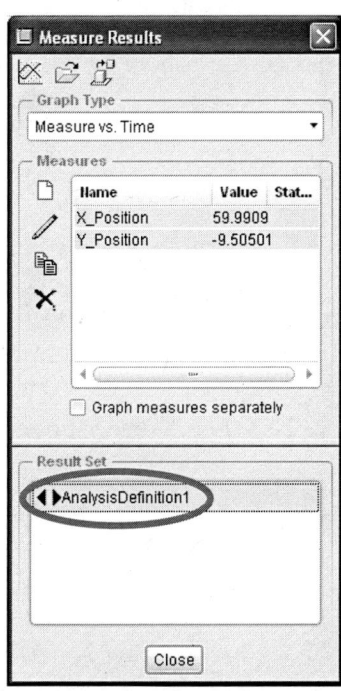

Figure 2-24 The *Measure Results* Dialog Box After

Repeat the same steps to define the *Y_Positon* measure. After that, you should see both measures are listed in the *Measure Results* dialog box (Figure 2-24).

Select *AnalysisDefinition1* under *Result Set*. (If you changed the result set name, select the respective name). The *Graph Type* should be *Measure vs. Time* (on top) and the measure values at the current status will appear in the *Measure* table. More about the measures in *Mechanism Design* can be found in Appendix B.

Choose both measures by clicking them while pressing the *Shift* key. Click on the top left corner to show a graph for the measures. The graph should be similar to that of Figure 2-25.

As shown in Figure 2-25, the *X*-position of the ball is represented in a straight line with a slope of 100 in/sec, which is the *X*-component of the initial velocity. The *Y*-position is a parabolic curve. The ball will hit the ground (when *Y*-position is zero) around 0.52 seconds. This is why we entered 0.6 seconds for the analysis duration. Unfortunately, *Mechanism Design* does not provide the functionality to terminate the analysis when the ball reaches the ground. You will have to specify a reasonably large duration value to cover the entire simulation period. You may make an adjustment on the analysis duration after reviewing the first analysis results. Close the *Graph* window and the *Measure Results* dialog box.

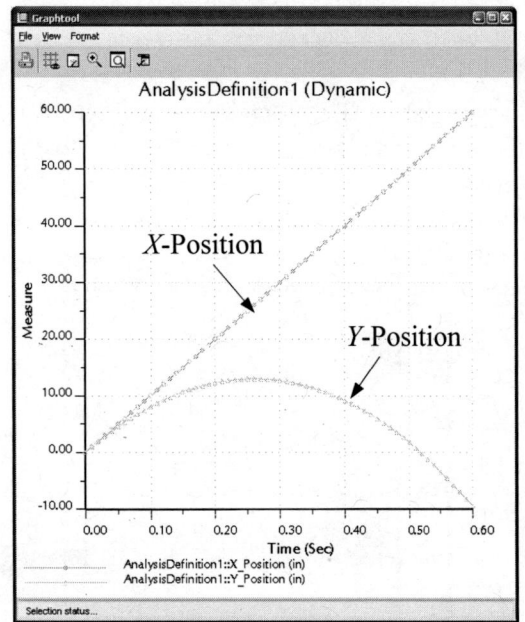

Figure 2-25 The *X*- and *Y*-Position Graphs

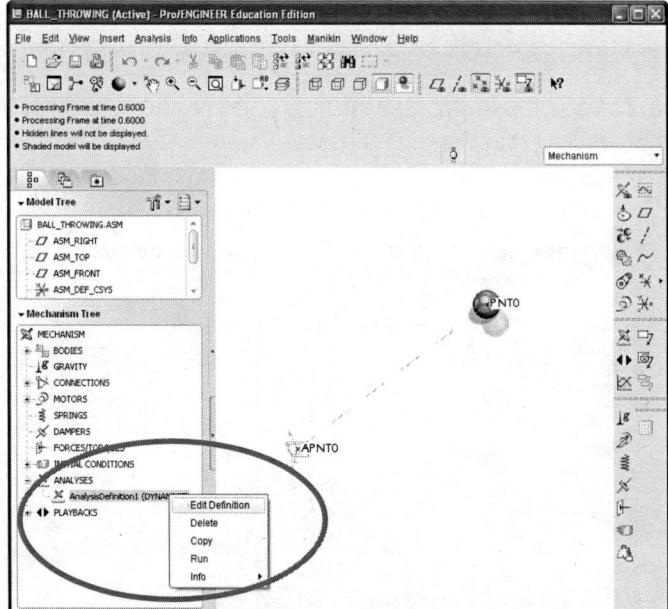

Figure 2-26 The Motion Model Entities Listed in the *Model Tree* Window

Reviewing and Changing the Dynamic Model

From time to time you may need to review or modify a given simulation model. Reviewing and changing the motion model is straightforward in *Mechanism Design*. The best way to do so is using the *Model Tree*. In the *Model Tree* window, you should see that the entities created for the motion model are listed in the lower half of the window (Figure 2-26).

In order to review or change an entity, simply click the entity name listed in the *Model Tree* window, and use the right mouse button to bring up the *Edit Definition* option (among others). For example, you may bring up the *Analysis Definition* dialog box (Figure 2-17a) by clicking the *Analyses* (to expand its contents), clicking *AnalysisDefinition1* using the right mouse button, and then choosing *Edit Definition* (see Figure 2-26).

Exporting the Graph

You may export data shown in a graph to a text file or an *Excel* spreadsheet. All you have to do is to use the *File* pull-down menu of the graph (for example, Figure 2-25), and choose either *Export Excel* or *Export Text*.

Going back to *Pro/ENGINEER* (standard mode) is straightforward. Simply choose *Applications > Standard* from the pull-down menu.

Make sure to save your model before exiting from *Pro/ENGINEER* by choosing *File > Save* from the pull-down menu.

2.4 Result Verifications

In this section, we will verify analysis results obtained from *Mechanism Design* using particle dynamics theory you learned in high school *Physics*.

There are two assumptions that we have to make in order to apply the particle dynamics theory to this ball-throwing problem:

(i) The ball is of a concentrated mass, and
(ii) No air friction is present.

Equation of Motion

It is well-known that the equations that describe the position and velocity of the ball are, respectively,

$$P_x = V_{0_x} t \qquad (2.1a)$$

$$P_y = V_{0_y} t - \frac{1}{2} g t^2 \qquad (2.1b)$$

and

$$V_x = V_{0_x} \qquad (2.2a)$$

$$V_y = V_{0_y} - gt \qquad (2.2b)$$

where P_x and P_y are the *X*- and *Y*-positions of the ball, respectively; V_x and V_y are the *X*- and *Y*-velocities, respectively; V_{0x} and V_{0y} are the initial velocities in the *X*- and *Y*-directions, respectively; and g is the gravitational acceleration.

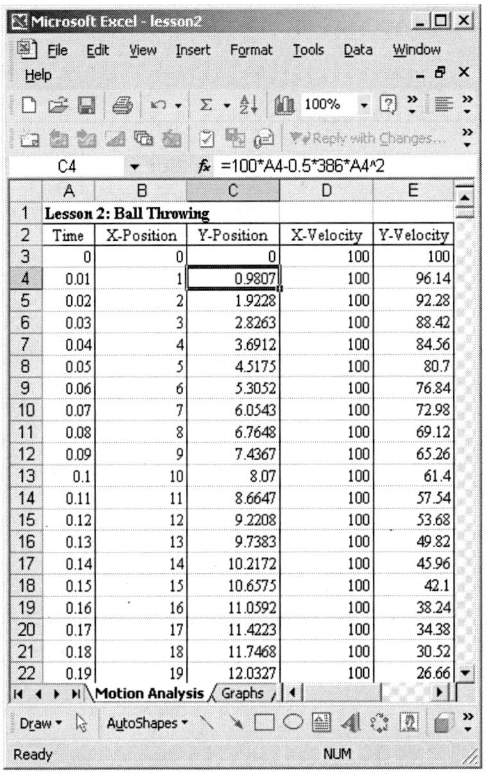

	A	B	C	D	E
1	Lesson 2: Ball Throwing				
2	Time	X-Position	Y-Position	X-Velocity	Y-Velocity
3	0	0	0	100	100
4	0.01	1	0.9807	100	96.14
5	0.02	2	1.9228	100	92.28
6	0.03	3	2.8263	100	88.42
7	0.04	4	3.6912	100	84.56
8	0.05	5	4.5175	100	80.7
9	0.06	6	5.3052	100	76.84
10	0.07	7	6.0543	100	72.98
11	0.08	8	6.7648	100	69.12
12	0.09	9	7.4367	100	65.26
13	0.1	10	8.07	100	61.4
14	0.11	11	8.6647	100	57.54
15	0.12	12	9.2208	100	53.68
16	0.13	13	9.7383	100	49.82
17	0.14	14	10.2172	100	45.96
18	0.15	15	10.6575	100	42.1
19	0.16	16	11.0592	100	38.24
20	0.17	17	11.4223	100	34.38
21	0.18	18	11.7468	100	30.52
22	0.19	19	12.0327	100	26.66

Figure 2-27 The *Excel* Spreadsheet

The above equations can be implemented using, for example, *Microsoft Excel* shown in Figure 2-27, for numerical solutions.

As shown in Figure 2-27, Columns B and C show the results of Eqs. 2.1a and b, respectively; with a time interval from 0 to 0.52 seconds and increment of 0.01 seconds. Also, Columns D and E show the results of Eqs. 2.2a and b, respectively. Data in columns B and C are graphed in Figure 2-28. Also, columns D and E are graphed in Figure 2-29. Comparing Figure 2-28 with Figure 2-25, the results obtained from theory and *Mechanism Design* are very close (they are virtually identical), which means the dynamic model has been created properly in *Mechanism Design*, and *Mechanism Design* does its job and gives us good results. Note that the solution spreadsheet can be found at the publisher's website (filename: *lesson2.xls*).

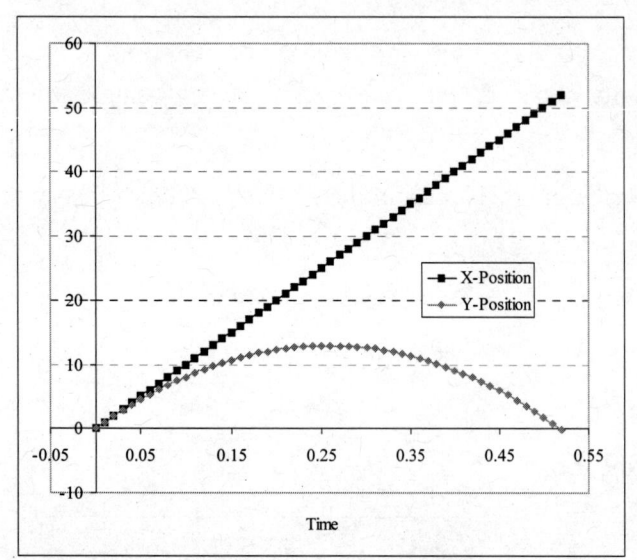

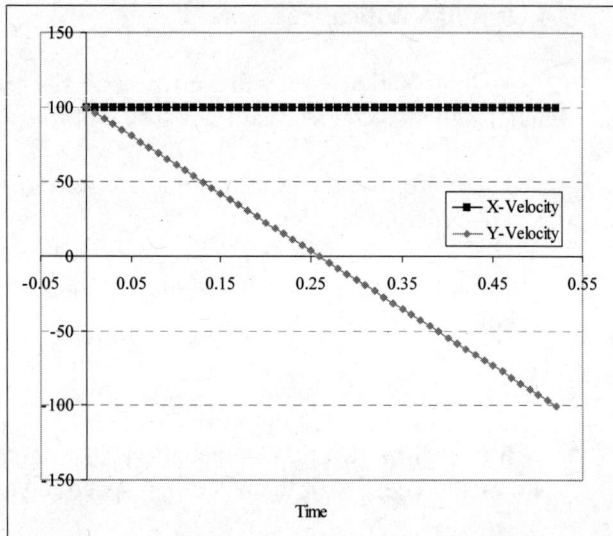

Figure 2-28 Graph of the *X*- and *Y*-Positions of the Ball Obtained from Spreadsheet Calculations

Figure 2-29 Graph of the *X*- and *Y*-Velocities of the Ball Obtained from Spreadsheet Calculations

Lesson 2: The Ball Throwing Example

Exercises:

1. A ball is thrown at an initial velocity of V_{0_x} = 100 in/sec from a stand that is 100 in. above the ground, as shown in Figure E2-1. The radius of the ball is 0.1 in., and the material is steel.

    (i) Create a dynamic simulation model using *Mechanism Design* to simulate the trajectory of the ball. Report position, velocity, and acceleration of the ball at 0.1 seconds in both vertical and horizontal directions obtained from *Mechanism Design*.

    (ii) Derive and solve the equations that describe the position and velocity of the ball. Compare your solutions with those obtained from *Mechanism Design*.

    (iii) Calculate the time for the ball to reach the ground. Compare your calculation with the simulation obtained from *Mechanism Design*.

2. A 1"×1"×1" block slides from top of a 45° slope (due to gravity) without friction, as shown in Figure E2-2. The material of the block is *AL2014*.

    (i) Create a dynamic simulation model using *Mechanism Design* to analyze motion of the block. Report position, velocity, and acceleration of the block in both vertical and horizontal directions at 0.5 seconds obtained from *Mechanism Design*.

    Hint: create a planar joint between the block and the slope face.

    (ii) Derive and solve the equation of motion for the system. Compare your solutions with those obtained from *Mechanism Design*.

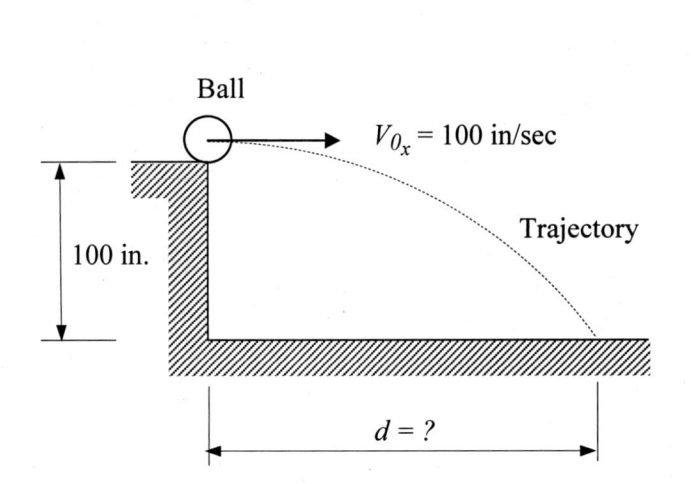

Figure E2-1 The Ball Throwing Problem

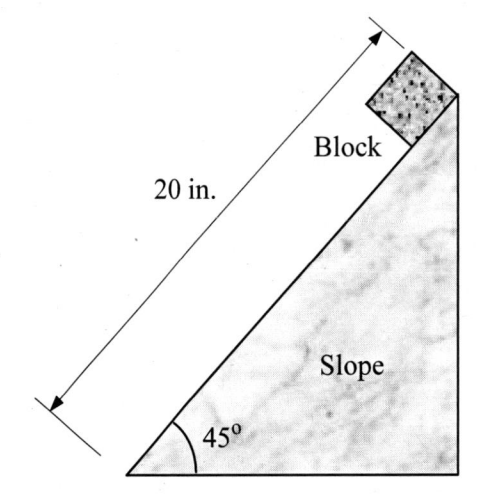

Figure E2-2 The Block Sliding Problem

Notes:

Lesson 3: A Spring-Mass System

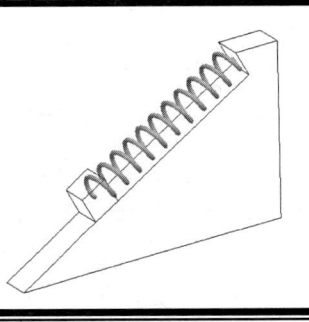

3.1 Overview of the Lesson

In this lesson, we will create a simple spring-mass system and simulate its dynamic responses. A schematics of the system is shown in Figure 3-1, in which a steel block of *1"×1"×1"* is sliding along a 30° slope with a spring connecting it to the top end of the slope. The block will slide back and forth along the slope under different scenarios. In this lesson, you will learn how to create the spring-mass model, run a motion analysis, and visualize the analysis results. The analysis results of the spring-mass example can be verified using particle dynamics theory. Similar to *Lesson 2*, we will formulate the equation of motion, solve the differential equations, graph positions of the block, and compare our calculations with results obtained from *Mechanism Design*.

3.2 The Spring-Mass System

Physical Model

Note that the default unit system in-lb_m-sec will be used for this example. The spring constant and unstretched length are (in the in-lb_m-sec unit system) $k = 20$ lb_m/sec² (which is different from lb_f/in we usually see) and $U = 3$ in., respectively. Please refer to Appendix C for more details regarding unit systems, especially, the mass and force units in the English system, lb_m and lb_f. No friction is assumed between the block and the slope.

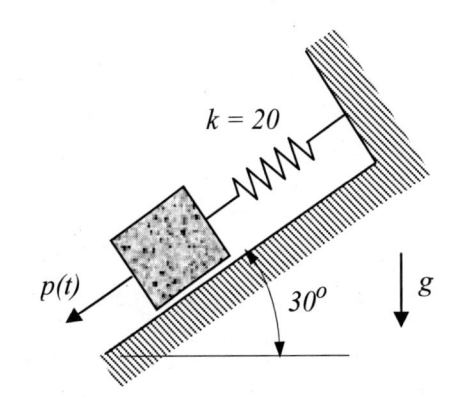

Figure 3-1 The Spring-Mass System

Three scenarios are included in this lesson. The first scenario assumes a free vibration, where the block is stretched 1 in. along the 30° slope, where no gravitational acceleration exists. The second scenario is identical to the first one except a gravitational acceleration $g = 386$ in/sec² is assumed. In the third scenario, an external force $p(t) = 10 \cos 2t$ lb_m in/sec² is applied to the block with the gravitational acceleration, as shown in Figure 3-1. Note that the force magnitude is very small (10 lb_m in/sec² = 0.00518 lb_f). All three scenarios will be simulated using *Mechanism Design*.

Pro/ENGINEER Parts

In this lesson, *Pro/ENGINEER* parts of the spring-mass example have been created for you. You can find the model files at publisher's web site (http://www.schroff1.com/). As mentioned in *Lesson 1*, datum features are extremely important in creating a successful motion model. In this lesson, we will use both datum points and datum axes to assist in creating the motion model.

The spring-mass system consists of two parts, the block (*block.prt*) and the ground (*ground.prt*), as shown in Figure 3-2. The *block* part has an extruded solid feature, a datum axis (A_1), three datum planes (*FRONT*, *TOP*, and *RIGHT*), a coordinate system (*PRT_CSYS_DEF*), and a datum point *PNT0* at the origin of the coordinate system.

Similarly, the ground part has an extruded solid feature, a datum axis (A_1), three datum planes (*FRONT*, *TOP*, and *RIGHT*), a coordinate system (*PRT_CSYS_DEF*), and two datum point *PNT1* and *PNT2*. Note that the datum axes are created to align the block properly to the ground as part of the initial conditions. The datum points *PNT0* of the block and *PNT1* of the ground are used to define the spring. In addition, *PNT0* of the block and *PNT2* (4 in. downward along the slope) of the ground are used to position the block before starting the simulation.

We will create a new assembly called *spring_mass* and bring in these two parts. In the new assembly, you will be given three datum planes (*ASM_RIGHT*, *ASM_TOP*, and *ASM_FRONT*), and an assembly coordinate system (*ASM_DEF_CSYS*). The ground part will be brought into the assembly by aligning their coordinate systems. The block will be brought in by creating a planar joint between the block and the ground. Note that the planar joint will be defined by aligning the bottom face of the block with the slope face of the ground, as shown in Figure 3-2. As a result, the block is free to move on the face of the slope. We will then align the two datum axes in order to restrict the motion of the block, as shown in Figure 3-3. We will use the current configuration as initial condition for motion analysis.

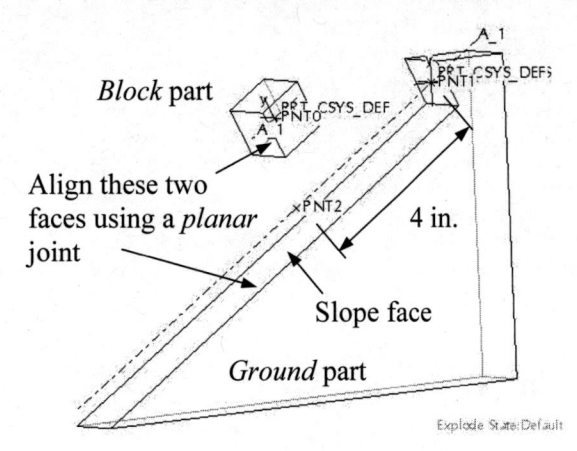

Figure 3-2 The Block and Ground Parts

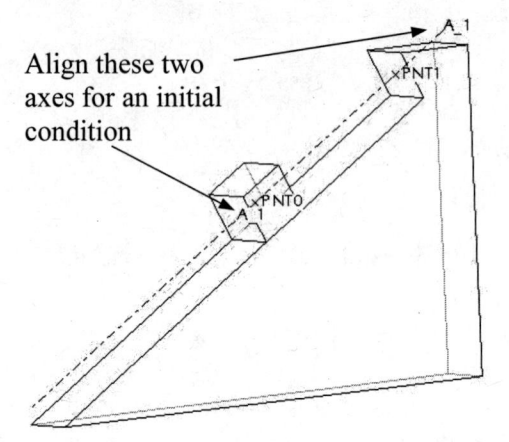

Figure 3-3 Spring Mass Assembly

Motion Model

In this example, the block will be the only movable body. A planar joint will be defined between the block and the ground body (*ground.prt*), as shown in Figure 3-4. The planar joint that is co-planar with the slope face will restrain the block to move along the 30° plane. A spring is defined by connecting datum points *PNT0* of the block and *PNT1* of the ground. As mentioned earlier, the spring has an unstretched length $U = 3$ in. The block will be stretched further down to the slope 1 in. from the unstretched configuration. This will be defined by aligning *PNT0* of the block and *PNT2* of the ground (4 in. from *PNT1* along the slope, see Figure 3-2).

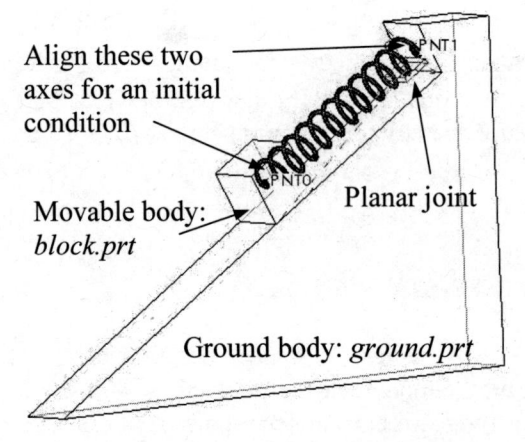

Figure 3-4 Spring Mass Dynamic Model

Lesson 3: A Spring-Mass System

The spring will be released with zero initial velocity. In the first scenario, no gravity exists. Gravitational acceleration and an external force will be added for the remaining two scenarios.

3.3 Using *Mechanism Design*

Creating an Assembly

Start *Pro/ENGINEER*, set the working directory, and create a new assembly: *spring_mass.asm* (or any assembly name you prefer). You should see three assembly datum planes (*ASM_FRONT*, *ASM_TOP*, and *ASM_FRONT*) and one coordinate system (*ASM_DEF_CSYS*).

Click the *Add component* shortcut button on the right of the *Graphics* window or choose from the pull-down menu

Insert > Component > Assemble > [choose ground.prt].

The *ground* part will appear in the *Graphics* window. We will assemble the ground part by aligning two datum coordinate systems, *PRT_CSYS_DEF* of the ground part and *ASM_CSYS_DEF* of the assembly. In the *Component Placement* dashboard (upper left) click the *Placement* button, and choose *Coord Sys* from the *Automatic Constraint* list, as shown in Figure 3-5. Click the datum coordinate systems, *PRT_CSYS_DEF* (*ground.prt*) and *ASM_DEF_CSYS* (assembly) from the *Graphics* window. Click the ✓ button at right of the *Component Placement* dashboard to accept the definition.

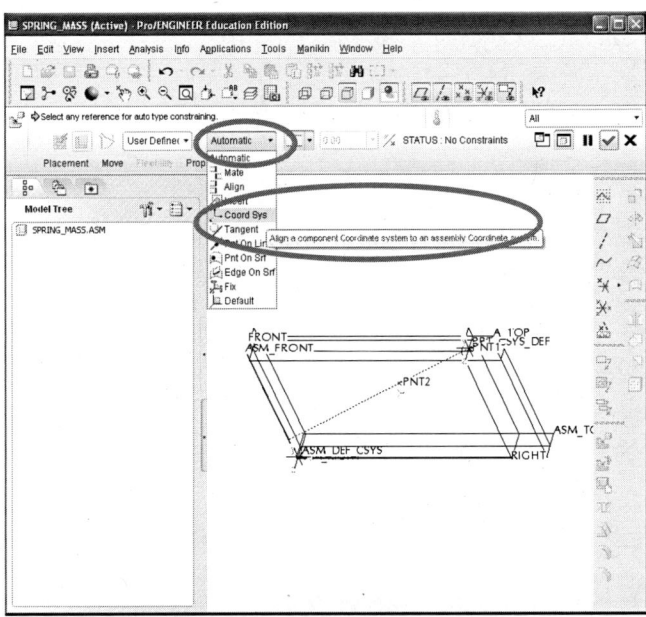

Figure 3-5 Choosing *Coord Sys* from the *Component Placement* Dashboard

Next, we will assemble the block to the ground by defining a planar joint.

Click the *Add component* shortcut button and choose the block part. The block will be brought into the *Graphics* window. Note that you may want to turn off some datum feature displays (for examples, datum planes) to see or pick the datum entities. Move and orient the block to a configuration similar to that of Figure 3-6 using the *Move* option (next to the *Placement* button in the *Component Placement* dashboard shown in Figure 3-5). Most importantly, orient the block so that the two axes *A_1* are roughly aligned (similar to those of Figure 3-6).

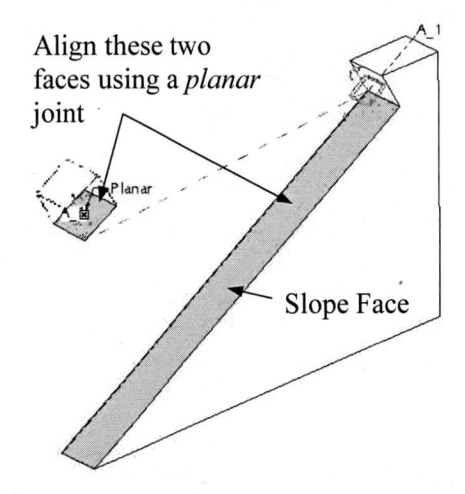

Figure 3-6 Defining a *Planar* Joint

Choose the planar joint from the *User Defined* list of the *Component Placement* dashboard (similar to *Lesson 2*). Choose the slope face of the ground and the bottom face of the block (right-click to choose the bottom face) for the planar joint. The planar joint symbol will appear.

Note that the block can now be dragged freely on the 30° plane (for example, using the *Drag Packed Components* button), which is not quite yet what we are looking for. In order to constrain the block motion along the slope face, we will align axes *A_1* in the block and *A_1* in the ground next.

Note that after using the *Drag* option to move the object, you will have to click the *Play* button ▶ at the right of the *Component Placement* dashboard to accept the configuration and continue the modeling process. Click the ✓ button to the right of the *Component Placement* dashboard to accept the definition.

Creating a Dynamic Simulation Model

From the pull-down menu, choose

Applications > Mechanism.

We will first define a spring and set the initial conditions for the simulation model.

Click the *Springs* shortcut button; a new set of selections will appear at the top of the *Graphics* window for defining the spring (Figure 3-7). Choose *Extension or compression spring* button (the first button from the left, should have been selected by default). Activate the *Select items* field by clicking it. Turn on the datum point display. Then, pick *PNT0* of the block. Drag the handle appeared in the *Graphics* window (Figure 3-8) and overlap it with *PNT1* (release the mouse button when *PNT1* is highlighted). A spring will appear, connecting *PNT0* (block) and *PNT1* (ground). However, the spring may not align properly with the slope face (or datum axis *A_1* of the ground).

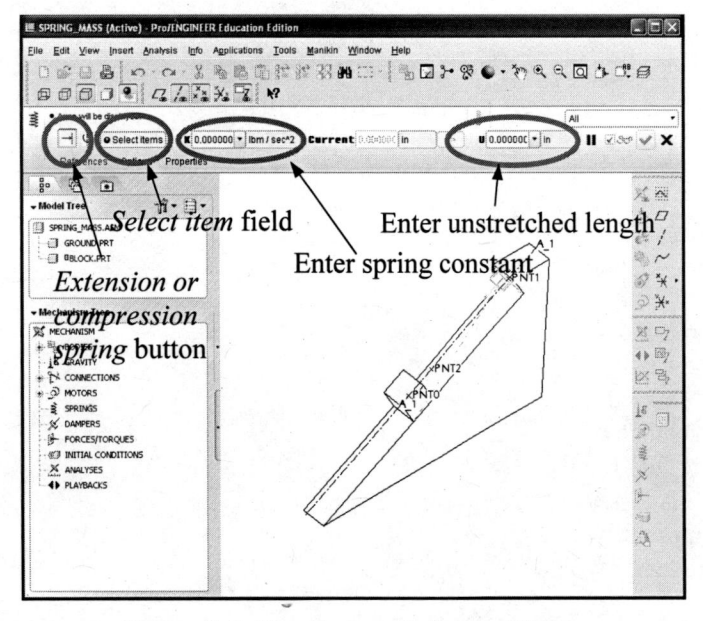

Figure 3-7 The *Spring Definition* Field

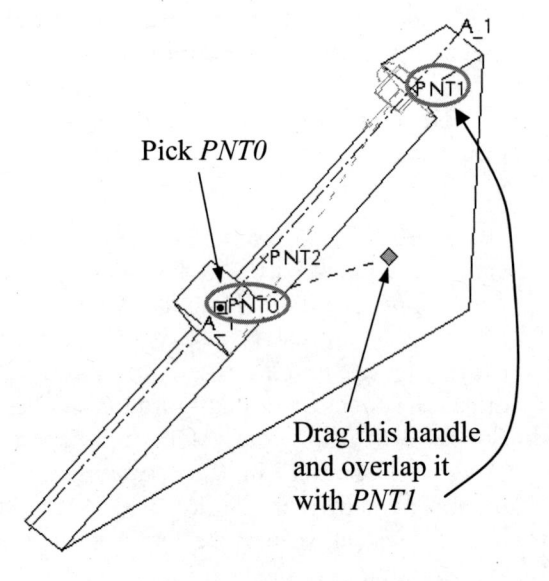

Figure 3-8 Defining the Spring

Lesson 3: A Spring-Mass System

Next, enter *20* for spring constant *K* and *3* for the unstretched spring length *U* from the text fields at the top of the *Graphics* window (see Figure 3-7). Note that the spring constant we enter is very small. The constant $K = 20$ $lb_m/sec^2 = 20/386$ $lb_f/in = 0.0518$ lb_f/in. It is a very soft spring. We expect to see a relatively small vibration frequency.

Note that you may adjust the spring diameter (only for visual effect) by clicking the *Options* button below the *Select item* field (Figure 3-9). Also, you may change the spring name by using the *Properties* button.

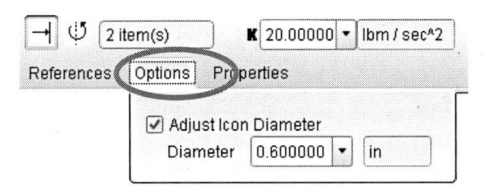

Figure 3-9 Adjust the Spring Diameter

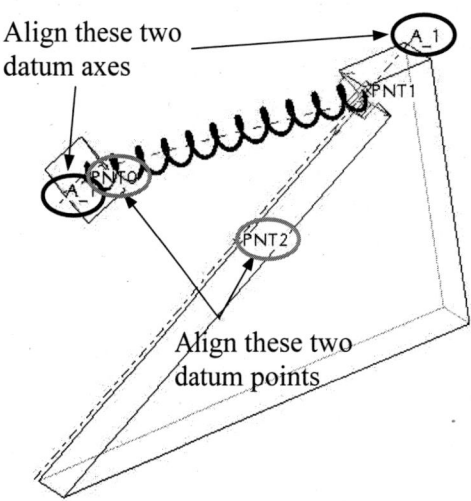

Figure 3-10 Align the Spring

Click the ✓ button on the right to accept the definition.

In order to properly align the block, we will use the *Drag* command to align the two *A_1* axes, as shown in Figure 3-10. We will also align two datum points, *PNT0* of the block and *PNT2* of the ground to set up the initial position for the block.

Click the *Drag Packed Components* button at the top of the *Graphics* window, and the *Drag* dialog box appears (Figure 3-11, similar to what we learned in *Lesson 2*). Click the *Constraints* tab, and choose the *Align Two Entities* button (first on the left). Choose two datum axes *A_1* (see Figure 3-10). The *block* should now be sitting on top of the slope face and the spring should align properly with the slope face.

Repeat the same process and pick two datum points, *PNT0* (block) and *PNT2* (ground) for aligning points. The block should be placed at its start position (see Figure 3-4), which is 4 in. from the top of the slope; i.e., the spring is stretched 1 in. from its unstretched length of 3 in.

Click the *Current Snapshots* button to create a snapshot *Snapshot1*, as shown in Figure 3-11.

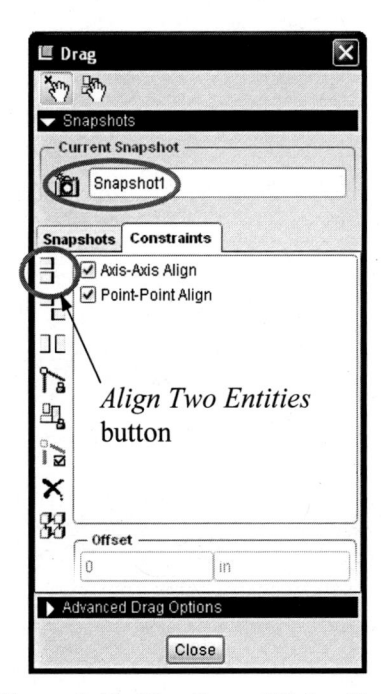

Figure 3-11 The *Drag* Dialog Box

Note that since the initial velocity is zero, we do not need to use the *Define Initial Conditions* button for any initial velocity. The motion model is now completely defined. We are ready to create and run a dynamic analysis.

Creating and Running a Dynamic Analysis

From the button list on the right, click the *Mechanism Analysis* shortcut button to define an analysis. In the *Analysis Definition* dialog box (Figure 3-12) appearing, leave the default name, *AnalysisDefinition1*, and enter:

Type: *Dynamic*
Duration: *3*
Frame Rate: *100*
Minimum Interval: *0.01*
Initial Configuration: *Current*

Click *Run*. The progress of the analysis is shown at the top of the *Graphics* window, and the block starts sliding back and forth along the slope. Click *OK* to save the analysis definition.

Saving and Reviewing Results

Click the *Replay* button on the right (the same steps discussed in *Lesson 2*) to bring up the *Playbacks* dialog box and repeat the motion animation. On the *Playbacks* dialog box, click the *Save* button to save the results as a *.pbk* file.

Note that we want to create a measure to monitor the position of the block. We will choose the center point *PNT0* of the block and magnitude of the point position for the measure. To do so, click the *Generate Measure Results of Analyses* shortcut button on the right.

Figure 3-12 The *Analysis Definition* Dialog Box

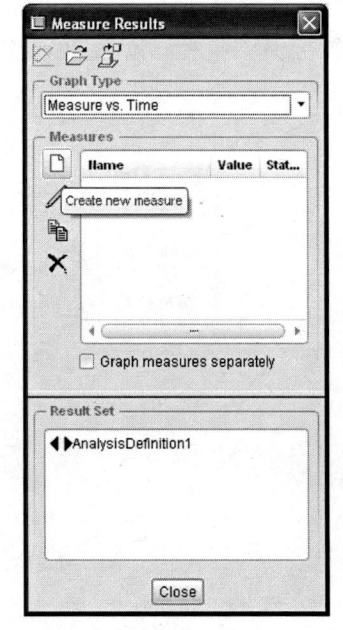

Figure 3-13 The *Measure Results* Dialog Box

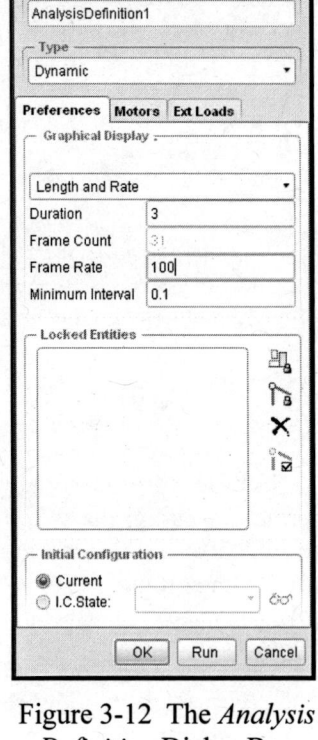

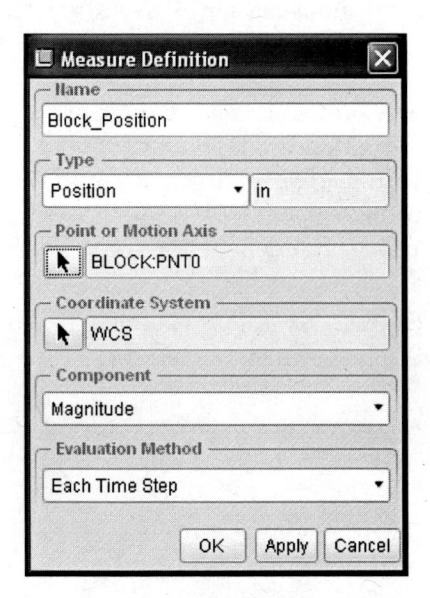

Figure 3-14 The *Measure Definition* Dialog Box

Lesson 3: A Spring-Mass System 3-7

In the *Measure Results* dialog box (Figure 3-13), click the *Create New Measure* button. The *Measure Definition* dialog box opens (Figure 3-14). Enter *Block_Position* for *Name*. Under *Type*, select *Position*. Select *PNT0* in the block part for *Point or Motion Axis*. Leave *WCS* as the *Coordinate System* (default). Choose *Magnitude* as the *Component* (default). Under *Evaluation Method*, leave *Each Time Step*. Click *OK* to accept the definition.

In the *Measure Results* dialog box (Figure 3-13) choose *AnalysisDefinition1* in the *Result Set* and click the *Graph* button on the top left corner to graph the measure.

The graph should be similar to that of Figure 3-15. Note that from the graph, the block will move along the slope face between 2 and 4 in. This is because the unstretched length of the spring is 3 in. and we stretched the spring 1 in. to start the motion. Also, it takes about 0.75 seconds to complete a cycle (for example, the time interval between peaks in Figure 3-15), which is large. This can be attributed to the fact that the spring is very soft (a very small spring constant was defined). We will carry out some calculations to verify these results. Before we do that, we will work on two more scenarios: with gravity and with the addition of an external force. Save your model before moving to the next scenario.

Figure 3-15 The *block* Position Graph

Scenario 2: With Gravity

We will add a gravitational acceleration and repeat the simulation. Do you expect to see any different results? Will the block move faster due to gravity?

Click the *Define Gravity* shortcut button on the right to bring up the *Gravity* dialog box (Figure 3-16, same as *Lesson 2*). Again, the default values of acceleration (386.088) and direction (0,−1,0) are what we need. No change is necessary. An arrow will appear in the *Graphics* window indicating the gravity.

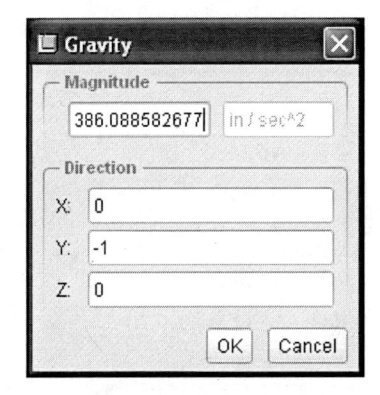

Figure 3-16 The *Gravity* Dialog Box

Simply click *OK* in the *Gravity* dialog box. You will need to activate the gravity when you define a dynamic analysis.

Before running the analysis again, we will move the block back to its initial position; i.e., aligning *PNT0* and *PNT2*. This can be done by imposing the snapshot *Snapshot1* we created earlier.

Click the *Drag Packed Components* button at the top of the *Graphics* window. In the *Drag* dialog box (Figure 3-17), the snapshot *Snapshot1* is listed. Choose *Snapshot1* and click the *Display* button (the first on the left). The *block* should be placed in the desired initial position. Close the *Drag* dialog box.

We will define a new dynamic analysis to include the gravity. Click the *Mechanism Analysis* shortcut button [icon] to define a new analysis. In the *Analysis Definition* dialog box, use the default name *AnalysisDefinition2*, enter the same parameters as those of *Scenario 1*. Choose the *Ext Loads* tab, select *Enable Gravity*, and click *Run* (see Figure 3-18).

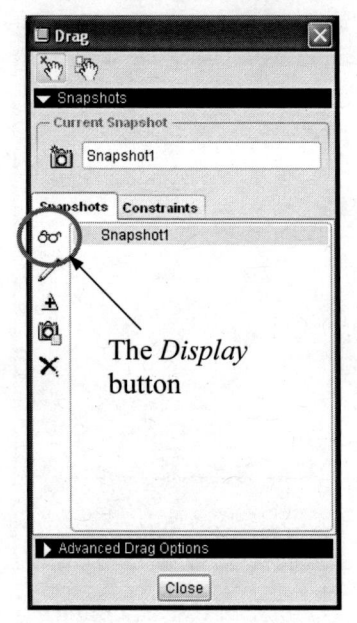

Figure 3-17 The *Drag* Dialog Box

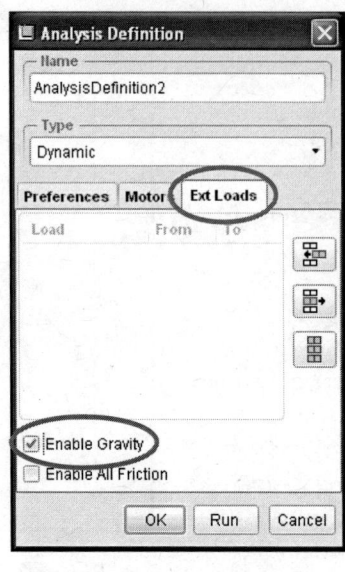

Figure 3-18 The *Analysis Definition* Dialog Box

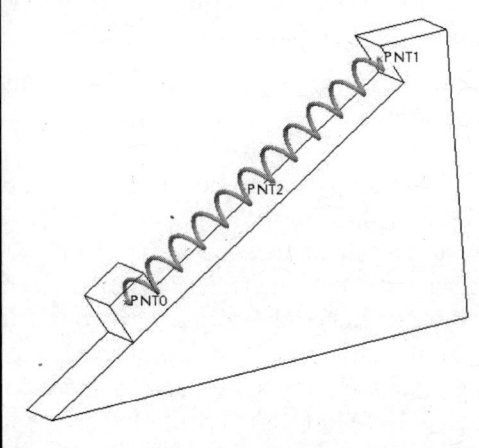

Figure 3-19 The *block* Motion of Scenario 2

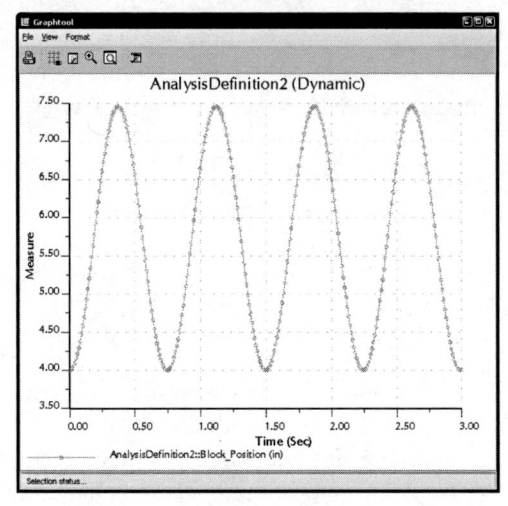

Figure 3-20 The *block* Position Graph of Scenario 2

The block will start moving. It will move further downward (see Figure 3-19) due to gravity. Click *OK* to save the analysis definition. Note that you may graph the position of the block. The graph should be like that of Figure 3-20. In case you see something different, you may need to re-set the unstretched length of the spring to 3.

Note that from the graph, the *block* will move along the slope between 4 and roughly 7.5 in. The vibration period is still about 0.75 seconds as it should be (why?). Save your model.

Scenario 3: With Gravity and External Force

In this scenario we will add an external force $p(t) = 10 \cos 2t$ at the center of the *block* in the downward direction along the slope. Note that the parameter in the cosine function of the external force must be converted from radian to degrees, as is assumed by *Mechanism Design*. Therefore, the force equation to enter becomes $p(t) = 10 \cos(2t \times 180/\pi)$; i.e., $10 \cos(114.59t)$.

Click the *Define Force/Torque* button [icon] or *Insert > Force/Torque* to access the *Force/Torque Definition* dialog box. In the *Force/Torque Definition* dialog box, enter *Force1* for *Name*, choose *PNT0* of the block from the *Graphics* window, and choose *User Defined* for the force function magnitude

Lesson 3: A Spring-Mass System 3-9

(default is *Constant*). Click the *Add expression* button (first on the right, see Figure 3-21), a function *t* will appear in the left cell of the first row under the *Expression*. Select the function *t*, and click the *Edit expression segment* button (3rd on the right). In the *Expression Definition* dialog box (Figure 3-22), enter *10*cos(114.59*t)*, enter *0* and *6.28* for the domain lower and upper limits, and click *OK*. As a result, the force will be applied for two complete cycles during the 6.28 second period. The expression and domain limits will appear in the *Force/Torque Definition* dialog box (Figure 3-21). In this case, we will also specify the analysis duration as 6.28 (seconds). Note that you may choose the buttons at the top of the *Expression Definition* dialog box (Figure 3-22) to see more predefined expressions in *Mechanism Design*.

Figure 3-21 The *Force/Torque Definition* Dialog Box

Figure 3-22 The *Expression Definition* Dialog Box

Add expression button

Edit expression segment button

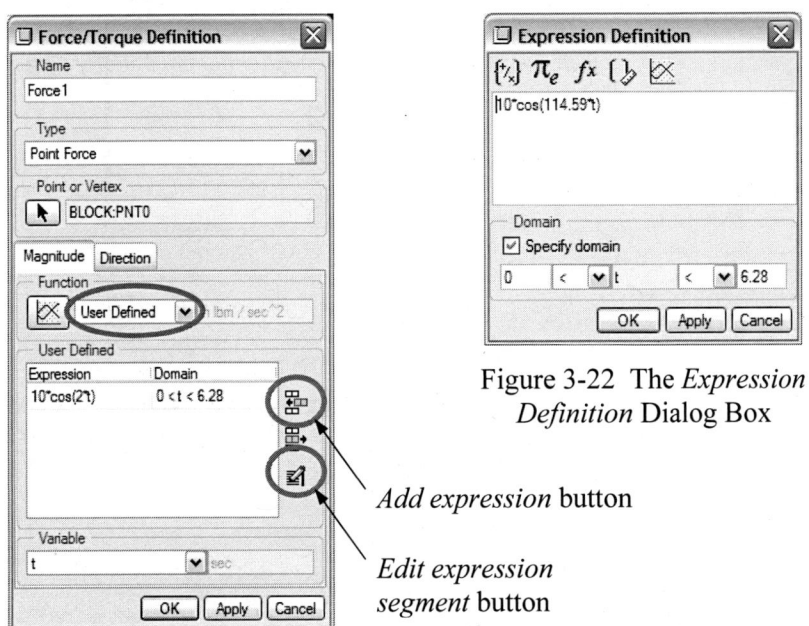

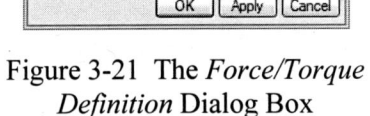

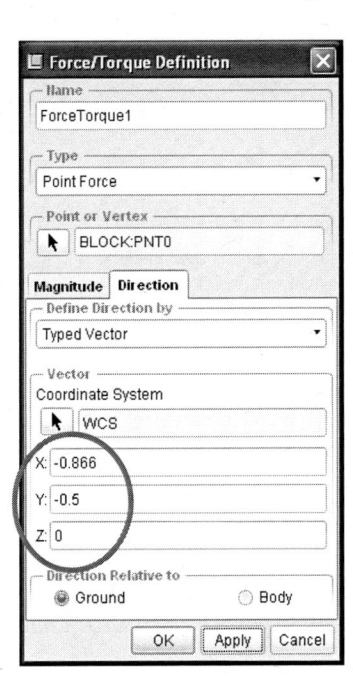

Figure 3-23 The *Direction* Tab in the *Force/Torque Definition* Dialog Box

Next, we will define the force direction; i.e., downward along the slope. Choose the *Direction* tab in the *Force/Torque Definition* dialog box (Figure 3-23); and enter *–0.866*, *–0.5*, and *0* for *X*, *Y*, and *Z*, respectively (these values define a unit vector along the 30° slope) and click *OK*. A force symbol will appear in the *Graphics* window, as shown in Figure 3-24.

Create a new dynamic analysis *AnalysisDefinition3* by entering *6.28* for *Duration* and *100* for *Frame Rate*. Choose the *Ext Loads* tab, and ensure *ForceTorque1* is listed under *Load* (Figure 3-25). Make sure the *Enable Gravity* is selected, and click *Run*.

The block will start moving. It will move further downward along the slope due to both the external force and gravity.

Note that you may graph the position of the block. The graph should be like that of Figure 3-26. From the graph, the block travels along the slope roughly 4.5 in., and the envelope of the motion amplitude varies. The result shows different patterns compared to those of *Scenarios 1* and *2*. Does the result make sense to you? Save your model. We will verify the simulation results next.

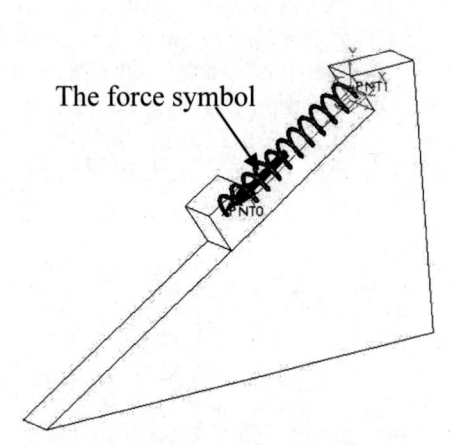

Figure 3-24 The Force Symbol

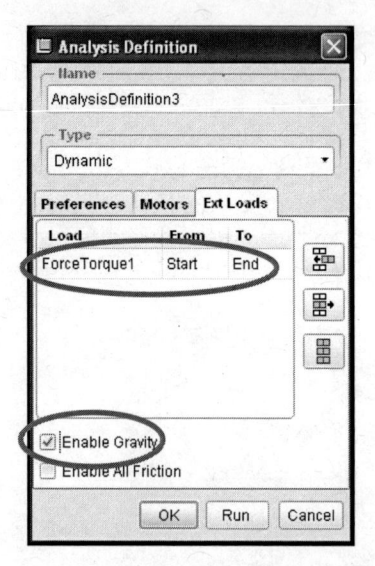

Figure 3-25 Force1 Listed in the Analysis Definition Dialog Box

3.4 Result Verifications

In this section, we will verify analysis results obtained from *Mechanism Design*.

There are two assumptions that we have to make in order to apply the particle dynamics theory to this spring-mass example:

(i) The block is of a concentrated mass, and
(ii) No friction is present between the block and the slope face of the ground part.

We will start with the case of *Scenario 2* for equation of motion (i.e., with gravity), and then solve for both *Scenarios 1* and *2*. Note that *Scenario 1* is simply a special case of *Scenario 2* where gravity is turned off.

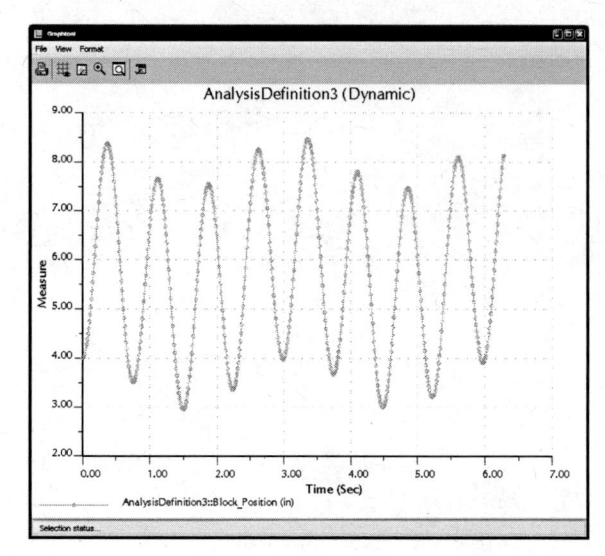

Figure 3-26 The Block Position Graph of *Scenario 3*

Equation of Motion: Scenarios 1 and 2

From the free-body diagram shown in Figure 3-27, applying Newton's Second Law and force equilibrium along the *X*-direction (i.e., the 30° slope), we have

$$\sum F_x = mg\sin\theta - k(x-U) = m\ddot{x} \qquad (3.1)$$

Therefore,

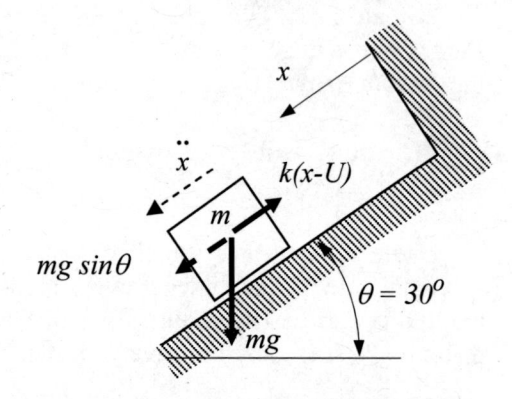

$$m\ddot{x} + k(x-U) = mg\sin\theta \qquad (3.2)$$

Figure 3-27 The Free-Body Diagram

Lesson 3: A Spring-Mass System

where m is the mass of the block, U is the unstretched length of the spring, x is the distance between the block and the top of the slope, measured from the top of the slope. The double dots on top of x represent the second derivative of x with respect to time. Rearrange Eq. 3.2, we have

$$m\ddot{x} + kx = mg\sin\theta + Uk \tag{3.3}$$

where the terms on the right hand side are constant.

This is a second-order ordinary differential equation. It is well known that the general solution of the differential equation is

$$x_g = A_1 \cos\omega_n t + A_2 \sin\omega_n t \tag{3.4}$$

where $\omega_n = \sqrt{\dfrac{k}{m}}$, and A_1 and A_2 are constants to be determined with initial conditions. Note that the mass of the steel block is 0.2828 lb$_m$. This can be obtained from *Pro/ENGINEER* by choosing, from the pull-down menu, *Analysis > Model > Mass Properties*. Therefore, $\omega_n = \sqrt{\dfrac{k}{m}} = \sqrt{\dfrac{20}{0.2828}} = 8.410$ rad/sec, and the natural frequency of the system is $f_n = \omega_n/2\pi = 1.338$ Hz. The period for a complete cycle $T = 1/f_n = 0.747$ seconds, which is close to the figure shown in all graphs (for example, see Figure 3-15).

The particular solution of Eq. 3.3 is

$$x_p = \frac{mg\sin\theta}{k} + U \tag{3.5}$$

Therefore the total solution is

$$x = x_g + x_p = A_1 \cos\omega_n t + A_2 \sin\omega_n t + \frac{mg\sin\theta}{k} + U \tag{3.6}$$

The initial conditions for the spring-mass system are $x(0) = x_0 = 4$ in., and $\dot{x}(0) = 0$ in/sec. Plugging the initial conditions into Eq. 3.6 (you will have to take the derivative of Eq. 3.6 as well), we have

$$A_1 = x_0 - \left(\frac{mg\sin\theta}{k} + U\right), \text{ and}$$

$$A_2 = 0.$$

Hence, the overall solution is

$$x = \left(x_0 - \frac{mg\sin\theta}{k} - U\right)\cos\omega_n t + \frac{mg\sin\theta}{k} + U \tag{3.7}$$

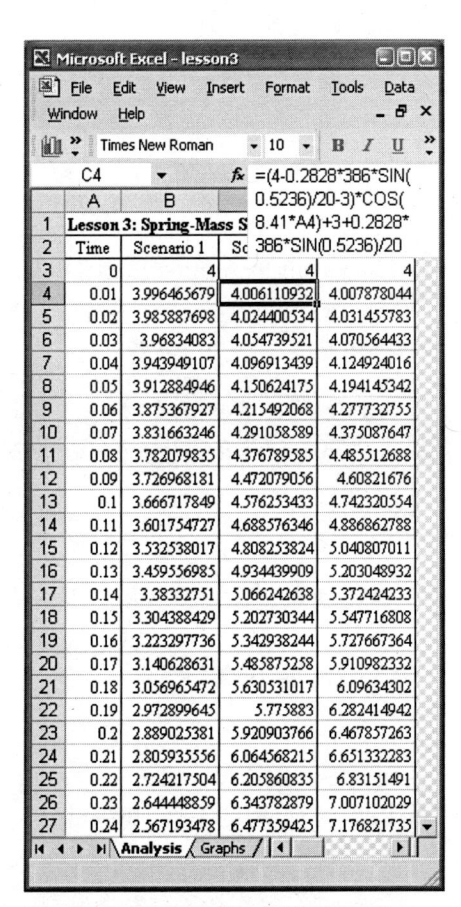

Figure 3-28 The *Excel* Spreadsheet

Note that Eq. 3.6 gives results for *Scenario 2*. For *Scenario 1*, simply set gravity g to *0*; i.e.,

$$x = (x_0 - U)\cos\omega_n t + U \tag{3.8}$$

Equations 3.7 and 3.8 can be implemented into *Microsoft Excel* shown in Figure 3-28.

Note that Columns B and C in the spreadsheet show the results of Eqs. 3.8 and 3.7, respectively. Data in Column B are without gravity; i.e., Eq. 3.8 representing *Scenario 1*. Column C is for Eq. 3.7; i.e., *Scenario 2*.

Data in these two columns are graphed in Figures 3-29 and 3-30, respectively. Comparing Figures 3-29 and 3-30 with Figures 3-15 and 3-20, the results obtained from theory and *Mechanism Design* agree very well, which means the motion model has been properly defined, and *Mechanism Design* gives us good results.

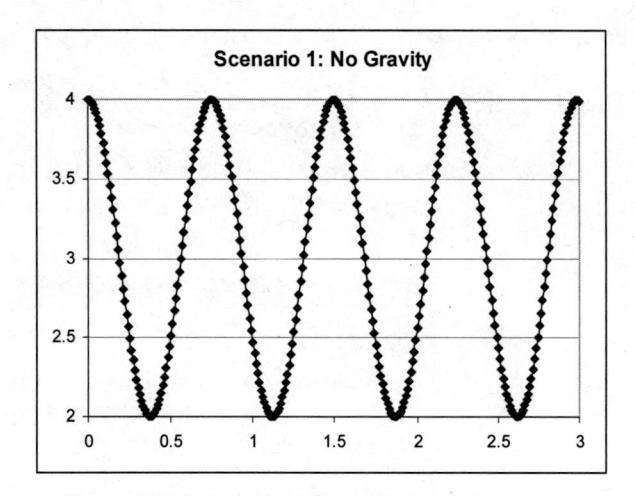

Figure 3-29 Solution from Theory: *Scenario 1*

Figure 3-30 Solution from Theory: *Scenario 2*

Equation of Motion: Scenario 3

From the free-body diagram shown in Figure 3-27, for force equilibrium of *Scenario 3*, we must include the force $p = 10 \cos(2t)$ along the *X*-direction; i.e.,

$$m\ddot{x} + k(x - U) = mg\sin\theta + f_0 \cos(\omega t) \tag{3.9}$$

where $f_0 = 10$ lb$_m$ in/sec^2 and $\omega = 2$ rad/sec. Rearrange Eq. 3.9, we have

$$m\ddot{x} + kx = mg\sin\theta + Uk + f_0 \cos(\omega t) \tag{3.10}$$

where the right-hand side consists of constant and time-dependent terms. For the constant term, the particular solution is identical to the previous case; i.e., Eq. 3.5. For the time-dependent term; i.e., $p = f_0 \cos(\omega t)$, the particular solution is

$$x_{p_2} = \frac{f_0}{k - \omega^2 m} \cos\omega t \tag{3.11}$$

Lesson 3: A Spring-Mass System

Therefore, the overall solution of Eq. 3.9 is

$$x = x_g + x_p + x_{p_2} = A_1 \cos\omega_n t + A_2 \sin\omega_n t + \frac{mg\sin\theta}{k} + U + \frac{f_0}{k-\omega^2 m}\cos\omega t \qquad (3.12)$$

Plugging the initial conditions into the solution, we have

$$A_1 = x_0 - \left(\frac{mg\sin\theta}{k} + U + \frac{f_0}{k-\omega^2 m}\right), \text{ and } A_2 = 0.$$

Hence, the complete solution is

$$\begin{aligned}
x &= \left(x_0 - \frac{mg\sin\theta}{k} - U - \frac{f_0}{k-\omega^2 m}\right)\cos\omega_n t + \frac{mg\sin\theta}{k} + U + \frac{f_0}{k-\omega^2 m}\cos\omega t \\
&= \left[\left(x_0 - \frac{mg\sin\theta}{k} - U\right)\cos\omega_n t + \frac{mg\sin\theta}{k} + U\right] + \frac{f_0}{k-\omega^2 m}(\cos\omega t - \cos\omega_n t)
\end{aligned} \qquad (3.13)$$

Note that terms grouped in the first bracket of Eq. 3.13 are identical to those of Eq. 3.7; i.e., *Scenario 2*. The second term of Eq. 3.13 graphed in Figure 3-31 represents the contribution of the external force *p(t)* to the block motion. The graph shows that the amplitude of the block vibration should vary in time.

The overall solution of *Scenario 3*; i.e., Eq. 3.13, is a combination of graphs shown in Figures 3-30 and 3-31. In fact, Eq. 3.13 has been implemented in Column C of the spreadsheet. The data are graphed in Figure 3-32. As expected, the amplitude of the vibration is not constant. The vibration amplitude depends on time.

Comparing Figure 3-32 with Figure 3-26, the results obtained from theory and *Mechanism Design* are identical. Note that the spreadsheet shown in Figure 3-29 can be found at the publisher's website (filename: *lesson3.xls*).

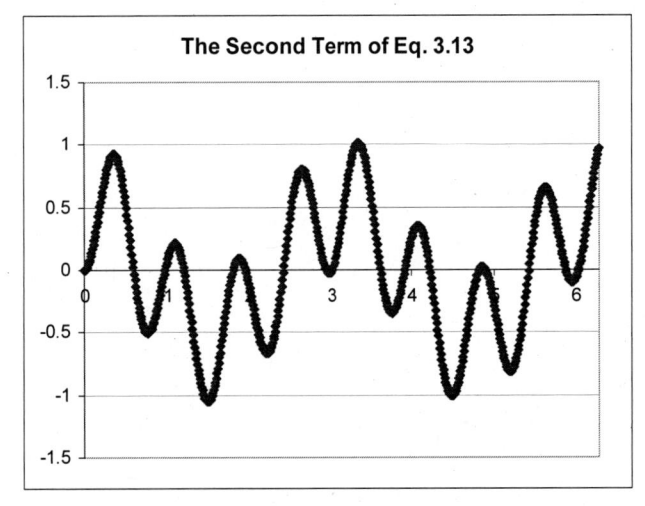

Figure 3-31 Graph of the Second Term of Eq. 3.13

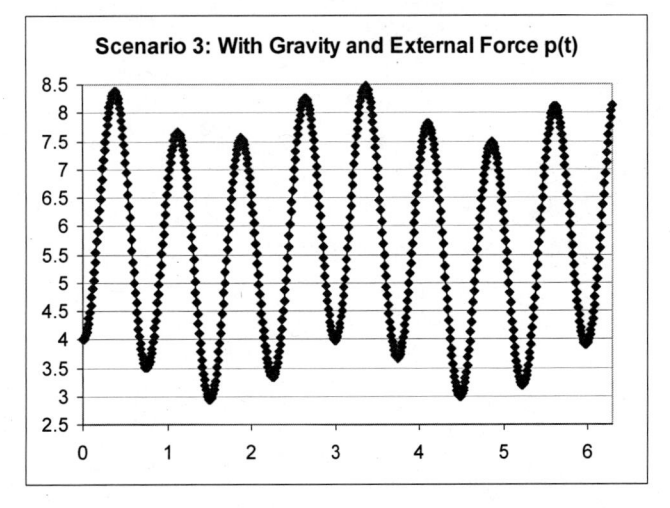

Figure 3-32 Solution from Theory: *Scenario 3*

Exercises:

1. Create and run a static analysis for Scenario 2. Where will the block be resting on the slope face due to gravity? Formulate a force equilibrium equation to solve for the resting position for the block. Is your result consistent with that of *Mechanism Design*?

2. Show that Eq. 3.13 is the correct solution of *Scenario 3* governed by Eq. 3.9 by simply plugging Eq. 3.13 into Eq. 3.9.

3. Repeat the *Scenario 3* of this lesson, except changing the external force to *p(t) = 10 cos 8.41t* lb_m in/sec^2. Will this external force change the vibration amplitude of the system? Can you simulate this resonance scenario in *Mechanism Design*?

4. Add a damper with damping coefficient *C* = 1 lb_m/sec and repeat the *Scenario 1* simulation using *Mechanism Design*.

    (i) Calculate the natural frequency of the system and compare your calculation with that of *Mechanism Design*.

    (ii) Derive and solve the equations that describe the position and velocity of the mass. Compare your solutions with those obtained from *Mechanism Design*.

Lesson 4: A Simple Pendulum

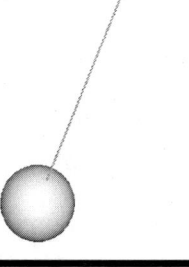

4.1 Overview of the Lesson

In this lesson, we will create a simple pendulum model using *Mechanism Design*. The pendulum will be released from a position slightly off the vertical line. The pendulum will then rotate freely due to gravity. In this lesson, we will learn how to create the pendulum motion model, run a dynamic analysis, and visualize the analysis results. The dynamic analysis results of the simple pendulum example can be verified easily using particle dynamics theory. Similar to *Lessons 2* and *3*, we will formulate the equation of motion; calculate the angular position, velocity, and acceleration of the pendulum; and compare our calculations with results obtained from *Mechanism Design*.

4.2 The Simple Pendulum Example

Physical Model

The physical model of the pendulum is composed of a sphere and a rod rigidly connected, as shown in Figure 4-1. The radius of the sphere is 10 mm. The length and radius of the thin rod are 90 mm and 0.5 mm, respectively. The top of the rod is connected to the wall with a pin joint. This pin joint allows the pendulum to rotate. The rod and sphere are made of aluminum and steel, respectively. Note that from the *Pro/ENGINEER* material library the *AL2014* and *STEEL* material types have been selected for the rod and sphere, respectively. The *mmNs* system is selected for this example (millimeter for length, Newton for force, and second for time). In the *mmNs* unit system, the gravitational acceleration is 9,806 mm/sec^2.

The pendulum will be released from an angular position of 10 degrees from the vertical position along the pin joint. The rotation angle is intentionally kept small so that the particle dynamics theory can be applied to verify the simulation result.

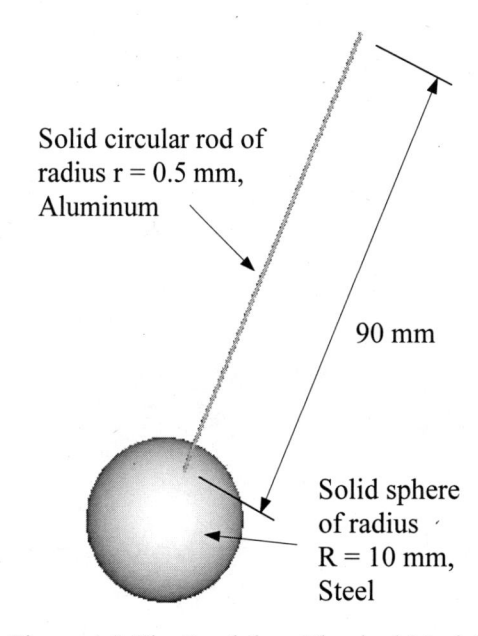

Figure 4-1 The Pendulum Physical Model

In this lesson, *Pro/ENGINEER* parts of the pendulum example have been created for you. A partial assembly model with datum features required for this lesson has also been created. You can find the model files at publisher's web site (http://www.schroff1.com/). As mentioned in *Lesson 1*, datum features are extremely important in creating a successful motion model. In this lesson, we will use datum axis and datum points to define the pin joint. An additional datum axis will be used for defining the initial position of the pendulum. In this lesson, no solid part will be used for ground (unlike what we did in *Lesson 3*).

The assembly datum features will be grouped for the ground body. Again, the datum coordinate system of the root assembly will be converted into the World Coordinate System (*WCS*) for the motion model.

Pro/ENGINEER Parts and Assembly

The pendulum assembly consists of two parts, rod (*rod.prt*) and sphere (*sphere.prt*), as well as one assembly (*pendulum_partial.asm*) with only datum features. Note that you will need to open this assembly and assemble rod and sphere for a complete assembly. The exploded views shown in Figure 4-2 are from the complete assembly. They serve the purpose of illustration. In this lesson we will learn to create two new joints: the pin joint, and the rigid joint. A pin joint allows rotation in one direction only. A rigid joint fixes all relative motion between parts. Obviously, a rigid joint will be defined between the rod and the sphere, and the pin joint will connect the top of the rod with the ground, allowing rotational motion along the *Y*-direction of the assembly datum coordinate system *ASM_DEF_CSYS* (Figure 4-2b), which is *WCS*.

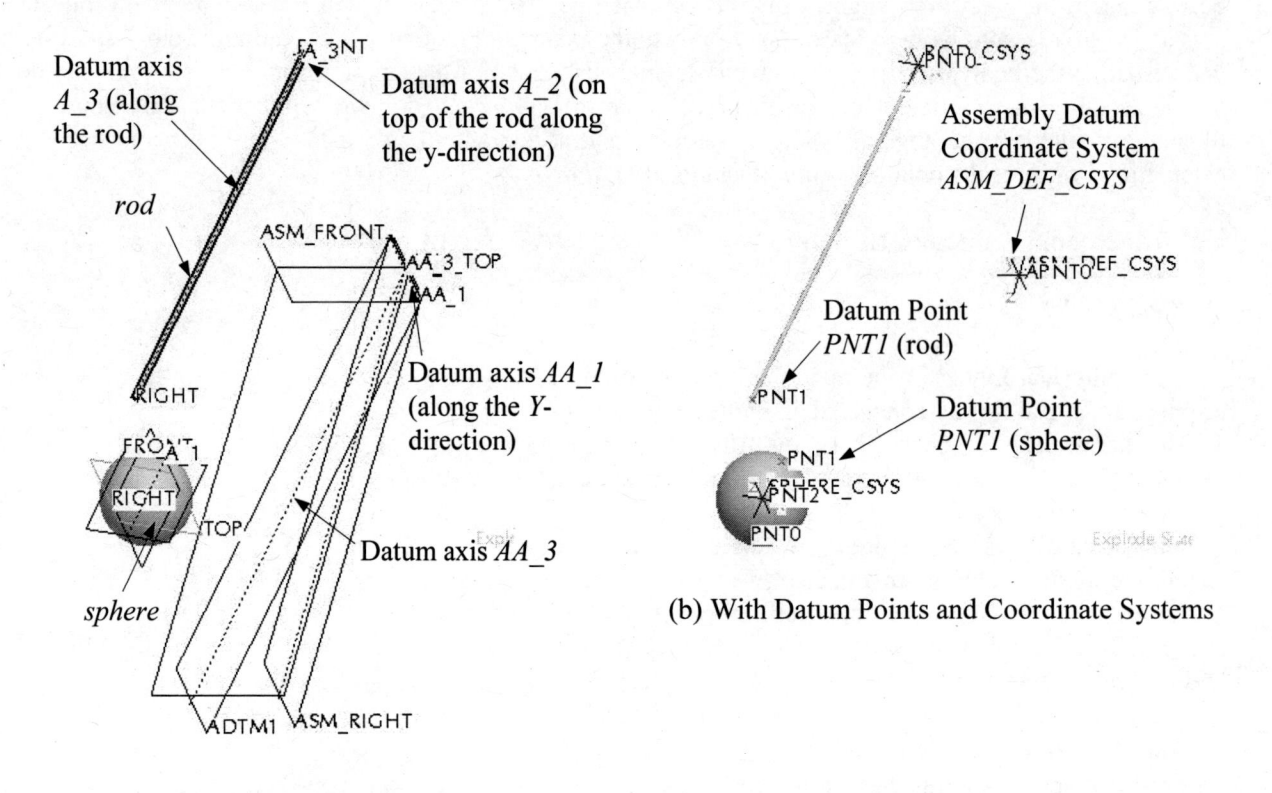

(a) With Datum Planes and Axes

(b) With Datum Points and Coordinate Systems

Figure 4-2 The Pendulum Assembly (Exploded View)

As shown in Figure 4-2a, the assembly *pendulum_partial.asm* consists of four datum planes. Note that the datum plane *ADTM1* was created by rotating *ASM_RIGHT* along the axis *AA_1* in a 10-degree angle, where the datum axis *AA_3* resides. The datum axis *AA_3* will be used to align with the datum axis *A_3* of the rod for defining the initial position of the pendulum. The datum axis *AA_1* aligns with the *Y*-axis of the assembly datum coordinate system (*ASM_DEF_CSYS*). Note that the datum axis *AA_1* and *A_2* of the rod will be aligned to define the rotational direction of the pin joint. In addition, datum points *APNT0* and *PNT0* (rod) are used to restrain the translation of the pin joint. The rigid joint will be defined by aligning datum axes *A_1* of the sphere with *A_3* of the rod, and the datum points *PNT1* of the rod and *PNT1* of the sphere.

Lesson 4: A Simple Pendulum   4-3

You may access the pendulum assembly by:

- Copying the *lesson4* folder that you downloaded from the publisher's web site to your hard drive;
- Starting *Pro/ENGINEER* and changing the working directory to *lesson4* folder; and
- Opening the pendulum assembly by choosing, from the pull-down menu, *File > Open*.

Figure 4-3 The Partial Assembly to Start With

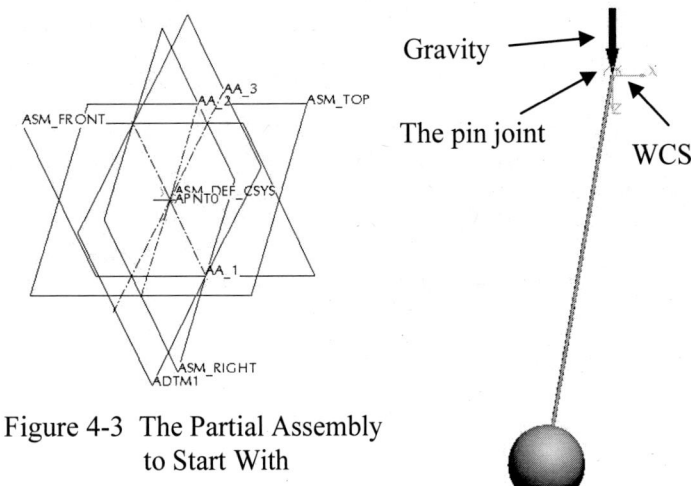

Figure 4-4 The Simulation Model

In the file open dialog box, choose *pendulum_partial.asm*. You should see, in the *Graphics* window, the partial pendulum assembly similar to the one shown in Figure 4-3.

Motion Model

As discussed, the rod and the sphere are connected by a rigid joint. Therefore, there is only one moveable body, which is free to rotate along the *Y*-direction due to gravity. Note that the gravity is pointing in the positive *Z*-direction. A complete view of the dynamic simulation model is given in Figure 4-4 shown in the *TOP* view (one of the saved views in the *Pro/ENGINEER* model). Friction between the pendulum and the ground is assumed zero.

4.3 Using *Mechanism Design*

Creating a Complete Pendulum Assembly

Start *Pro/ENGINEER*, set working directory, and open the assembly model: *pendulum_partial.asm* as discussed. Before you proceed further, you may want to make sure that the unit system is properly chosen for the parts and assembly. Check the units by choosing from the pull-down menu

File > Properties.

In the *Model Properties* dialog box, *millimeter Newton Second (mmNs)* is listed, as shown in Figure 4-5).

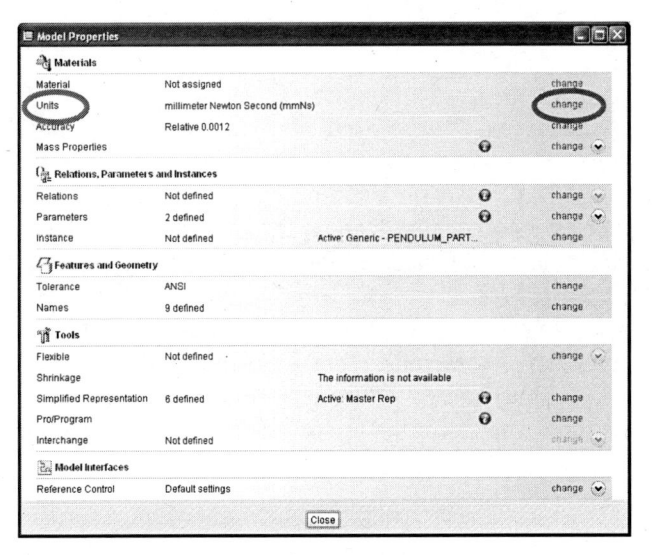

Figure 4-5

If this is not the case, click *change* for *Units* (Figure 4-5). The *Units Manager* dialog box will appear (Figure 4-6).

In the *Units Manager* dialog box, choose *millimeter Newton Second (mmNs)*, then click the *Set* push button.

In the *Changing Model Units* dialog box appearing (Figure 4-7), choose:

Interpret dimensions (for example 1" becomes 1mm), then click *OK*. The red arrow should point to the unit system that you intend to use, as shown in Figure 4-6. Close the *Units Manager* dialog box, and then the *Model Properties* dialog box. You may want to open individual parts and check on their units before you proceed.

Figure 4-6 *Units Manager* Dialog Box

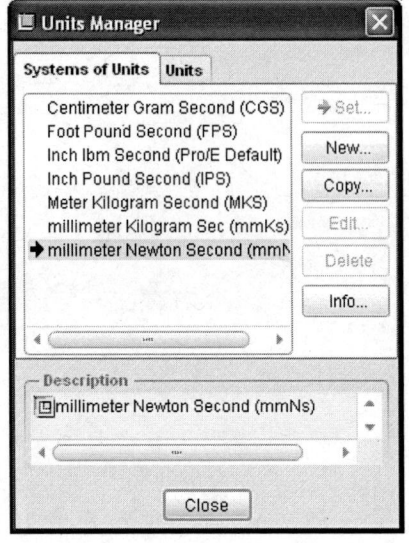

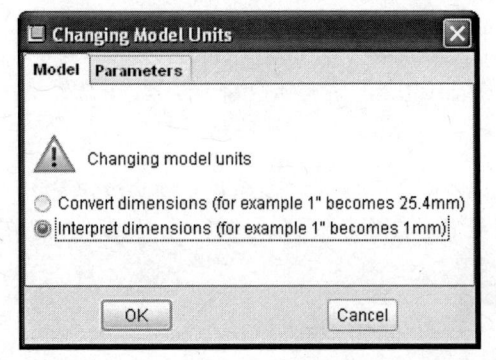

Figure 4-7 *Changing Model Units* Dialog Box

Now, we are ready to bring in the rod. Before we do that, keep in mind that we will define a pin joint by aligning *AA_1* (assembly) with *A_2* (rod) and *APNT0* (assembly) with *PNT0* (rod). Click the *Add component* shortcut button on the right of the *Graphics* window and choose *rod.prt*. As soon as the rod appears, *Pro/ENGINEER* assumes a configuration like the one shown in Figure 4-8a (you may see a different configuration), in which the datum features we are looking for are not quite visible. You may want to turn off the datum plane and the datum coordinate system display, and move the rod away from the assembly datum feature, for example, to the location similar to the one shown in Figure 4-8b. Zoom in the area as indicated in Figure 4-8b. Stay with the default view orientation for the time being.

In the *Component Placement* dashboard (upper left) choose the *Pin* joint (from *User Defined)*, and pick *AA_1* (assembly) and *A_2* (rod) for defining the rotational axis of the pin joint, then pick *APNT0* (assembly) and *PNT0* (rod) to restrain the translational movement of the rod. You should see a pin joint symbol appears at the top of the rod like that of Figure 4-9.

Click the ✓ button to the right of the *Component Placement* dashboard to accept the definition.

Next, we will bring in the sphere and define a rigid joint to "glue" it to the end face of the rod. We will align axes *A_1* (rod) with *A_1* (sphere) and *PNT1* (rod) with *PNT1* (sphere).

Click the *Add component* button and choose *sphere.prt*. In the *Component Placement* dashboard choose *Rigid* (from *User Defined*), and pick *A_1* (rod) and *A_1* (sphere), then pick *PNT1* (rod) and *PNT1* (sphere). Note that no rigid joint symbol will be shown. The joint status (middle of the *Component*

Lesson 4: A Simple Pendulum 4-5

Placement dashboard) should be *Partially Constrained*. This is fine since the only free degree of freedom between the rod and the sphere is the rotation along the common axis (*A_1* axes in rod and sphere, respectively). Click the ✓ button at right of the *Component Placement* dashboard to accept the definition.

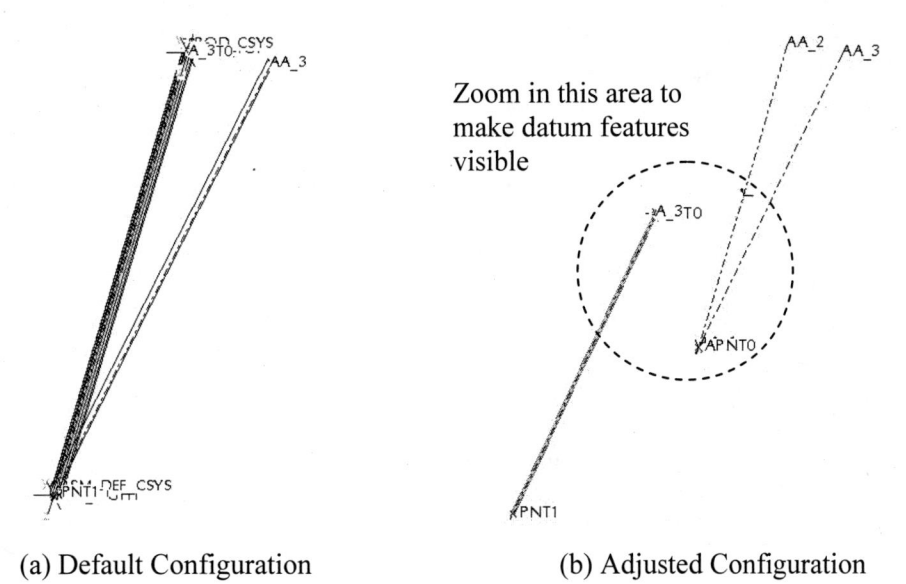

(a) Default Configuration   (b) Adjusted Configuration

Figure 4-8 Screen Captures of Rod Brought into Assembly

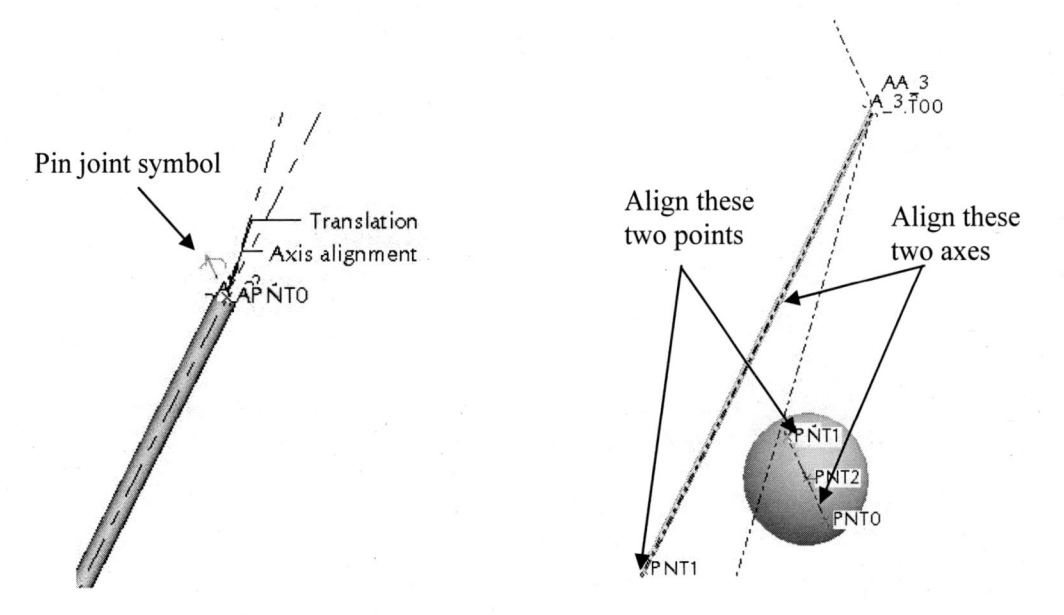

Figure 4-9 Pin Joint Defined for Rod   Figure 4-10 Defining a Rigid Joint

Creating a Dynamic Simulation Model

We are now ready to enter *Mechanism Design*. From the pull-down menu, choose

Applications > Mechanism

We will define the gravitational acceleration and orient the rod to its initial configuration.

A_1 of Click the *Define Gravity* shortcut button on the right. In the *Gravity* dialog box, the default value of acceleration (386.088) and default direction (0,0,1) appear. Keep the direction, change the *Magnitude* to 9806, then click *OK*.

Click the *Drag Packed Components* button at the top of the *Graphics* window, and the *Drag* dialog box appears (same as previous lessons). Click the *Constraints* tab, and choose the *Align Two Entities* button (first on the left). Pick datum axes *A_1* of rod (or *A_1* of sphere) and *AA_3* (assembly). The pendulum should now align with the inclined datum axes *AA_3* that is 10 degree rotated from the vertical axes *AA_2* (or Z-direction). Click the *Current Snapshots* button to create a snapshot (*Snapshot1*). You may want to choose the *TOP* view from the saved views list (click the Sa*ved View List* button at the top of the *Graphics* window) to see the pendulum model similar to that of Figure 4-11.

Creating and Running a Dynamic Analysis

Similar to previous lessons, we will create a dynamic simulation. Click the *Mechanism Analysis* shortcut button . In the *Analysis Definition* dialog box, select *Dynamic* for *Type*. Leave the default name, *AnalysisDefinition1*. Enter:

Duration: *1.5*
Frame Rate: *100*
Minimum Interval: *0.01*

Click the *Ext. Loads* tab, click *Enable Gravity*, and then click *Run*. You should see the pendulum start swinging back and forth along the pin joint in the *Graphics* window. Click *OK* to close the *Analysis Definition* dialog box.

Saving and Reviewing Results

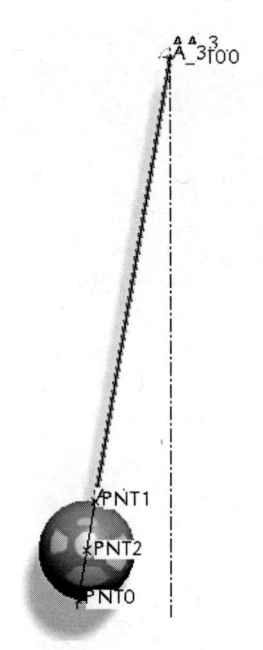

Figure 4-11 The Pendulum Model

Click the *Replay* button on the right (the same steps discussed in previous lessons) to bring up the *Playbacks* dialog box and repeat the motion animation. In the *Playbacks* dialog box, click the *Save* button to save the results as a *.pbk* file.

Note that we want to create a measure to monitor the position, velocity, and acceleration of the pendulum. We will choose the rotating axis of the pin joint for the measure. To do so, click the *Generate Measure Results of Analyses* button . In the *Measure Results* dialog box, click the *Create New Measure* button . The *Measure Definition* dialog box opens (Figure 4-12). Enter *angular_position* for *Name*. Under *Type*, select *Position*. Pick the pin joint symbol from the *Graphics* window for *Motion Axis*. A double arrow symbol will appear (Figure 4-13), indicating that the rotational axis is selected. Note that the axis name may be different from what was listed in Figure 4-12. Leave *WCS* as the *Coordinate System* (default). Under *Evaluation Method*, leave *Each Time Step*. Click *OK* to accept the definition.

Lesson 4: A Simple Pendulum

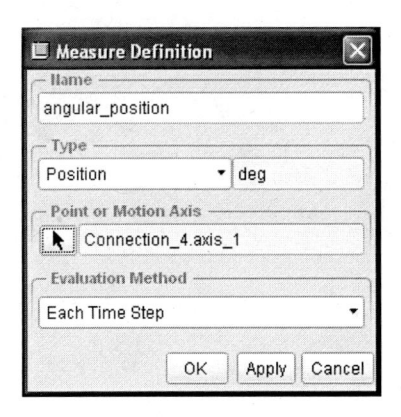

Figure 4-12 The *Measure Definition* Dialog Box

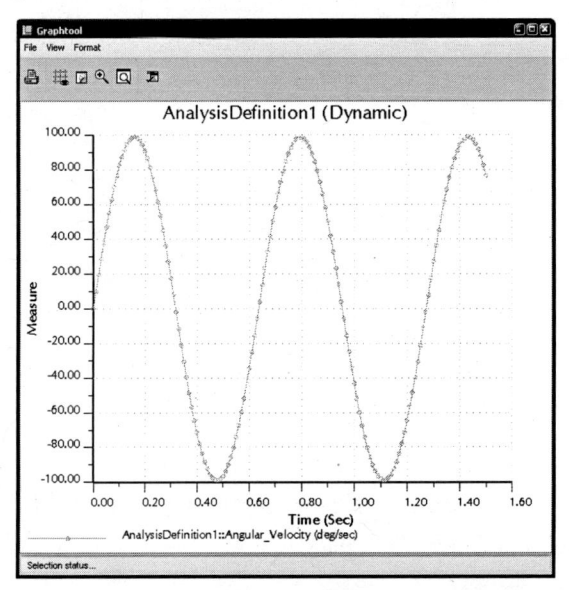

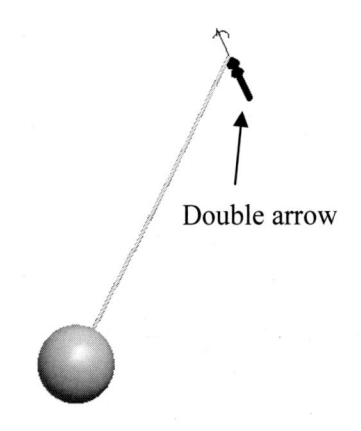

Figure 4-13 The Double Arrow Symbol

In the *Measure Results* dialog box choose *AnalysisDefinition1* in the *Result Set* and click the *Graph* button at the top left corner to graph the measure. The graph should be similar to that of Figure 4-14, which is a sinusoidal function with amplitude between −10 and 10 degrees, as expected.

You may repeat the same steps to define angular velocity and acceleration measures for the pendulum (define the measures at the motion axis; i.e., the rotation axis of the pin joint). You should see graphs of the angular velocity and acceleration similar to those of Figures 4-15 and 4-16. Note that in this example the counterclockwise direction is positive as expected.

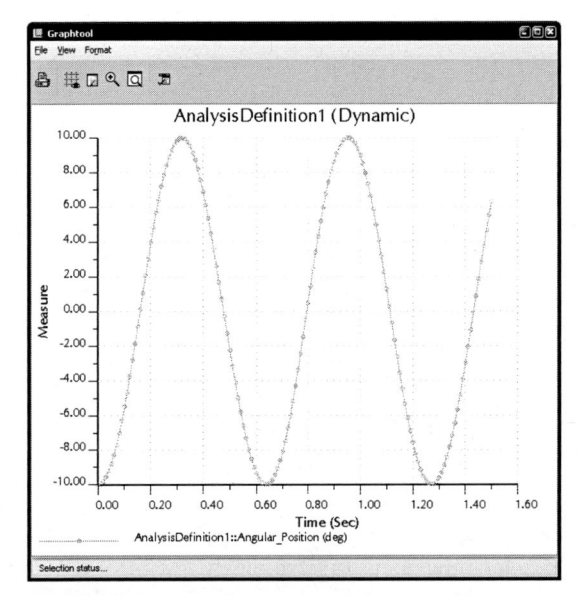

Figure 4-14 Angular Position of the Pendulum

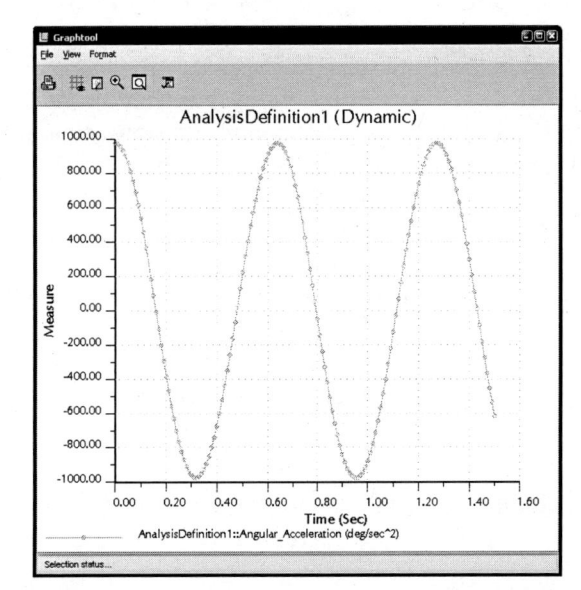

Figure 4-15 Angular Velocity of the Pendulum

Figure 4-16 Angular Acceleration of the Pendulum

Create Additional Datum Point for Displaying Results

We want to also display the velocity magnitude at the rod mass center. Since there is no reference point (datum point) at the rod mass center, we will have to first create a datum point for rod. The datum point will be created in the rod, along the axis *A_1* 45 mm from the top face of the rod (which is the *FRONT* datum plane, see Figure 4-17).

To create a datum point, we will have to open the rod part model. The rod part model will be opened in a different window.

To insert a datum point choose from the pull-down menu (you may also choose the shortcut button on the right of the *Graphics* window),

Insert > Model Datum > Point > Point.

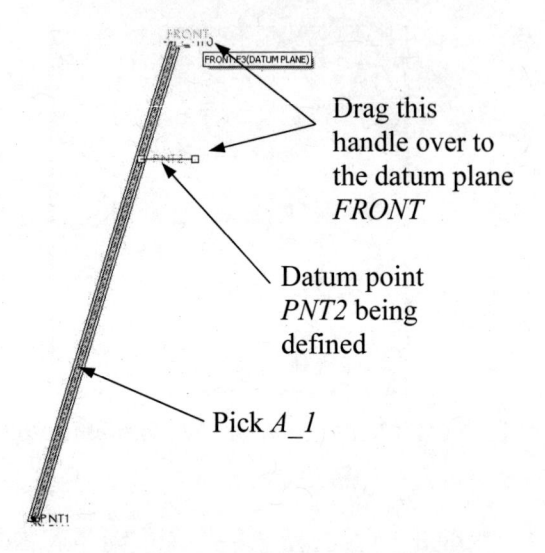

Figure 4-17 Creating New Datum Point

The *Datum Point* dialog box will appear (see Figure 4-18) where the *References* field is active and waiting for you to make selection. Pick datum axis *A_1* in rod. A temporary datum point *PNT2* will appear in the rod with one handle (small square box) aligning with the axis (see Figure 4-17), indicating that the datum point will stay on the axis.

In the *Datum Point* dialog box (Figure 4-18), the selected datum axis *A_1* will appear in the *References* field. Drag the dangling handle toward the datum plane on top; i.e., *FRONT*, until the datum plane label is highlighted, as shown in Figure 4-17. Then, release the mouse button. A dimension will appear in the rod indicating the distance of *PNT2* to the reference *FRONT*. Also in the *Datum Point* dialog box (Figure 4-18), an offset value appears with a number consistent to the dimension value in the *Graphics* window.

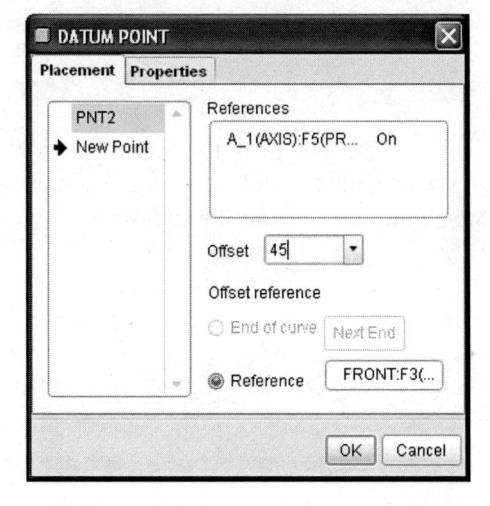

Figure 4-18 The *Datum Point* Dialog Box

Change the *Offset* value to 45, and click *OK*. The datum point *PNT2* is created. Be sure to turn on the datum point display to see the datum point. Save the rod model and close the rod model window. Back to the pendulum model, you should see that the newly created datum point *PNT2* appears in the rod.

Since there is no analysis result recorded for this new datum point, we will have to run the analysis again to generate analysis data for the datum point. Note that it is better to create datum points before the dynamic analysis to ensure you have complete results the first time.

Before you rerun the analysis, be sure to reset the configuration using the snapshot *Snapshot1* saved earlier, where the axis *A_1* of the rod is aligned with *AA_3*. Re-run the analysis

Lesson 4: A Simple Pendulum

After rerunning the analysis, define a new measure at *PNT2*. In the *Measure Definition* dialog box (Figure 4-19), enter *rod_center_pos* for *Name*, pick *PNT2* from the *Graphics* window, and leave everything else as default. Click *OK*. Note that the *Component* field is left as *Magnitude*. If you graph this measure, what do you expect to see? (A straight line? Why?)

Choose the *rod_center_pos* measure from the *Measure Results* dialog box (Figure 4-20), and click the *Edit* button (right below the *New* on the left). In the *Measure Definition* dialog box, choose *X-component* in the *Component* field (that is, the horizontal direction), and click *OK*. Graph the measure. You should see a sinusoidal curve similar to that of Figure 4-21.

Note that the pendulum is initially positioned to the left of the vertical axis. Therefore, the *X*-position of *PNT2* in the rod is on the negative side of the *X*-coordinate of the *WCS* (*ASM_DEF_CSYS*). The *X*-position of *PNT2* will vary between roughly −8 and 8 mm, as shown in Figure 4-21.

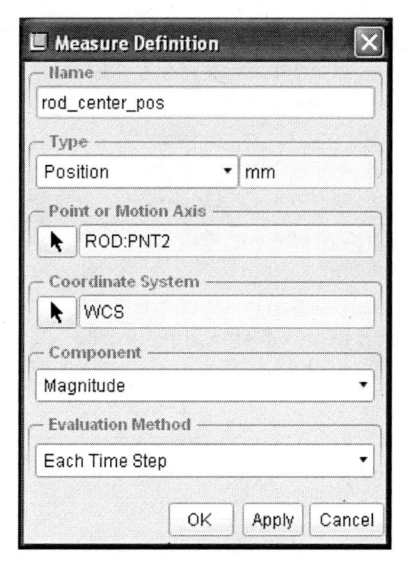

Figure 4-19 The *Measure Definition* Dialog Box

Figure 4-20 *Measure Results* Dialog Box

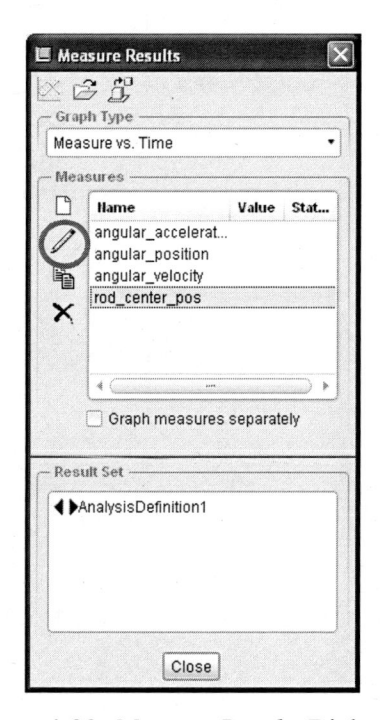

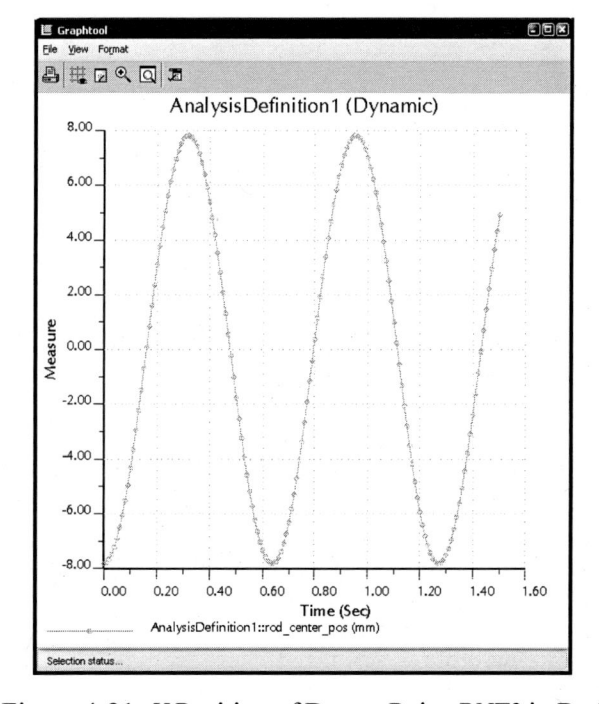

Figure 4-21 *X*-Position of Datum Point *PNT2* in Rod

4.4 Result Verifications

In this section, we will verify the analysis results obtained from *Mechanism Design* using particle dynamics theory.

There are four assumptions that we have to make in order to apply the particle dynamics theory to this simple pendulum problem:

(i)   Mass of the rod is negligible (this is why we chose *AL2014* for rod and *STEEL* for sphere),
(ii) The sphere is of a concentrated mass,
(iii) Rotation angle is small (remember the initial conditions we defined?), and
(iv) No friction is present.

The pendulum model has been created to comply with these assumptions as much as possible. We expect that the particle dynamics theory will give us results close to those obtained through simulation. Two approaches will be presented to formulate the equations of motion for the pendulum: energy conservation and Newton's law.

Energy Conservation

Referring to Figure 4-22, the kinetic energy and potential energy of the pendulum can be written, respectively, as

$$T = \frac{1}{2} J \dot{\theta}^2 \qquad (4.1)$$

where J is the polar moment of inertia, i.e., $J = m\ell^2$;

and

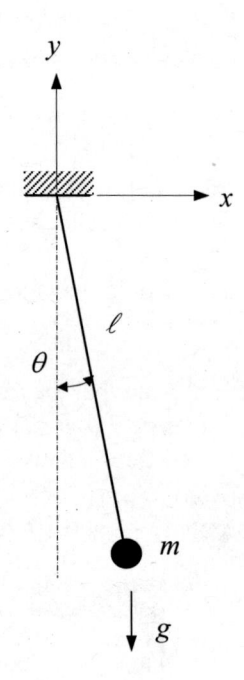

$$U = mg\ell(1 - \cos\theta) \qquad (4.2)$$

Figure 4-22 Particle Dynamics of Pendulum

According to the energy conservation theory, the total mechanical energy, which is the sum of the kinetic energy and potential energy, is a constant with respect to time; i.e.,

$$\frac{d}{dt}(T + U) = 0 \qquad (4.3)$$

where t represents time. Hence

$$\frac{d}{dt}\left(\frac{1}{2} m\ell^2 \dot{\theta}^2 + mg\ell(1 - \cos\theta)\right) = m\ell^2 \ddot{\theta} + mg\ell \sin\theta = 0 \qquad (4.4)$$

Therefore,

$$\ddot{\theta} + \frac{g}{\ell} \sin\theta = 0, \text{ and}$$

$$\ddot{\theta} + \frac{g}{\ell} \theta = 0 \qquad (4.5)$$

when $\theta \approx 0$.

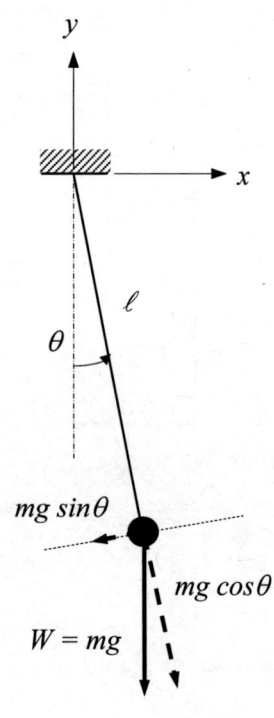

Figure 4-23 Free Body Diagram

Newton's Law

From the free-body diagram shown in Figure 4-23, the equilibrium equation of moment at the origin along the Z-direction (perpendicular to the paper) can be written as:

$$\sum M = -mg\ell \sin\theta = J\ddot\theta = m\ell^2 \ddot\theta \qquad (4.6)$$

Hence

$$\ddot\theta + \frac{g}{\ell}\sin\theta = 0, \text{ and}$$

$$\ddot\theta + \frac{g}{\ell}\theta = 0 \qquad (4.7)$$

when $\theta \approx 0$.

Note that the same equation of motion has been derived from two different approaches. The linear ordinary second-order differential equation can be solved analytically.

Solving the Differential Equation

It is well known that the solution of the differential equation is

$$\theta = A_1 \cos\omega_n t + A_2 \sin\omega_n t \qquad (4.8)$$

where $\omega_n = \sqrt{\frac{g}{\ell}}$, and A_1 and A_2 are constants to be determined by initial conditions. Note that $\omega_n = \sqrt{\frac{g}{\ell}} = \sqrt{\frac{9806}{100}} = 9.903$ rad/sec, and the natural frequency of the system is $f_n = \omega_n/2\pi = 1.576$ Hz. The time period for a complete cycle $T = 1/f_n = 0.634$ seconds, which is very close to that shown in all graphs (for example, Figure 4-14).

The initial conditions for the pendulum are $\theta(0) = \theta_0 = -10$ degrees, and $\dot\theta(0) = 0$ degree/sec. Plugging the initial conditions into the solution, we have

$A_1 = \theta_0 = -10$ degrees, and $A_2 = 0$.

Hence, the solutions are

$$\theta = \theta_0 \cos\omega_n t \qquad (4.9a)$$
$$\dot\theta = -\theta_0 \omega_n \sin\omega_n t \qquad (4.9b)$$
$$\ddot\theta = -\theta_0 \omega_n^2 \cos\omega_n t \qquad (4.9c)$$

The above equations represent angular position, velocity, and acceleration of the pin joint. These equations can be implemented into, for example, *Microsoft Excel* shown in Figure 4-24, for numerical solutions. Columns B, C, and D in the spreadsheet show the results of Eqs. 4.9a, b, and c, respectively, between 0 and 1.5 seconds with an increment of 0.005 seconds. Data in these three columns are graphed in Figures 4-25, 26, and 27, respectively. Comparing Figures 4-25 to 27 with Figures 4-14 to 16, the results obtained from theory and simulation are very close, which means the motion model has been properly defined, and *Mechanism Design* gives us good results.

However, these results are not completely identical. This is because that the *Mechanism Design* model is not really a simple pendulum since mass of the rod is non-zero. If you reduce the diameter of the rod, the *Mechanism Design* results should approach those obtained through theory calculations.

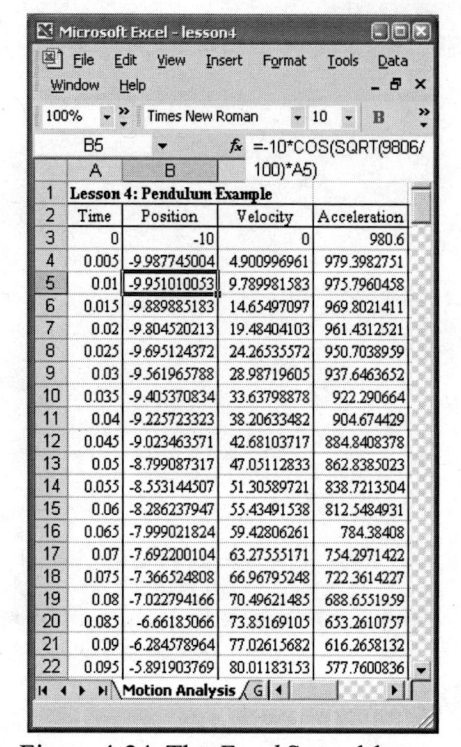

Figure 4-24 The *Excel* Spreadsheet

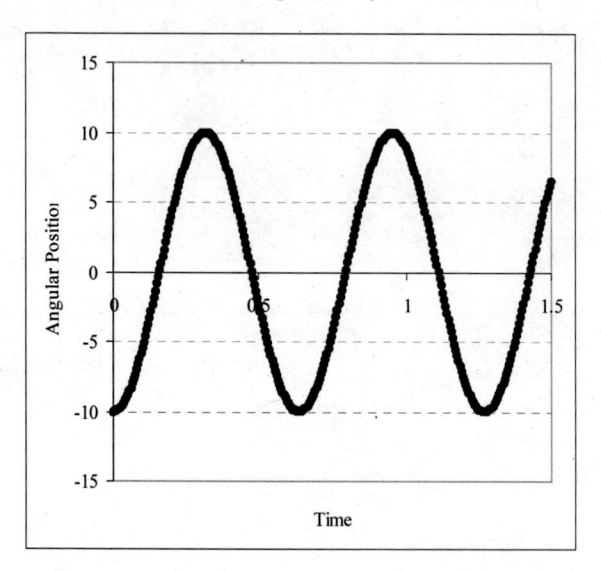

Figure 4-25 Angular Position from Theory

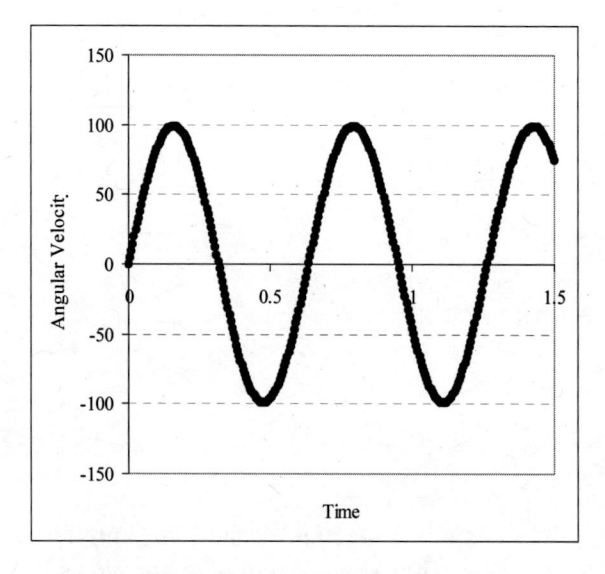

Figure 4-26 Angular Velocity from Theory

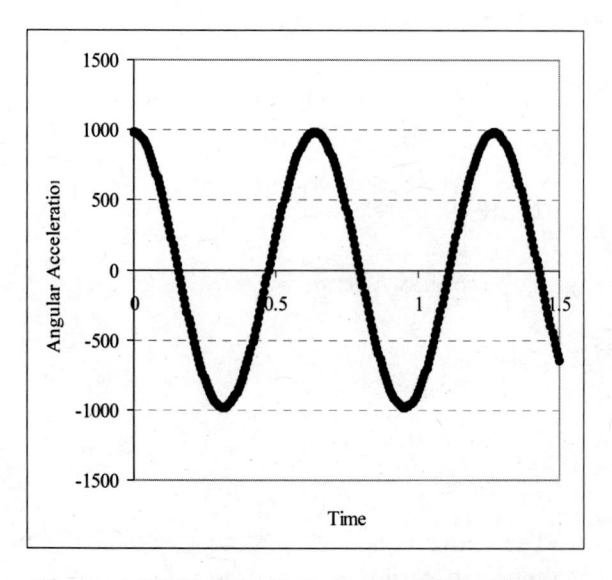

Figure 4-27 Angular Acceleration from Theory

Lesson 4: A Simple Pendulum

Exercises:

1. Define a measure and graph the maximum angular velocity of the pendulum. Also, calculate the maximum angular velocity of the pendulum from theory and compare your results with those obtained from *Mechanism Design*.

2. Create a spring-damper-mass system, as shown in Figure E4-1, using *Mechanism Design*. Note that the unstretched spring length is 3 in. The radius of the ball is 0.5 in. and the material is steel (mass density: 0.2637 lb_m/in^3)..

    (i) Find the spring length in the equilibrium condition using *Mechanism Design*. Hint: define a *Static* analysis to simulate the equilibrium position of the mass.

    (ii) Solve the same problem using Newton's laws. Compare your results with those obtained from *Mechanism Design*.

3. If a force $p = 2$ lb_f is applied to the ball as shown in Figure E4-1, repeat both (i) and (ii) of Problem 2.

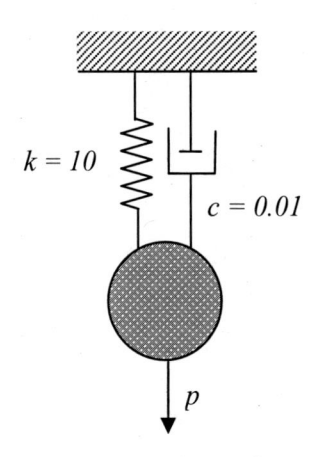

Figure E4-1 The Spring-Mass-Damper System

Notes:

Lesson 5: A Slider-Crank Mechanism —Static and Motion Analyses

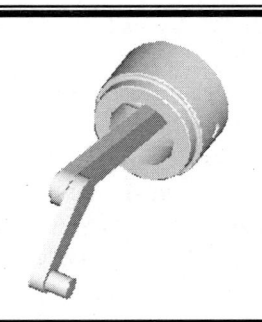

5.1 Overview of the Lesson

In this lesson you will learn how to create simulation models for a slider-crank mechanism and conduct three analyses. More joint types will be introduced in this lesson. You will learn how to select proper joint types together with placement constraints to connect parts. First, we will conduct a position analysis to check if initial positions of the bodies are adequately defined so that the mechanism can be assembled properly. Initial assembly may be straightforward for this slider-crank mechanism. When a mechanism involves more bodies with a complicated configuration, a physically meaningful initial assembly is essential for all subsequent analyses. While conducting the position analysis, we will turn on *Interference Checking* to see if parts collide. It is very important to make sure no interference exists between parts while the mechanism is in motion. The second analysis will be kinematic. A kinematic analysis will calculate velocity and acceleration data instead of just positional data. The final analysis will be dynamic, where we will add a firing force to the piston for a dynamic analysis. This lesson will start with a brief overview about the slider-crank assembly created in *Pro/ENGINEER*. At the end we will verify the kinematic simulation results using theory and computational methods employed for mechanism designs.

5.2 The Slider-Crank Example

Physical Model

The slider-crank mechanism shown in Figure 5-1 is essentially a four-bar linkage. They are commonly found in mechanical systems; e.g., internal combustion engine and oil-well drilling equipment. For the internal combustion engine, the mechanism is driven by a firing load that pushes the piston (slider), converting the reciprocal motion into rotational motion at the crank.

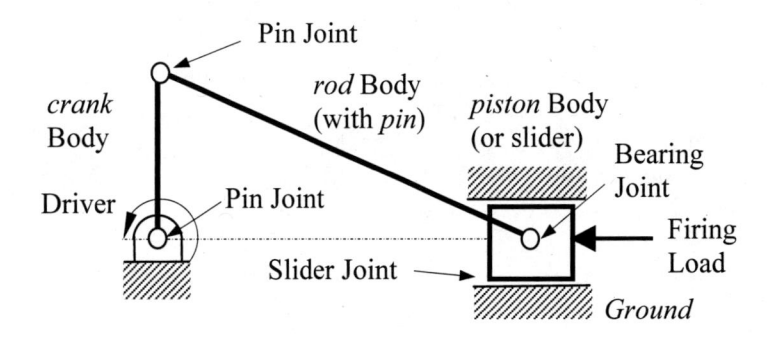

Figure 5-1 Schematic View of the Slider-Crank Mechanism

In the oil-well drilling equipment, a torque is applied at the crank. The rotational motion is converted to a reciprocal motion at the slider or piston that digs into the ground. Note that in any case the length of the crank must be smaller than that of the rod in order to allow the mechanism to operate (Grashof's law).

Note that the unit system chosen for this example is *IPS* (in-lb_f-sec). No friction is assumed between any pair of bodies.

Pro/ENGINEER Parts and Assembly

The slider-crank system consists of four parts, crank (*crank.prt*), rod (*rod.prt*), pin (*pin.prt*), and piston (*piston.prt*), as shown in the exploded view in Figure 5-2. Figure 5-2 also shows datum points in both parts and assembly. As discussed earlier, assembly datum features will be converted into ground body. Datum points (and datum axes) created in parts and assembly will be used to define connections (joints) between bodies as well as serve as the application points of forces.

In this lesson, we will start with a partial assembly, *slider_crank_partial.asm*. The partial assembly consists of datum planes, datum axes, and datum points, as shown in Figure 5-3. Note that the datum axes *AA_1* and *AA_2* and datum point *APNT0* will be used for creating joints—specifically, the pin joint between the ground and the crank, and the slider joint between the ground and the piston. Note that datum axis *AA_1* is offset 0.4 in. along the negative *Z*-direction of the assembly coordinate system *ASM_DEF_CSYS*. This is necessary for creating the slider joint between the piston and the ground since we would like to have the joint lined up parallel to the *X*-axis.

Simulation Model

In this example, we will define a pin joint (*Pin1*) that allows one rotational motion between the crank and the ground body. The second pin joint (*Pin2*) will be created to allow rotation motion between the crank and the rod. After assembling the crank and the rod, the system should have two degrees of freedom, allowing the crank and rod to rotate along their respective pin joints independently.

Next, the pin part will be assembled to the rod rigidly using placement constraints, still maintaining two dof's. Then, the piston will be assembled to the pin by defining a bearing joint (aligning axis *A_1* in pin with datum point *PNT2* in piston). The piston will be free to translate along the axis *A_1* (pin) and rotate in all three directions. The total dof's will now increase to six.

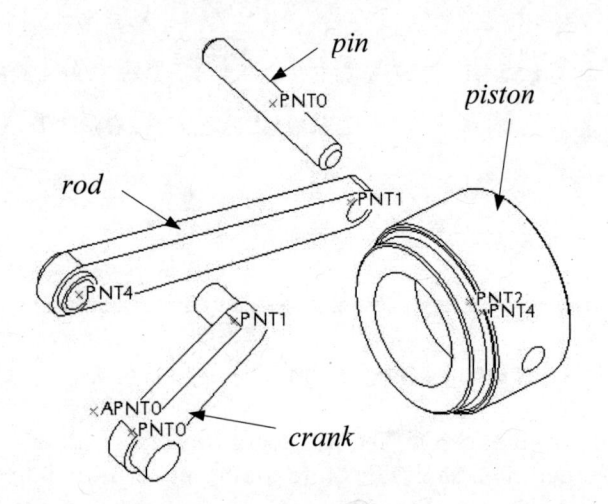

Figure 5-2 Slider-Crank Assembly (Exploded View)

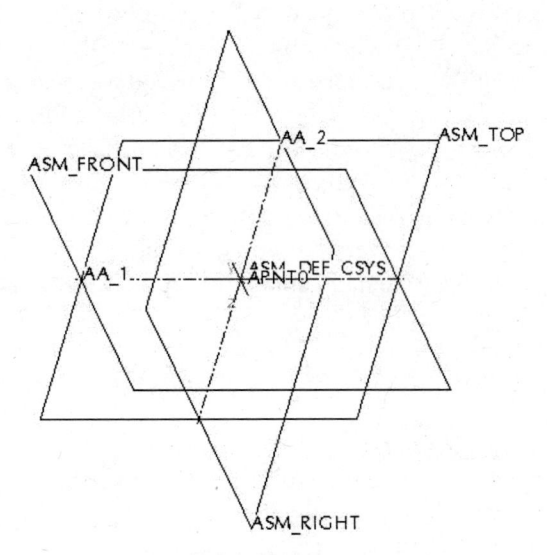

Figure 5-3 The Partial Assembly

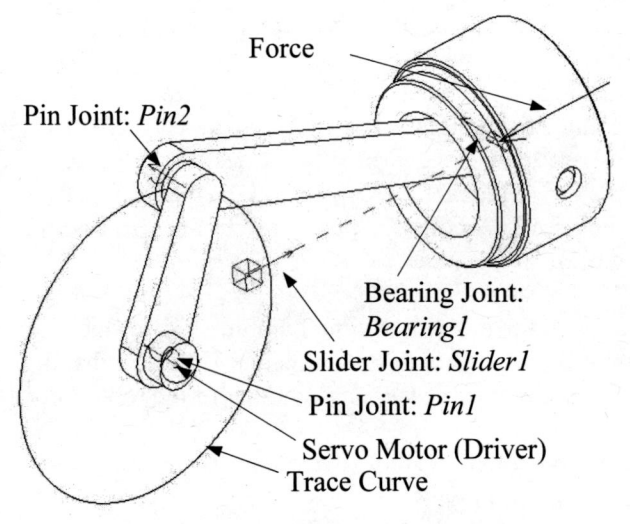

Figure 5-4 The Simulation Model

Lesson 5: A Slider-Crank Mechanism

Finally, the *piston* will be assembled to the ground body by defining a slider joint. The slider joint will be created by aligning two parallel axes (*A_1* in piston and *AA_1* in the assembly) and two datum planes (*DTM3* in piston and *ASM_TOP* in the assembly). The slider joint will allow only one translation movement between the piston and the assembly (ground); i.e., along the common axes without rotation; therefore, enforcing the bearing joint between the piston and pin to behave more like a pin joint, allowing only rotation along the common axes. The slider-crank mechanism is now restricted to planar motion, with three rotations (*Pin1*, *Pin2*, and *Bearing1*), and one translation (*Slider1*) motions. However, all three rotations and the translation motion are related to form a closed loop mechanism, leaving only one free dof, which can be any one of the rotations or the position of the piston.

The total number of degrees of freedom of the slider-crank mechanism can also be calculated as follows:

3 (bodies) × 6 (dof's/body) − 2 (pins) × 5 (dof's/pin) − 1 (slider joint) × 5 (dof's/slider) − 1 (bearing joint) × 2 (dof's/bearing) = 18 − 17 = 1

This calculation gives consistent result as discussed earlier. However, the way the joints are defined is not unique. One would probably create three pin joints (replacing the bearing joint with a pin joint between the piston and the pin) and one slider joint, which is still physically meaningful. However, the total dof's will become −2. This is because there are three redundant dof's created in the system. This is fine since *Mechanism Design* filters out the redundant dof's. You may want to check the redundancy following steps shown in Appendix A. For this slider-crank mechanism there is only one dof remaining, which means one single driver or force will move the mechanism and uniquely define the mechanism in time domain. Joints defined in this simulation model are summarized in Table 5-1.

Table 5-1 Joints Defined in the Simulation Model

	Ground Body	crank	rod/pin	piston
crank	*Pin1* *A_1* (crank)/*AA_2* and *PNT0*/*APNT0*		*Pin2* *A_2* (crank)/*A_1* (rod) and flat faces	
rod/pin		*Pin2* *A_2* (crank)/*A_1* (rod) and flat faces		*Bearing1* *PNT2* (piston)/*A_1* (pin)
piston	*Slider1* *A_1* (piston)/*AA_1* and *DTM3* (piston)/ *ASM_TOP*		*Bearing1* *PNT2* (piston)/*A_1* (pin)	

The pairs of datum points and datum axes created in the parts and assembly for defining these four joints can be seen in the top and front views of the mechanism, as shown in Figure 5-5.

To go through this lesson, you need to download the *lesson5* folder from the publisher's web site to your hard drive. Before going forward, please spend a few minutes to review the parts and assembly, especially paying close attention to the datum axes and datum points.

We need to also define a servo motor (driver) that will rotate the crank through the rotation axis of the joint *Pin1* (between the crank and the ground body). As a result, the motor will drive the slider-crank mechanism. The driver will rotate the crank at a constant angular velocity of 360 degrees/sec. The joints and driver defined in this example are shown in Figure 5-4. We will first conduct a position analysis and check interferences. Then, we will carry out a kinematic analysis for the slider-crank mechanism and later add a force for dynamic analysis.

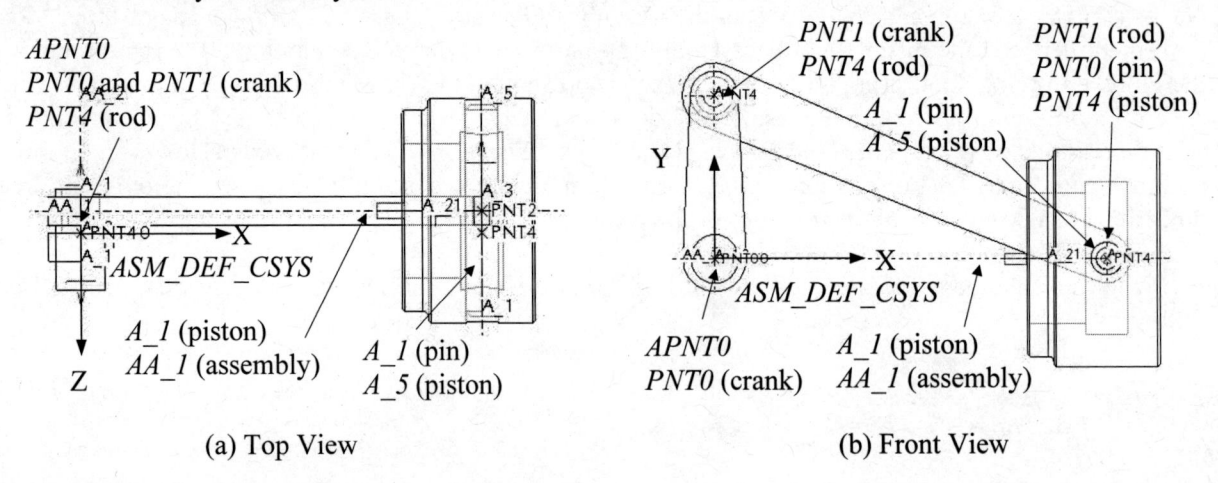

Figure 5-5 Locations of Datum Points and Datum Axes

5.3 Using *Mechanism Design*

Creating an Assembly

In the *lesson5* folder, you should see the following files:

lesson5\slider_crank_partial.asm
lesson5\crank.prt
lesson5\rod.prt
lesson5\pin.prt
lesson5\piston.prt

Start *Pro/ENGINEER*, change the working directory, and open the assembly model: *slider_crank_partial.asm*. You should see an assembly with numerous datum features, as shown in Figure 5-2. Before we proceed, you may want to make sure that the unit system is properly chosen for the part. The unit system for all four parts and the assembly should be *IPS* (in-lb_f-sec).

Now, we are ready to bring in the crank. Before we do that, please note that we will define a pin joint by aligning axis *A_1* (crank) with *AA_1* (assembly) and *PNT0* (crank) with *APNT0* (assembly). The pin joint will allow one rotation dof along the Z-direction of the assembly coordinate system.

Click the *Add component* shortcut button and choose *crank.prt*. As soon as the crank appears, *Pro/ENGINEER* assumes a configuration like the one shown in Figure 5-6a (only show datum axes and datum points). You may want to turn off the datum plane and datum coordinate system display to show only datum axes and datum points.

In the *Component Placement* dashboard, choose the *Pin* joint from the *User Defined* list, and pick *A_1* (crank) and *AA_2* (assembly). The crank will be repositioned to a configuration where *A_1* aligns with *AA_2*. Next, pick *PNT0* (crank) and *APNT0* (assembly). A pin joint symbol appears (Figure 5-6b). You may want to use the *No Hidden* option to unshade the crank in order to see the pin joint symbol.

Lesson 5: A Slider-Crank Mechanism

Even though you could drag/rotate the crank, it is recommended that you stay with the current configuration and not drag the component. Click the ✓ button to accept the definition.

(a) Default Configuration   (b) Assembled Configuration

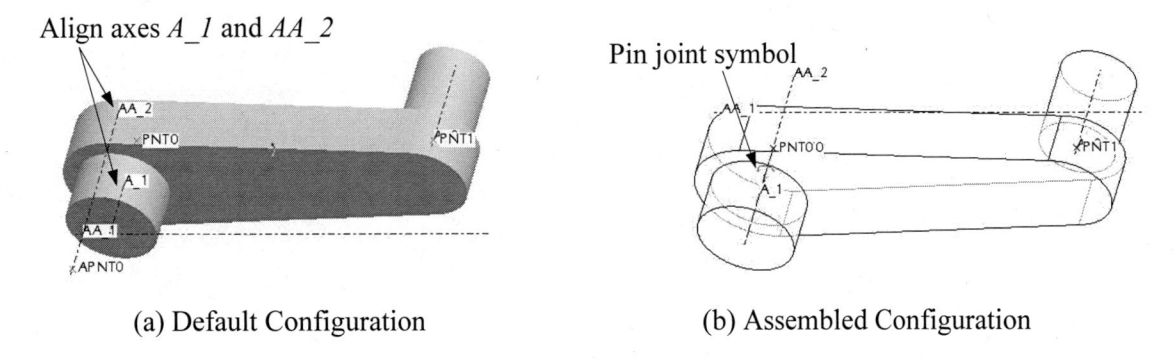

Figure 5-6 Assembling Crank to the Ground Body

(a) Aligning Datum Axes

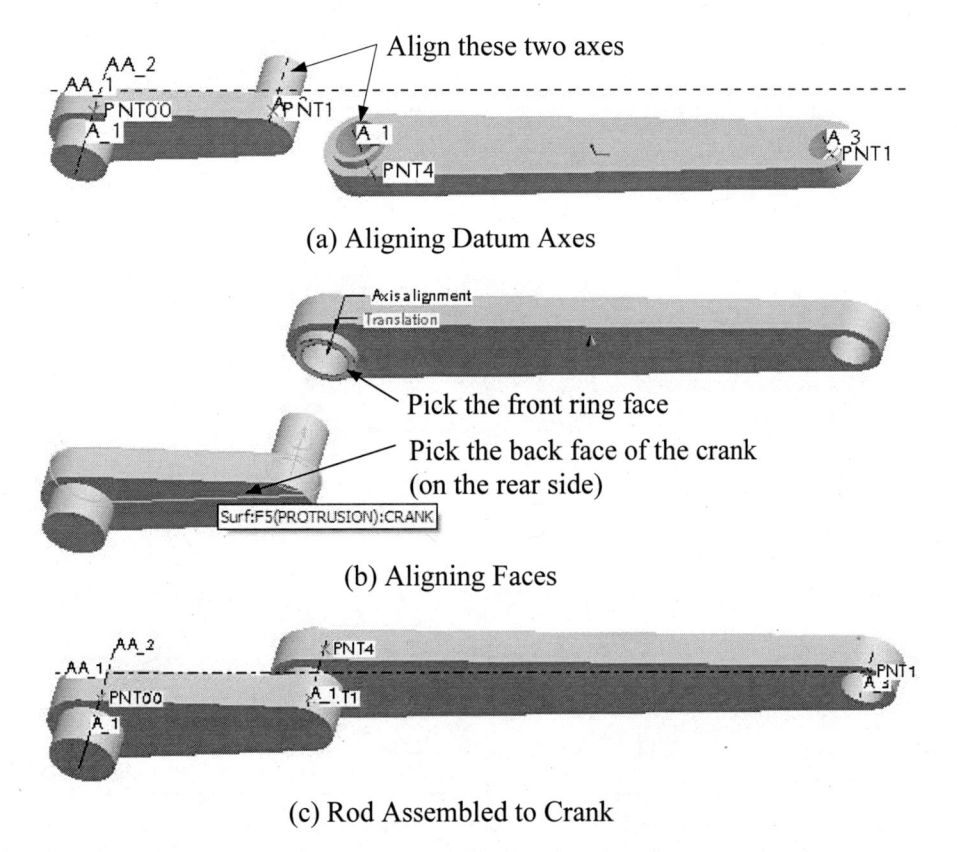

(b) Aligning Faces

(c) Rod Assembled to Crank

Figure 5-7 Assembling Rod to Crank

Next, we will bring in the rod and define a pin joint to connect it to the small end of the crank. We will align axes *A_1* (rod) with *A_2* (crank) and the front ring face of the rod with the back face of the crank. The rod will be shown in a default configuration, like that of Figure 5-7a when it is brought into the assembly. Use the *Move* option to orient the rod to a configuration similar to that of Figure 5-7b. Make sure *PNT4* (rod) is on the front side of the rod. In the *Component Placement* dashboard from the *Joint Type* list choose the *Pin* joint, and pick *A_1* (rod) and *A_2* (crank). Use the *Move* option to translate the rod away from the crank like the one shown in Figure 5-7b if necessary. Pick the front ring face of the rod and the back face of the crank (see Figure 5-7b), and you should see that the rod is properly assembled to the crank (Figure 5-7c). Click the ✓ button to accept the definition.

The next part we are brining in is the pin (*pin.prt*). Since the pin is connected to the rod rigidly, we will assemble the pin using standard placement constraints (*Automatic* type). We will align axes *A_1* (pin) with *A_3* (the small end of the rod) and *DTM2* (pin) with *DTM2* (rod), as shown in Figures 5-8a and 5-8b. The rod will be shown in a default configuration like that of Figure 5-8a. In the *Component Placement* dashboard click *Placement* then choose *Align* from the *Automatic* list. Pick *A_1* (pin) and *A_3* (rod). Next, pick *DTM2* (pin) and *DTM2* (rod) shown in Figure 5-8b, and you should see that the pin is properly assembled to the crank (Figure 5-8c). The message right below the *Graphics* window indicates that the part is *Fully Constrained* (with assumption; i.e., rotation along axis). Click the ✓ button to accept the definition.

(a) Aligning Datum Axes

(b) Aligning Datum Planes

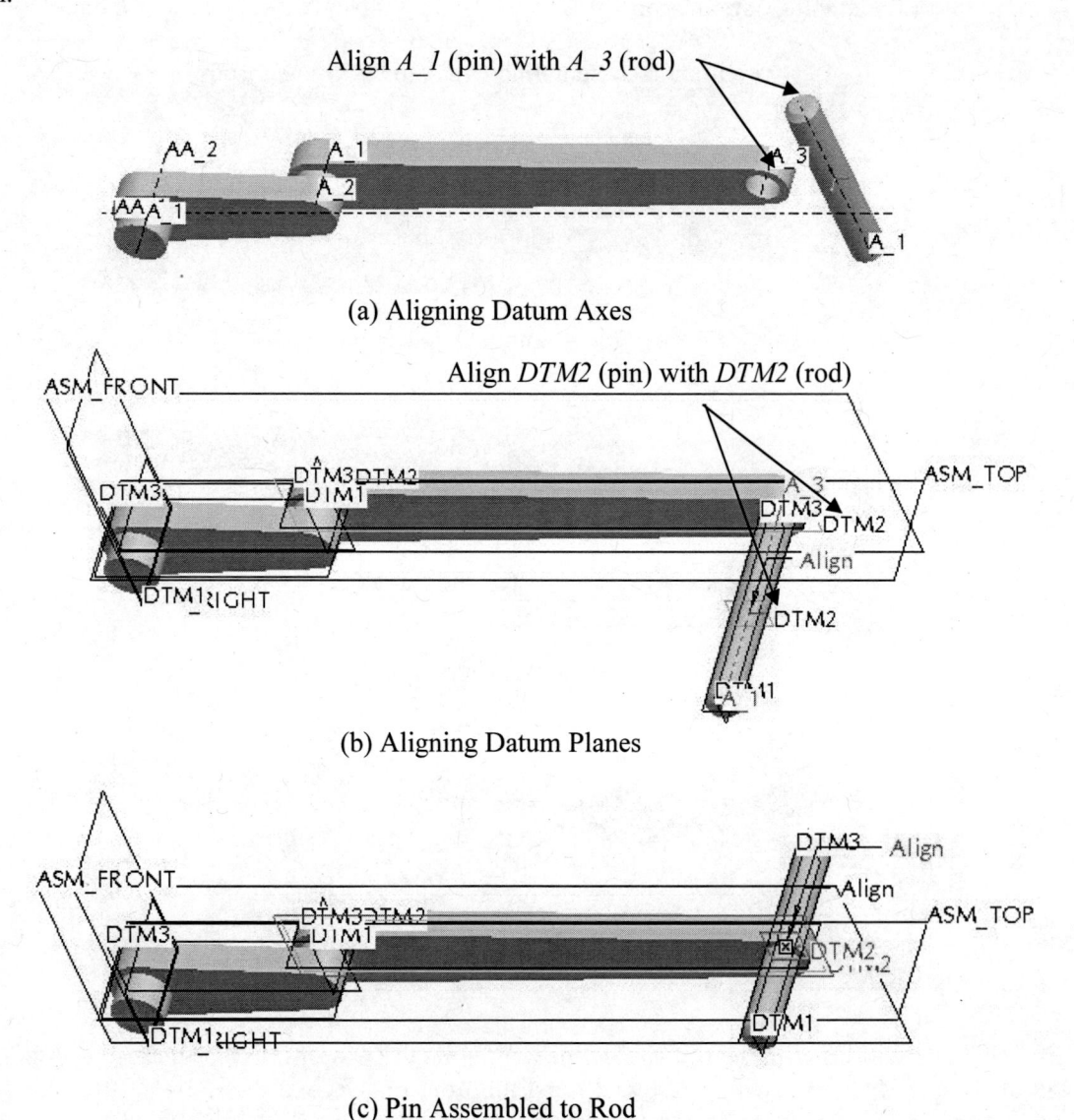

(c) Pin Assembled to Rod

Figure 5-8 Assembling Pin to Rod

The final part we are brining in is the piston. The piston will be assembled to the pin and the ground body using a slider and a bearing joint. The piston will be shown in a default configuration when it is

Lesson 5: A Slider-Crank Mechanism 5-7

brought into the assembly, similar to that of Figure 5-9a. In the *Component Placement* dashboard, click *Bearing* from the *User Defined* list. Pick *A_1* (pin) and *PNT2* (piston). *PNT2* is now allowed to move and rotate along axis *A_1*, therefore, a bearing joint. Next, we will define a slider joint.

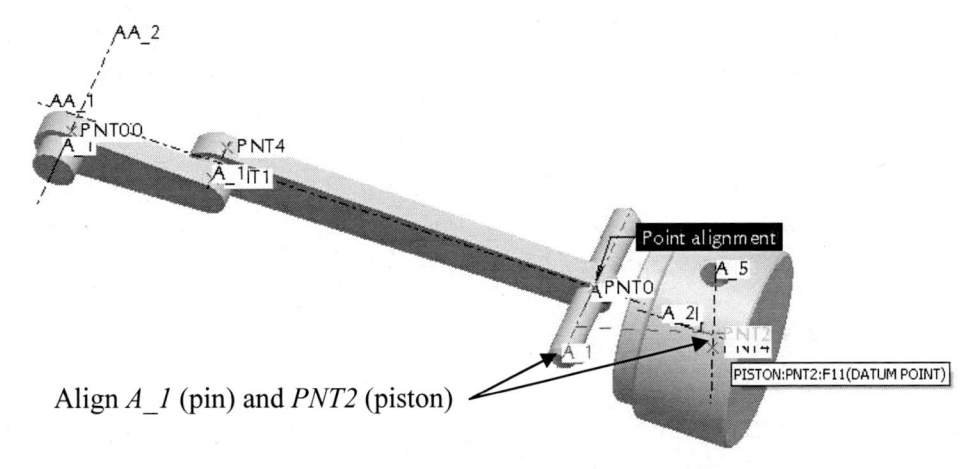

(a) Aligning Datum Point to Axis for Bearing Joint

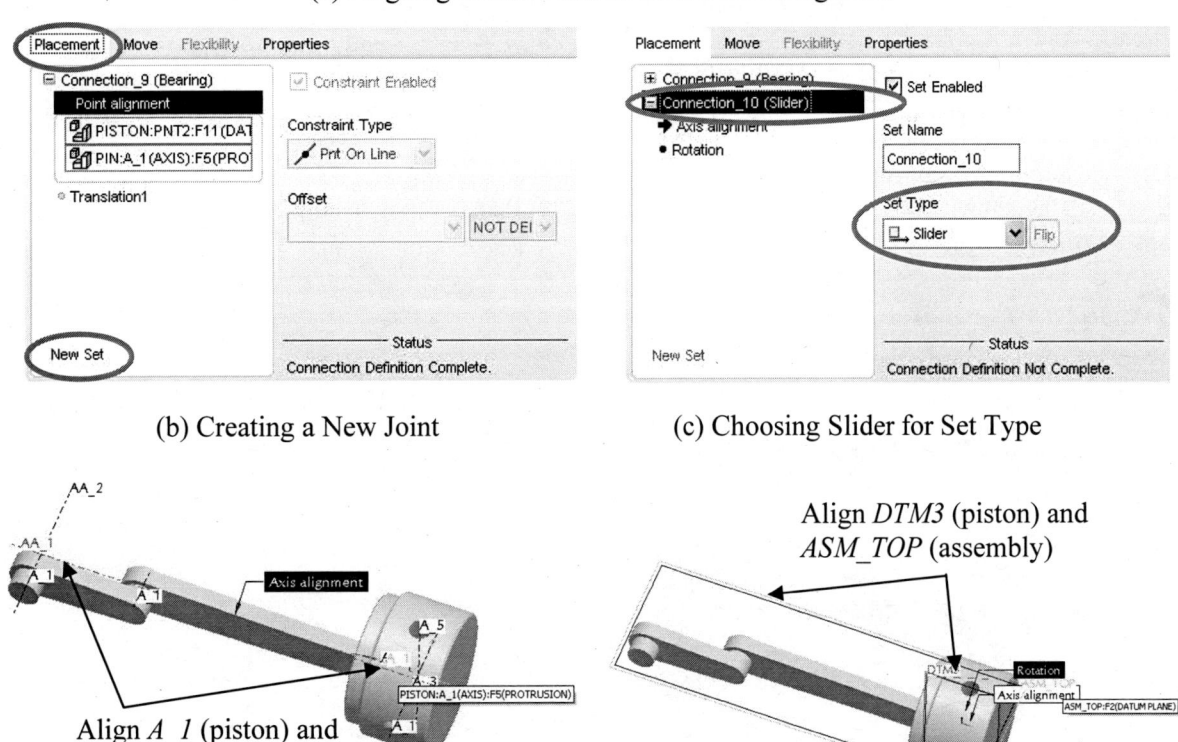

(b) Creating a New Joint

(c) Choosing Slider for Set Type

(d) Piston Assembled to Pin and Ground Body

Figure 5-9 Assembling Piston to Ground Body and Pin

Click the *Placement* button in the *Component Placement* dashboard, a bearing joint is now listed, as shown in Figure 5-9b. Click the *New Set* button (lower left corner) to cerate a new joint. Click the new joint label appearing in the *Component Placement* dashboard (see Figure 5-9c), choose *Slider* for *Set Type*. Pick *A_1* (piston) and *AA_1* (assembly), and *DTM3* (piston) and *ASM_TOP* (assembly), as shown in Figure 5-9d. Note that some datum planes were hid in Figure 5-9d for better illustration. You should see that the piston is properly assembled and a slider joint appears. Click the ✓ button to accept the definition.

Now, we have completely assembled the mechanism. You may want to use the *Drag* option (shortcut button at the top of the *Graphics* window) to move the mechanism. Simply click the crank and move the mouse. You should see the slider-crank mechanism moves as expected (Figure 5-10).

Creating Simulation Models

Now we are ready to enter *Mechanism Design*. From the pull-down menu, choose

Applications > Mechanism.

We will first define an initial condition for the simulation model. The initial condition will be defined similar to the sketch shown in Figure 5-1, where the crank is pointing vertically upward. Then, we will create a driver at joint *Pin1* to conduct position and kinematic analyses.

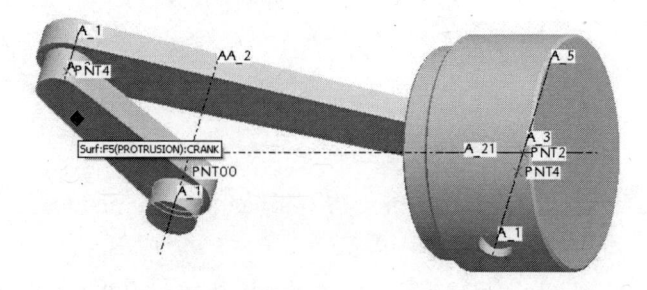

Figure 5-10 Move the Mechanism by Dragging the Crank

Two datum planes will be aligned for the initial configuration; *DTM1* (crank) and *ASM_TOP* (assembly), as shown in Figure 5-11a. We will use the *Drag* option to align the planes and create a snapshot of the configuration for future use.

Align *DTM1* (crank) and *ASM_TOP* (assembly)

(a) Selecting Two Datum Planes for Alignment

(b) Initial Configuration

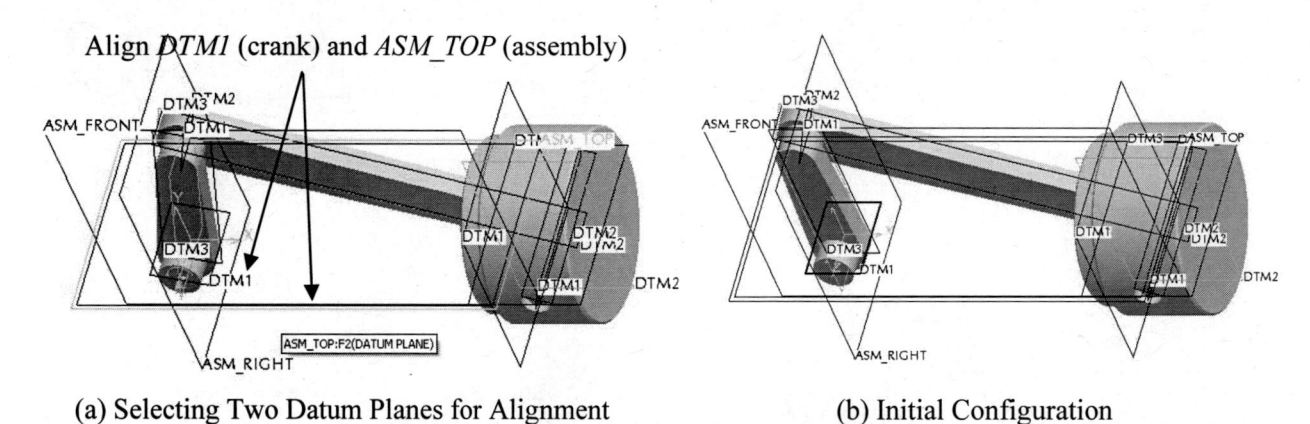

Figure 5-11 Defining Initial Configuration

Click the *Drag Packed Components* button at the top of the *Graphics* window, and the *Drag* dialog box appears. Click the *Constraints* tab, and choose the *Align Two Entities* button (first on the left). Choose two datum planes, *DTM1* (crank) and *ASM_TOP* (assembly), as shown in Figure 5-11a. The crank should now sit upright as that of Figure 5-11b. Click the *Current Snapshot* button on top, and a default name *Snapshot1* will appear. Click *Close*. The snapshot *Snapshot1* has been saved for future use. Before starting analysis, make sure you bring up this snapshot as the initial configuration for analysis.

Now we will create a driver at the rotational axis of the pin joint between the crank and the ground body (*Pin1*). The driver will rotate the crank at a constant angular velocity of 360 degrees/sec. From the

Lesson 5: A Slider-Crank Mechanism 5-9

shortcut buttons on the right, click *Define Servo Motors* (4th from the top), or choose from the pull-down menu

Insert > Servo Motors.

The *Servo Motor Definition* dialog box will appear (Figure 5-12a). Enter *Motor1* for *Name*, leave *Motion Axis* (default) for *Driven Entity* (under *Type* tab), then pick *Pin1* from the *Graphics* window. Note that you may want to turn off all datum features in order to see the pin joint (see Figure 5-12b for the pin joint location). Note that you may click the *Flip* button to make sure you pick the correct rotation axis. The axis must point in a direction like that of Figure 5-12b.

After picking the pin joint, a larger arrow appears to confirm your selection. The next step is to specify the profile of the motor. From the *Servo Motor Definition* dialog box, pick the *Profile* tab (Figure 5-12c), choose *Velocity* in *Specification*, and leave *Constant* (default) in *Magnitude*. Enter *360* for the constant *A*, and click *OK*. Please see Appendix D for more details regarding the magnitude settings. A driver symbol should appear at the pin joint in the *Graphics* window (Figure 5-12d).

(a) The *Servo Motor Definition* Dialog Box

(b) Pick the Pin Joint *Pin1*

(c) The *Servo Motor Definition* Dialog Box (*Profile* tab)

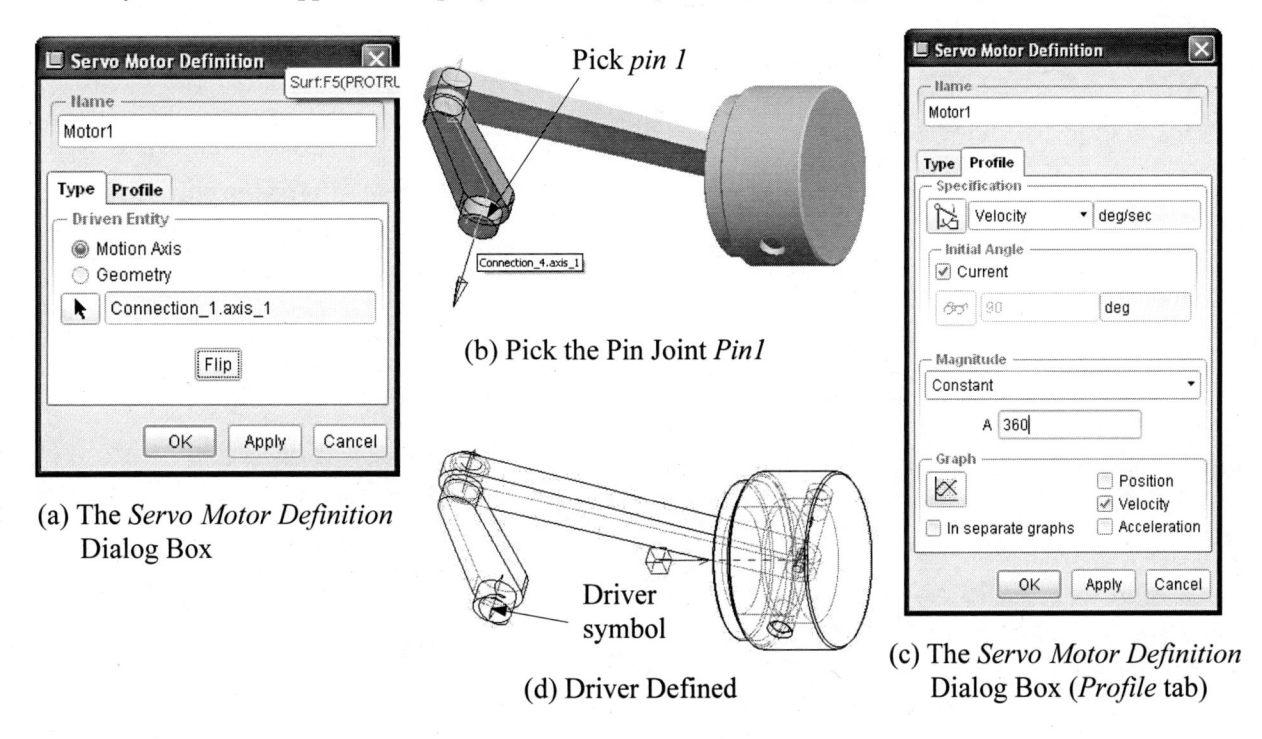

(d) Driver Defined

Figure 5-12 Defining a Servo Motor

Creating and Running a Position Analysis

Position analysis is also called *Kinematic* or *Repeated Assembly* analysis in *Mechanism Design*. It is a series of assembly analyses driven by servo motors.

A position analysis simulates the mechanism's motion, satisfying the requirements of the servo motors profiles and any joint (and cam-follower, slot-follower, or gear-pair connections), and records position data for the mechanism's various components. It does not take force and mass into account in performing the analysis. Therefore, you do not have to specify mass properties for your mechanism. Dynamic entities in the model, such as springs, dampers, gravity, forces/torques, and force motors, do not affect a position analysis. A position analysis gives you positions of components over time, trace curves of the mechanism's motion, and interference between components.

From the shortcut button list on the right, click the *Mechanism Analysis* shortcut button to define an analysis. In the *Analysis Definition* dialog box appearing, enter:

Name: *Position_Analysis*
Type: *Position*
Start Time: *0*
End Time: *1*
Frame Rate: *100*
Minimum Interval: *0.01*
Initial Configuration: *Current*

Click *Run* button. In the *Graphics* window, the mechanism starts moving. The crank rotates 360 degrees as expected (Figure 5-13). Click *OK* to save the analysis definition.

Saving and Reviewing Results

Click the *Playbacks* button on the right to bring up the *Playbacks* dialog box and repeat the motion animation. On the *Playbacks* dialog box, click the *Save* button to save the results as a *.pbk* file.

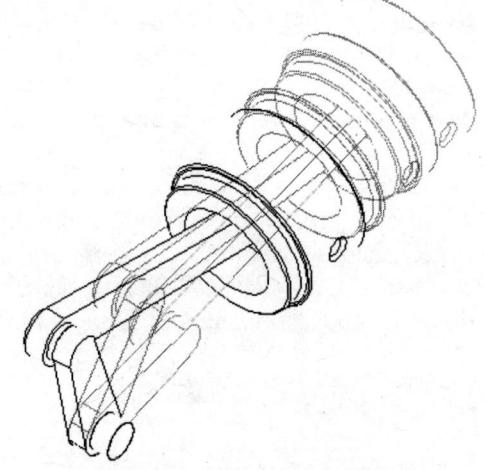

Figure 5-13 Animation

Note that we want to create a measure to monitor the position of the piston. We will choose the center point *PNT2* of the piston and magnitude of the point position for the measure. To do so, click the *Generate Measure Results of Analyses* button. In the *Measure Results* dialog box appearing, click the *Create New Measure* button. The *Measure Definition* dialog box opens (Figure 5-14). Enter *Piston_Position* for *Name*. Under *Type*, select *Position*. Pick *PNT2* in the *piston* part. Leave *WCS* as the *Coordinate System* (default). Choose *Magnitude* as the *Component* (default). Under *Evaluation Method*, leave *Each Time Step*. Click *OK* to accept the definition.

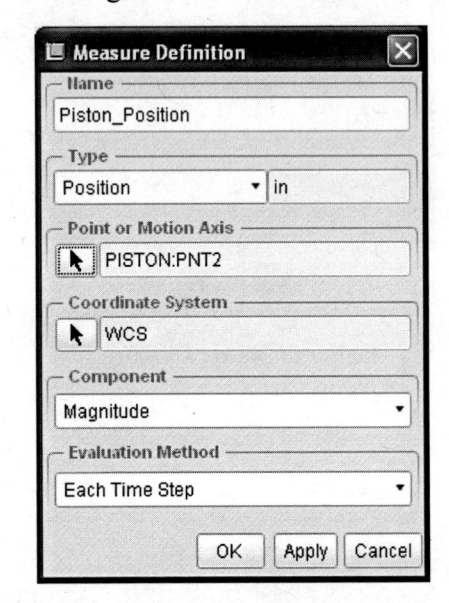

Figure 5-14 The *Measure Definition* Dialog Box

In the *Measure Results* dialog box, choose *Position_Analysis* in the *Result Set* and click the *Graph* button on the top left corner to graph the measure.

The graph should be similar to that of Figure 5-15. Note that from the graph, the piston moves between about 7 and 11 in. horizontally, in reference to the *WCS*. At the starting point, the crank is in the vertical position, and the piston is at 7.42 in. (that is, $\sqrt{8^2 - 3^2}$) to the right of *WCS*. Note that the lengths of the crank and rod are 3 and 8 in., respectively. When the crank rotates to 90 degrees counterclockwise, the

Lesson 5: A Slider-Crank Mechanism

position becomes 5 (which is 8–3). When the crank rotates 270 degrees, the piston position is 11 (which is 8+3).

Repeat the same steps to define a measure for the angular position of the pin joint *Pin1*. The graph of the angular position of *Pin1* should be similar to that of Figure 5-16. The graph shows a straight line between 90 and 450 degrees within the one second time period. Certainly, this is due to the fact that a driver of a constant angular velocity is employed to drive the mechanism.

Now we will create a trace curve to trace the location of pin joint *Pin2* (between crank and rod). What will the curve look like?

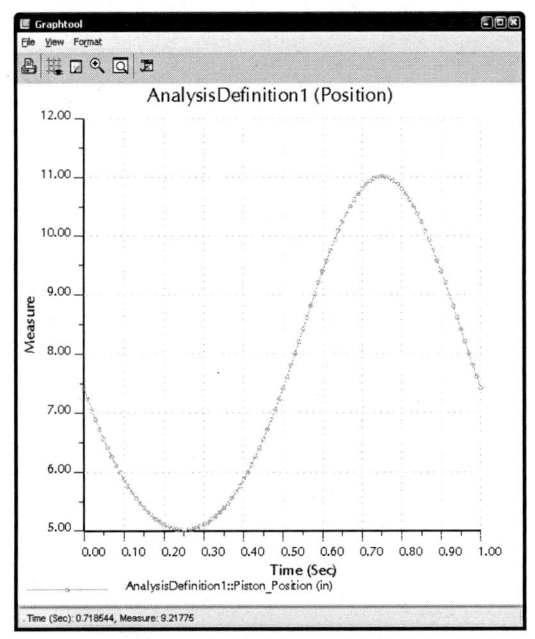

Figure 5-15 Position of the Piston

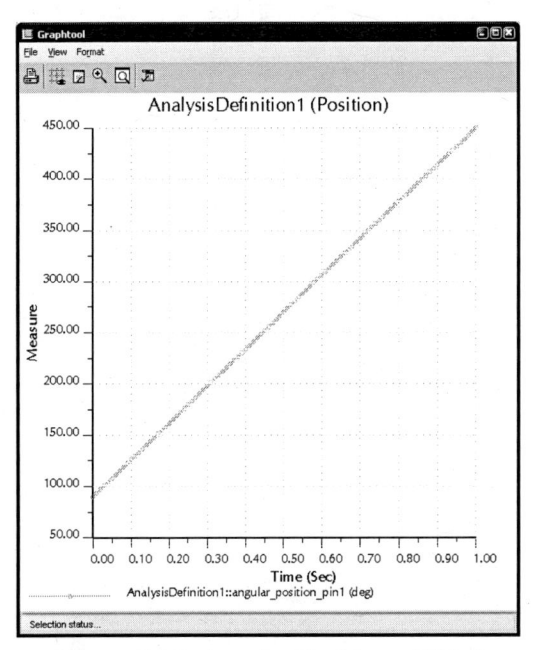

Figure 5-16 Angular Position of *Pin1*

A trace curve graphically represents the motion of a point or vertex relative to a part in your mechanism. This is especially useful for designing a cam profile.

When you select *Insert > Trace Curve* from the pull-down menu, the *Trace Curve* dialog box opens (Figure 5-17). Pick *SLIDER_CRANK_PARTIAL.ASM* from the *Model Tree* for *Paper Part* (that is, the reference), and *PNT1* (crank) for the trace point (under *Point, Vertex, or Curve Endpoint* in the *Trace Curve* dialog box). Leave *2D* for *Curve Type*, choose *Position_Analysis*, and click *Preview* (or *OK*). A circle centered at *APNT0* and passing through *PNT1* appears (Figure 5-18). This circle specifies the trace of point *PNT1* with respect to the ground body (*slider_crank_partial.asm*).

Interference Checking

Next we will learn how to perform interference checking during animation. In *Mechanism Design*, interference occurs when two parts collide, indicating that one part is interfering with another part's ability to move. You should check for interference if you are modeling the detailed geometry of the mechanism, like this slider-crank example. The interference checking is straightforward in *Mechanism Design*. The capability is built in playbacks.

Click the *Playbacks* button on the right to bring up the *Playbacks* dialog box (Figure 5-19). Click the *Collision Detection Settings* button. In the *Collision Detection Settings* dialog box (Figure 5-20), click *Global Collision Detection*, and then click *OK*. The *Global* option allows *Mechanism Design* to check for interference between all parts in the mechanism. You may choose to ring message bell or stop the animation when interference is detected. The *No Collision Detection* option (default) will turn off interference checking.

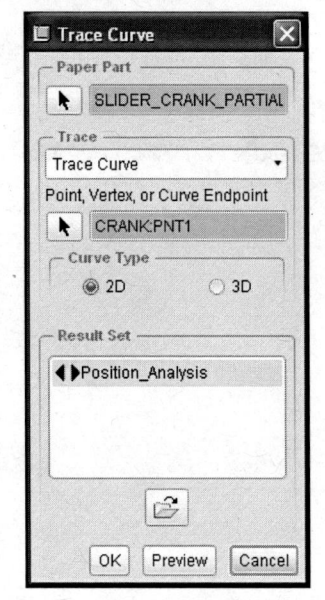

Figure 5-18 The Trace Curve of Datum Point *PNT1* (crank)

Figure 5-17 The *Trace Curve* Dialog Box

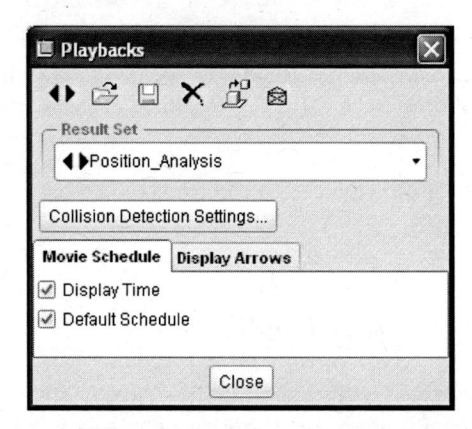

Figure 5-19 The *Playbacks* Dialog Box

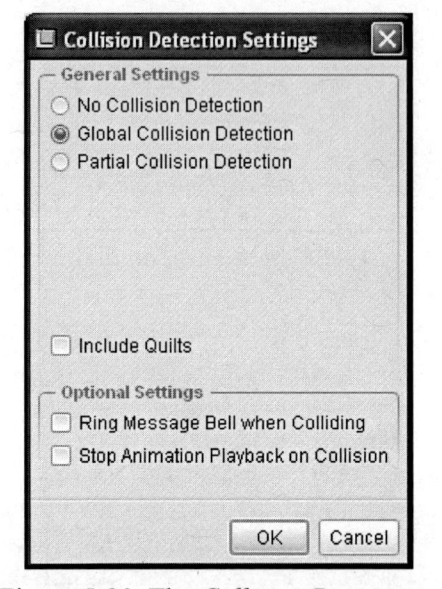

Figure 5-20 The *Collision Detection Settings* Dialog Box

From the *Playbacks* dialog box, click the *Animate* button (top left) to bring up the *Animate* dialog box. Note that it may take some time for *Mechanism Design* to calculate interference at each time frame. Click the *Play* button from the *Animate* dialog box to see the animation again.

You should see that a small portion of the exterior surfaces of the piston and the rod is highlighted in red (Figure 5-21a), meaning interference is detected between these two parts. You may re-orient the model view similar to that of Figure 5-21b to locate the interference more clearly.

Lesson 5: A Slider-Crank Mechanism   5-13

You may use a saved view or choose *View > Orientations* and pick planes (or datum planes) as references to create a desired view.

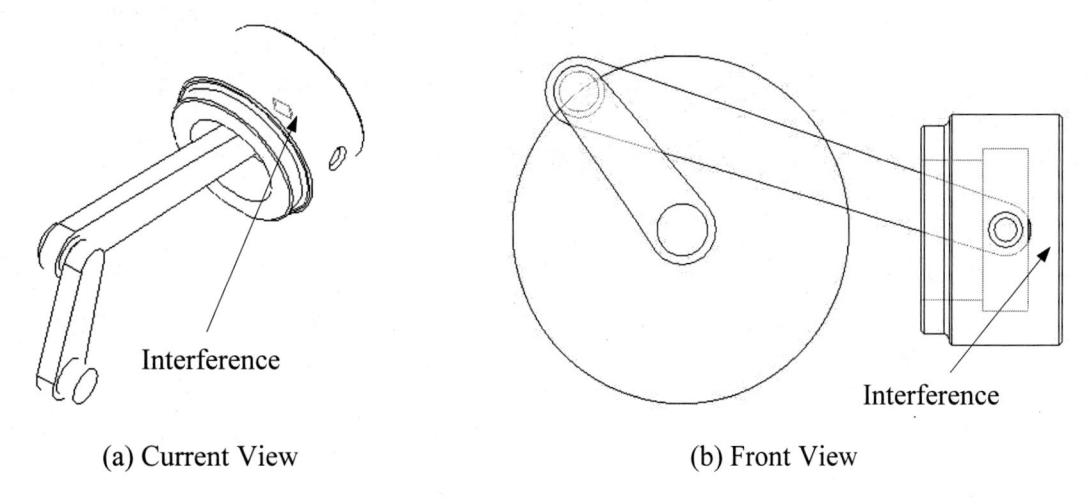

(a) Current View (b) Front View

Figure 5-21 Interference Checking

Creating and Running a Kinematic Analysis

We will define a kinematic analysis for the same slider-crank simulation model. The definition includes:

Name: *Kinematic Analysis*
Type: *Kinematic*
Start Time: *0*
End Time: *1*
Frame Rate: *100*
Minimum Interval: *0.01*
Initial Configuration: *Current*

The mechanism should be in its initial configuration; i.e., crank is in the upright position. If not, click the *Drag Packed Components* button at the top of the *Graphics* window, and the *Drag* dialog box appears (Figure 5-22). Choose *Snapshot1*, and click the *Display selected snapshot* button (first on the left). The mechanism will be restored to its initial configuration.

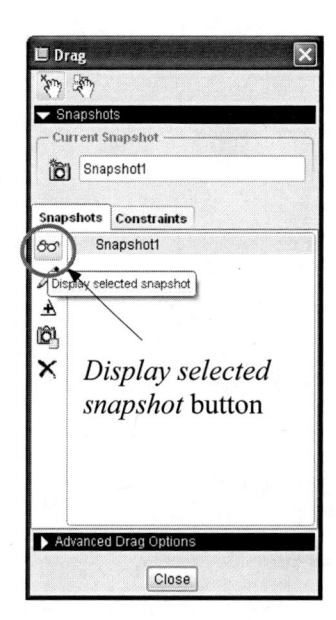

Figure 5-22 The *Drag* Dialog Box

Run the kinematic analysis. In the *Graphics* window, the mechanism starts moving. The crank rotates 360 degrees just like the position analysis. However, velocity and acceleration data are calculated. Define additional measures, for example, angular velocity of *Pin2*, and piston velocity in the *X*-direction (at *PNT2*). Graphs of the measures should be like those of Figures 5-23 and 24, respectively.

Creating and Running a Dynamic Analysis

A force simulating the engine firing load (acting along the negative *X*-direction of *ASM_DEF_CSYS*) will be added to the piston for a dynamic simulation. It will be more realistic if the force can be applied when the piston starts moving left and can be only applied for a short time. In order to do so, we will have to define measures that monitor the position of the piston for the firing load to be activated. Unfortunately, such a capability is not available in *Mechanism Design*. Therefore, the force is simplified as an impulse force with a triangular shape that has a peak of 1,000 lb$_f$ at 0.5 seconds, as shown in Figure 5-25. The force will be applied over a one-second period. This force will be defined as a point force at datum point *PNT2* in the piston (Figure 5-26).

From the shortcut buttons on the right, click *Define Force/Torque* (3rd from the bottom), or choose from the pull-down menu

Insert > Force/Torque.

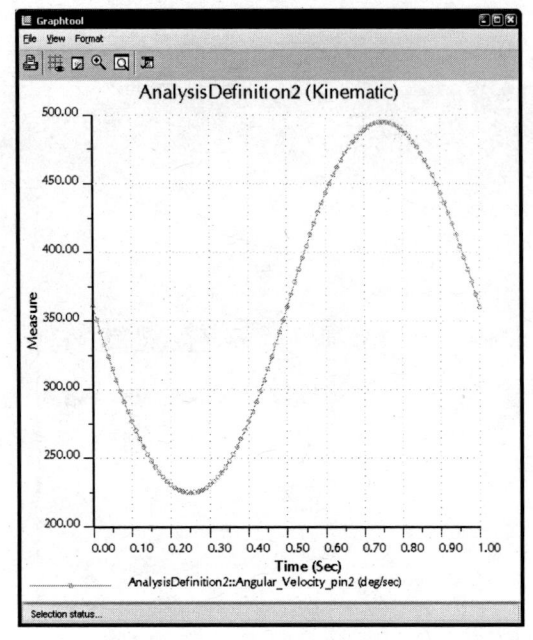

Figure 5-23 Angular Velocity of Pin Joint: *Pin2*

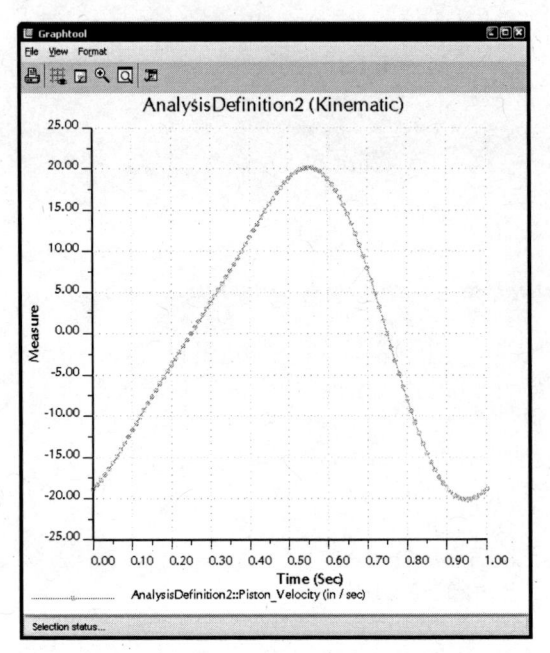

Figure 5-24 Piston Velocity in *X*-Direction (*PNT2*)

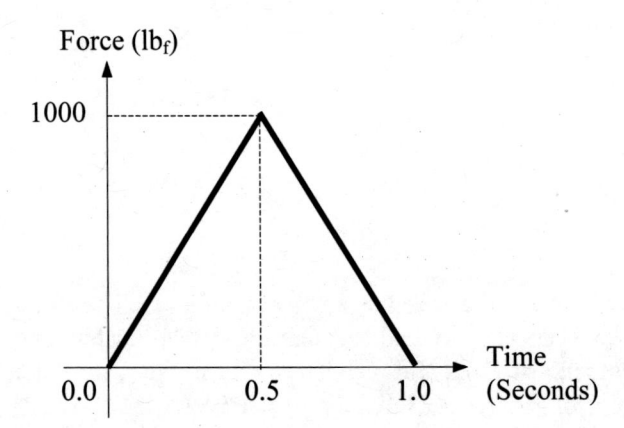

Figure 5-25 The Force Profile

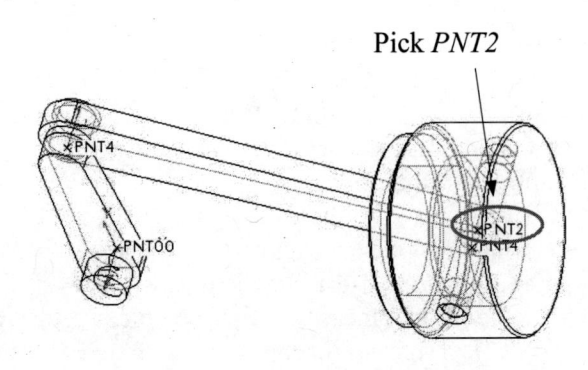

Figure 5-26 Pick Point for Force Application

Lesson 5: A Slider-Crank Mechanism

The *Force/Torque Definition* dialog box will appear (Figure 5-27). Enter *Firing_load* for *Name*, leave *Point Force* (default) for *Type*, and pick *PNT2* in piston. Note that you may want to turn off all datum features except datum points (see Figure 5-26). After picking the point, a larger arrow appears pointing along a default direction (Z-direction: 0, 0, 1). We will change it to (−1, 0, 0) later. For the time being, we will enter the load magnitude as a function as described in Figure 5-25. Under the *Magnitude* tab choose *Table* from the function list. Click the *Add rows to table* button (first of the two buttons on the right) three times to create three rows. Enter three pairs of data (*0, 0*), (*0.5, 1,000*), and (*1, 0*). Note that you must make sure that the unit system is in-lb$_f$-sec. If you are still using the default unit system, in-lb$_m$-sec, you will have to enter a peak force *386,000 lb$_m$ in/sec^2* at *0.5 second* (instead of 1,000 lb$_f$).

Now, we will define the direction of the force. Click the *Direction* tap, enter (−*1, 0, 0*), and click *Apply* (Figure 5-28). The arrow should turn horizontal toward the crank as desired. Click *OK* to accept the force. A force symbol should appear at *PNT2* in the piston in the *Graphics* window (Figure 5-29).

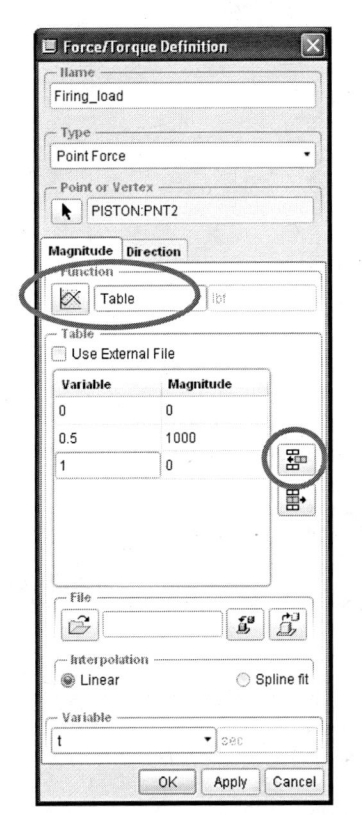

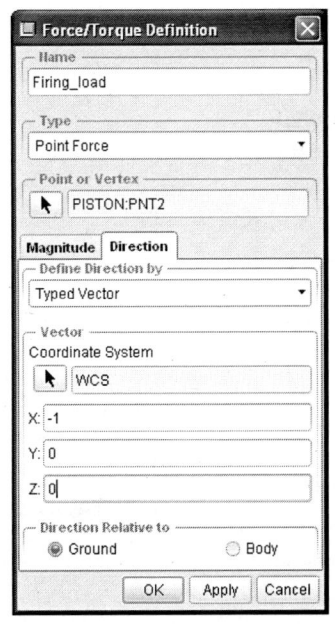

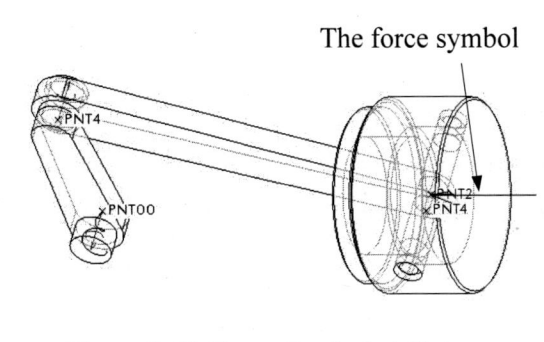

Figure 5-29 Force Symbol at Piston

Figure 5-28 The *Force/Torque Definition* Dialog Box (Direction)

Figure 5-27 The *Force/Torque Definition* Dialog Box

Now we are ready for the dynamic analysis. Before we proceed, we will reset the initial position. Click the *Drag Packed Components* button at the top of the *Graphics* window, and the *Drag* dialog box will appear. Click *Snapshot1*, and click the *Display selected snapshot* button (first on the left). The mechanism will be reset to the configuration where the crank is in the upright position.

Click the *Mechanism Analysis* shortcut button to define an analysis. In the *Analysis Definition* dialog box, leave the default name, *AnalysisDefinition2*, and enter:

Name: *Dynamic Analysis*
Type: *Dynamic*
Duration: *3*
Frame Rate: *100*
Minimum Interval: *0.01*
Initial Configuration: *Current*

We will have to delete the motor to comply with our scenario. To do so, click the *Motors* tab, select *Motor1*, then click the *Delete highlighted row(s)* button (2nd on the right). Click the *Ext Loads* tab just to make sure the *Firing_load* is included. Click *Run*. In the *Graphics* window, the mechanism starts moving. The crank rotates about one and half cycles. Click *OK* to save the analysis definition.

You may also see graphs for some of the measures; e.g., piston position as shown in Figure 5-30. Do not forget to save your model.

5.4 Result Verifications

In this section, we will verify the motion analysis results using kinematic analysis theory commonly found in mechanism design textbooks. Note that in kinematic analysis, position, velocity, and acceleration of given points or axes in the mechanism are analyzed.

In kinematic analysis, forces and torques are not involved. All bodies (or links) are assumed massless. Hence, mass properties defined for bodies are not influencing the analysis results.

The slider-crank mechanism is a planar kinematic analysis problem. A vector plot that represents the positions of joints of the planar mechanism is shown in Figure 5-31. The vector plot serves as the first step in computing position, velocity, and accelerations of the mechanism.

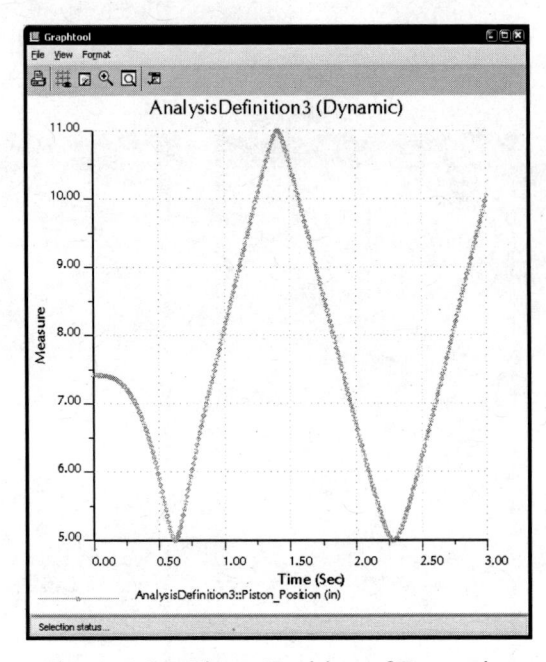

Figure 5-30 Piston Position of Dynamic Simulation

The position equations of the system can be described by the following vector summation,

$$Z_1 + Z_2 = Z_3 \quad (5.1)$$

where

$Z_1 = Z_1 \cos \theta_A + i Z_1 \sin \theta_A = Z_1 e^{i\theta_A}$
$Z_2 = Z_2 \cos \theta_B + i Z_2 \sin \theta_B = Z_2 e^{i\theta_B}$
$Z_3 = Z_3$, since θ_C is always 0.

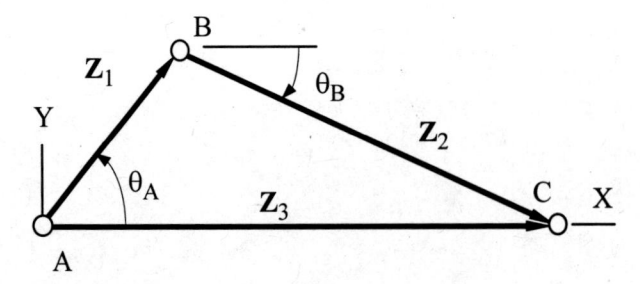

Figure 5-31 Vector Plot of the *slider-crank* Mechanism

The real and imaginary parts of Eq. 5.1, corresponding to the *X* and *Y* components of the vectors, can be written as

Lesson 5: A Slider-Crank Mechanism

$$Z_1 \cos \theta_A + Z_2 \cos \theta_B = Z_3 \tag{5.2a}$$

$$Z_1 \sin \theta_A + Z_2 \sin \theta_B = 0 \tag{5.2b}$$

In Eqs. 5.2a and 5.2b, Z_1, Z_2, and θ_A are given. We are solving for Z_3 and θ_B. Equations 5.2a and 5.2b are non-linear functions of Z_3 and θ_B. Solving them directly for Z_3 and θ_B is not straightforward. Instead, we will calculate Z_3 first, using trigonometric relations; i.e.,

$$Z_2^2 = Z_1^2 + Z_3^2 - 2Z_1 Z_3 \cos \theta_A$$

Hence,

$$Z_3^2 - 2Z_1 \cos \theta_A Z_3 + Z_1^2 - Z_2^2 = 0$$

Solving Z_3 from the above quadratic equation, we have

$$Z_3 = \frac{2Z_1 \cos \theta_A \pm \sqrt{(2Z_1 \cos \theta_A)^2 - 4(Z_1^2 - Z_2^2)}}{2} \tag{5.3}$$

where two solutions of Z_3 represent the two possible configurations of the mechanism shown in Figure 5-32. Note that point C can be either at C or C' for given Z_1 and θ_A.

From Eq. 5.2b, θ_B can be solved by

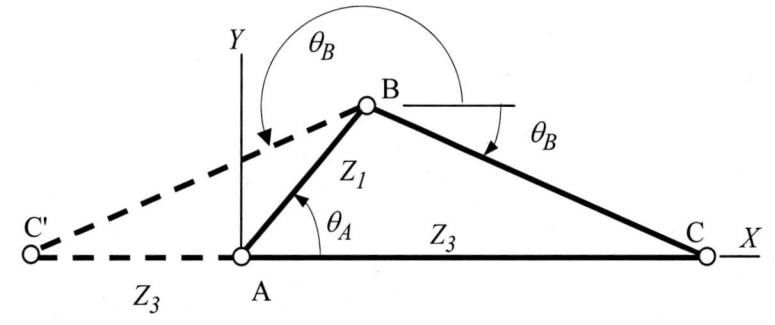

Figure 5-32 Two Possible Configurations

$$\theta_B = \sin^{-1}\left(\frac{-Z_1 \sin \theta_A}{Z_2}\right) \tag{5.4}$$

Similarly, θ_B has two possible solutions, corresponding to vector $\mathbf{Z}_3$.

Taking derivatives of Eqs. 5.2a and 5.2b with respect to time, we have

$$-Z_1 \sin \theta_A \, \dot{\theta}_A - Z_2 \sin \theta_B \, \dot{\theta}_B = \dot{Z}_3 \tag{5.5a}$$

$$Z_1 \cos \theta_A \, \dot{\theta}_A + Z_2 \cos \theta_B \, \dot{\theta}_B = 0 \tag{5.5b}$$

where $\dot{\theta}_A = \dfrac{d\theta_A}{dt} = \omega_A$ is the angular velocity of the driver, which is a constant. Note that Eqs. 5.5a and 5.5b are linear functions of $\dot{Z}_3$ and $\dot{\theta}_B$. Rewrite the equations in a matrix from; i.e.,

$$\begin{bmatrix} Z_2 \sin\theta_B & 1 \\ Z_2 \cos\theta_B & 0 \end{bmatrix} \begin{bmatrix} \dot{\theta}_B \\ \dot{Z}_3 \end{bmatrix} = \begin{bmatrix} -Z_1 \sin\theta_A \, \dot{\theta}_A \\ -Z_1 \cos\theta_A \, \dot{\theta}_A \end{bmatrix} \tag{5.6}$$

Equation 5.6 can be solved by

$$\begin{bmatrix} \dot{\theta}_B \\ \dot{Z}_3 \end{bmatrix} = \begin{bmatrix} Z_2 \sin\theta_B & 1 \\ Z_2 \cos\theta_B & 0 \end{bmatrix}^{-1} \begin{bmatrix} -Z_1 \sin\theta_A \, \dot{\theta}_A \\ -Z_1 \cos\theta_A \, \dot{\theta}_A \end{bmatrix}$$

$$= \frac{1}{-Z_2 \cos\theta_B} \begin{bmatrix} 0 & -1 \\ -Z_2 \cos\theta_B & Z_2 \sin\theta_B \end{bmatrix} \begin{bmatrix} -Z_1 \sin\theta_A \, \dot{\theta}_A \\ -Z_1 \cos\theta_A \, \dot{\theta}_A \end{bmatrix}$$

$$= \frac{1}{-Z_2 \cos\theta_B} \begin{bmatrix} Z_1 \cos\theta_A \, \dot{\theta}_A \\ Z_1 Z_2 \cos\theta_B \sin\theta_A \, \dot{\theta}_A - Z_1 Z_2 \sin\theta_B \cos\theta_A \, \dot{\theta}_A \end{bmatrix}$$

$$= \begin{bmatrix} -\dfrac{Z_1 \cos\theta_A \, \dot{\theta}_A}{Z_2 \cos\theta_B} \\ -\dfrac{Z_1 \left(\cos\theta_B \sin\theta_A \, \dot{\theta}_A - \sin\theta_B \cos\theta_A \, \dot{\theta}_A \right)}{\cos\theta_B} \end{bmatrix} \tag{5.7}$$

Hence

$$\dot{\theta}_B = -\frac{Z_1 \cos\theta_A \, \dot{\theta}_A}{Z_2 \cos\theta_B} \tag{5.8}$$

and

$$\dot{Z}_3 = Z_1 \left(\tan\theta_B \cos\theta_A \, \dot{\theta}_A - \sin\theta_A \, \dot{\theta}_A \right) \tag{5.9}$$

In this example, $Z_1 = 3$, $Z_2 = 8$, and the initial conditions are $\theta_A(0) = \pi/2$ and $\theta_B(0) = \sin^{-1}(3/8)$.

The solutions can be implemented using a spreadsheet. The *Excel* file, *lesson5.xls*, can be found at the publisher's web site. As shown in Figure 5-33, Columns A to I represent time, Z_1, Z_2, $\dot{\theta}_A$, θ_A, Z_3, θ_B, $\dot{Z}_3$, and $\dot{\theta}_B$, respectively. Note that in this calculation, $Z_3(0) > 0$ is assumed, hence $\dot{\theta}_B(0) < 0$, as illustrated in Figure 5-32. This is consistent with the initial conditions we defined for the motion model.

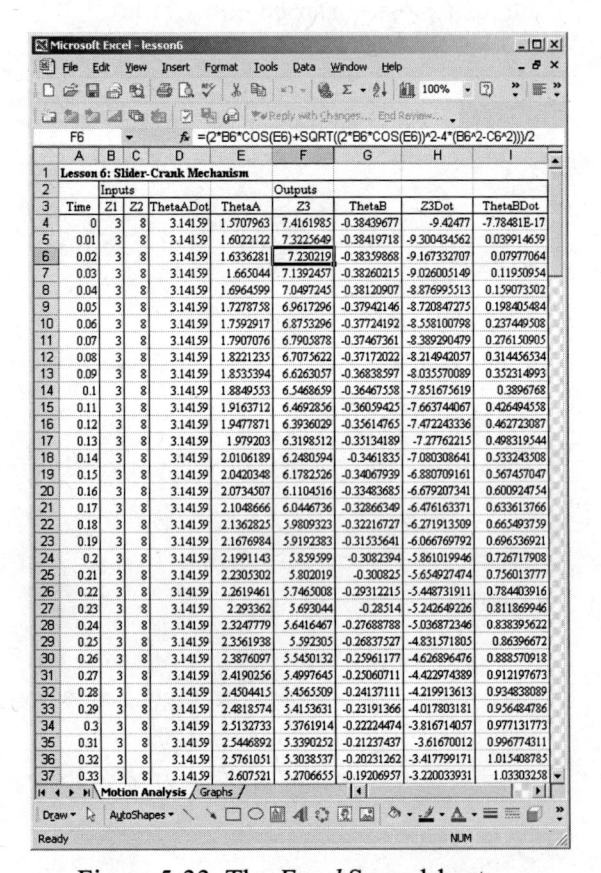

Figure 5-33 The *Excel* Spreadsheet

Figures 5-34 to 5-36 show the graphs of data in Columns F, G, and H. Comparing Figures 5-34 to 5-36 with Figures 5-15, 5-23, and 5-24, the simulation analysis results are verified.

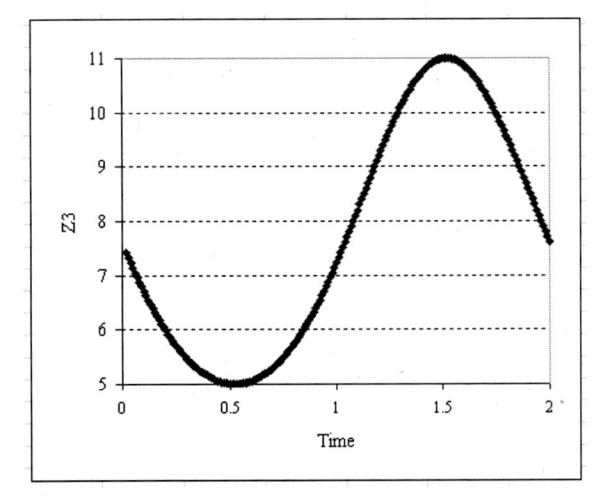

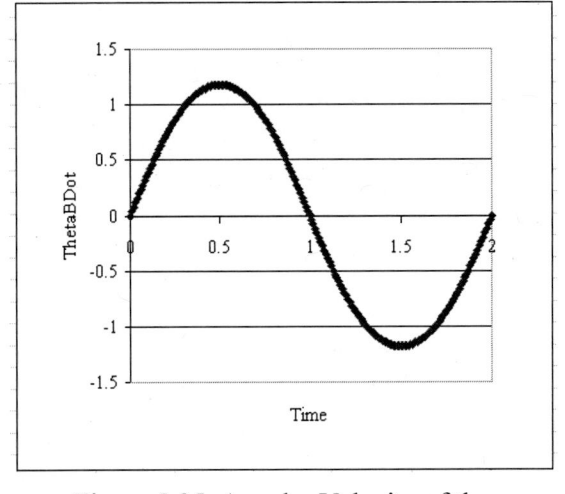

Figure 5-34 Position of the Piston

Figure 5-35 Angular Velocity of the Pin Joint: *Pin2*

Note that in Figures 5-23 and 5-35 the graphs are different in sign. This is because the direction of the pin joint, *Pin2*, is pointing in the negative Z-direction in *echanism Design*, which is different from what we assumed in our calculations. Also, the angle units are different.

Note that the accelerations of a given joint in the mechanism can be formulated by taking one more time derivative of Eqs. 5.5a and 5.5b. The resulting two linear equations can be solved using *Excel*. This is left as an exercise.

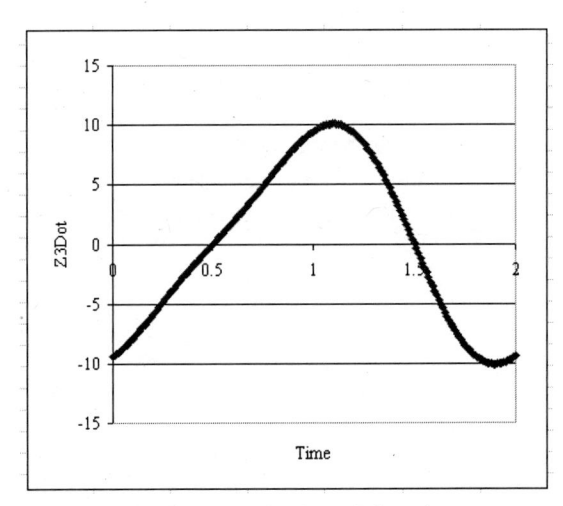

Figure 5-36 Velocity of the Piston

Exercises:

1. Derive the acceleration equations for the slider-crank mechanism, by taking derivatives of Eqs. 5.5a and 5.5b with respect to time. Solve these equations for the linear acceleration of the piston and the angular acceleration of the pin joint *Pin2*, using a spreadsheet. Compare your solutions with those obtained from *Mechanism Design*.

2. Use the same slider-crank model to conduct a static analysis using *Mechanism Design*. The static analysis in *Mechanism Design* should give you equilibrium configuration(s) of the mechanism due to gravity. Show the equilibrium configuration(s) of the mechanism and use the energy method you learned from *Statics* to verify the equilibrium configuration(s).

3. Change the length of the crank from 3 to 5 in. in *Pro/ENGINEER*. Repeat the kinematic analysis discussed in this lesson. In addition, change the crank length in the spreadsheet (*Microsoft Excel* file, *lesson5.xls*). Generate position and velocity graphs from both *Mechanism Design* and the spreadsheet. Do they agree with each other? Is the maximum slider velocity increase due to a longer crank? Is there interference occurring in the mechanism?

4. Download four *Pro/ENGINEER* parts from the publisher's web site to your computer (folder name: *Exercise 5-4*).

   (i) Use these four parts, i.e., crankshaft, connecting rod, piston pin, and piston (see Figure E5-1), to create an assembly like the one shown in Figure E5-2. Note that the crankshaft must be 45° CCW.

   (ii) Create a motion model for kinematic analysis. Conduct motion analysis by defining a driver that drives the crankshaft at a constant angular speed of 1,000 rpm.

   (iii) Use the spreadsheet *lesson5.xls* to calculate the piston velocity. Compare your calculations with those obtained from *Mechanism Design*.

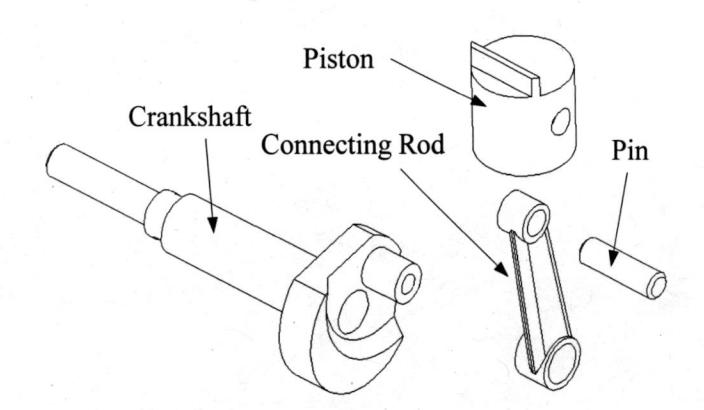

Figure E5-1 Four *Pro/ENGINEER* Parts

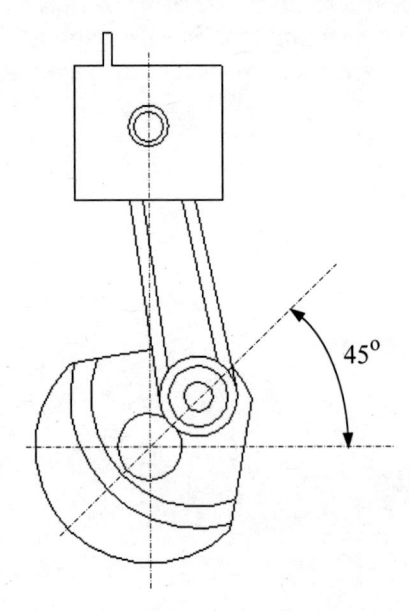

Figure E5-2 Assembled Configuration

Lesson 6: A Compound Spur Gear Train

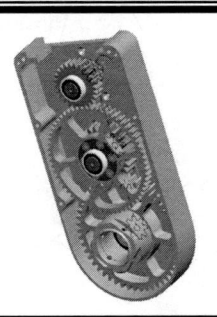

6.1 Overview of the Lesson

In this lesson we will discuss how to simulate motion of a spur gear train. A gear train is a set or system of gears arranged to transfer torque (or energy) from one part of a mechanical system to another. A gear train consists of a driving gear that is attached to the input shaft, a driven gear attached to the output shaft, and idler gears that interpose between the driving and driven gears in order to maintain the direction of the output shaft to be the same as the input shaft or to increase the distance between the driving and driven gears. There are different kinds of gear trains, such as simple gear train, compound gear train, epicyclic gear train, etc., depending on their functionality and how the gears are arranged. The gear train we are simulating in this lesson is a compound gear train, in which two or more gears are used to transmit torque (or energy). All gears included in this lesson are spur gears; therefore, the shafts that these gears mounted on are parallel.

In *Mechanism Design*, each gear in a gear train comprises one body, called gear, rack, or pinion, and a second body called the carrier (where the gear is mounted on), connected by a joint. One way to ensure that the geometry in your gear train maintains the desired spatial orientation during an analysis is to use the same body as the carrier body for both gears. This is usually the ground or can be another body in the mechanism. Figure 6-1 shows a simple standard gear train in which the two parts used for the carrier bodies (purple blocks) belong to the same body.

As shown in Figure 6-1, *Mechanism Design* simply uses cylinders or disks to represent the gears. No detailed tooth profile is necessary for any of the computations involved. Apparently, force and moment between a pair of teeth in contact will not be calculated in gear train simulations. However, there are other important data being calculated by *Mechanism Design*, such as reaction force exerting on the driven shaft (for a dynamic analysis), which is critical for mechanism design. Pitch circle diameters are critical for defining gear trains in *Mechanism Design*.

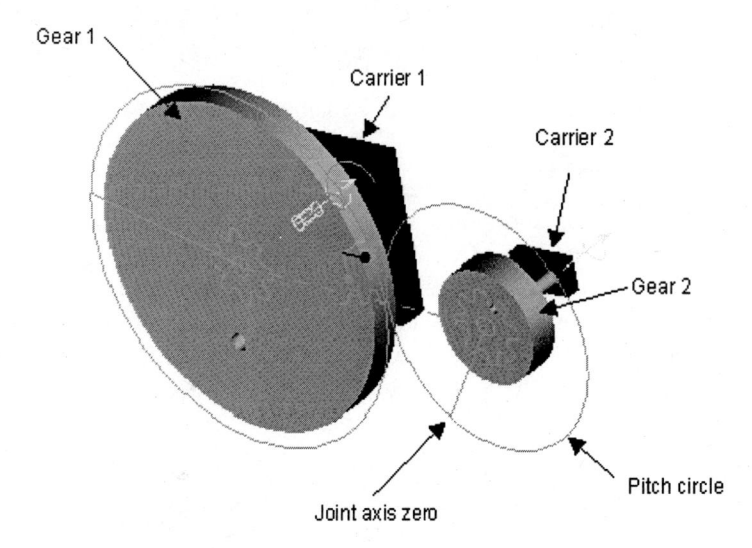

Figure 6-1 Gears and Carriers

Although cylinders or disks are sufficient to represent gears, we will use a more realistic gear train throughout this lesson. All gears in the example are shown with detailed geometric representation, including teeth. In addition, detailed parts, including shafts, bearing, screws and aligning pins are included for a realistic gear train system. In this gear train simulation, we will focus more on graphical animation, less on computations of physical quantities. We will add a servo motor to drive the input shaft, therefore, conducting a kinematic analysis.

6.2 The Gear Train Example

Physical Model

The gear train example we are using for this lesson is part of a gearbox designed for an experimental lunar rover. The gear train is located in a gear box which is part of the transmission system of the rover, driven by a motor powered by solar energy. The purpose of the gear train is to convert high speed and small torque generated by the motor to low speed and large torque output in order to drive the wheels of the rover. The gear train consists of four spur gears mounted on three parallel axes, as shown in Figure 6-2.

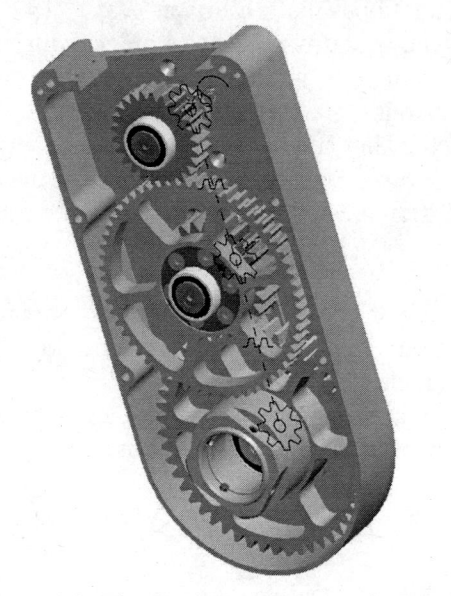

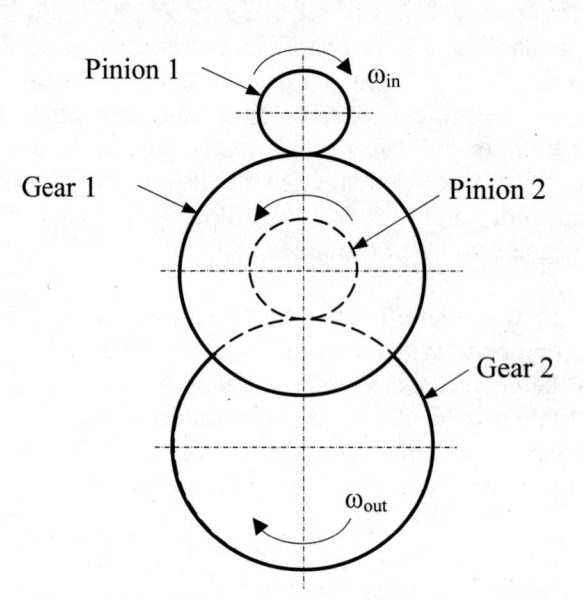

Figure 6-2 The Gear Train System in Rover

Figure 6-3 Schematic View of the Gear Train

The four spur gears form two gear pairs: *Pinion 1* and *Gear 1*, and *Pinion 2* and *Gear 2*, as illustrated in Figure 6-3. Note that *Pinion 1* is the driving gear that connects to the motor. The motor rotates in a clockwise direction, therefore, driving *Pinion 1*. *Gear 1* is the driven gear of the first gear pair, which is mounted on the same shaft as *Pinion 2*. Both rotate in a counterclockwise direction. *Gear 2* is driven by *Pinion 2*, and rotates in a clockwise direction. Note that the diameters of the pitch circles of the four gears are: 50, 120, 60, and 125 mm, respectively; and the numbers of teeth are 25, 60, 24, and 50, respectively. Therefore, the circular pitch P_c and module m of the two gear pairs are, respectively,

$$p_c = \frac{\pi d_{p1}}{N_{p1}} = \frac{\pi d_{g1}}{N_{g1}} = \frac{\pi(50)}{25} = \frac{\pi(120)}{60} = 6.283 \text{ mm}, \quad m = \frac{d_{p1}}{N_{p1}} = \frac{d_{g1}}{N_{g1}} = \frac{50}{25} = \frac{120}{60} = 2 \text{ mm} \quad (6.1\text{a})$$

$$p_c = \frac{\pi d_{p2}}{N_{p2}} = \frac{\pi d_{g2}}{N_{g2}} = \frac{\pi(60)}{24} = \frac{\pi(125)}{50} = 7.854 \text{ mm}, \quad m = \frac{d_{p1}}{N_{p1}} = \frac{d_{g1}}{N_{g1}} = \frac{50}{24} = \frac{125}{50} = 2.5 \text{ mm} \quad (6.1\text{b})$$

Lesson 6: A Compound Spur Gear Train 6-3

The gear ratio g_r of the gear train is:

$$g_r = \frac{\omega_{out}}{\omega_{int}} = \frac{d_{p1}}{d_{g1}}\frac{d_{p2}}{d_{g2}} = \frac{50}{120}\frac{60}{125} = \frac{1}{5} \qquad (6.2)$$

where ω_{out} and ω_{in} are the output and input angular velocities of the gear train system, respectively; and d_{p1}, d_{g1}, d_{p2}, and d_{g2} are the pitch diameters of the four gears. The gear ratio of the gear train is 1:5; i.e., the angular velocity is reduced 5 times at the output. Theoretically, the torque output will increase 5 times if there is no loss due to; e.g., friction. Note that we will use *mmNs* unit system for this lesson.

Pro/ENGINEER Parts and Assembly

The gear train assembly consists of one part and three subassemblies. You may want to open the final assembly, *gear_train_final.asm*, to check the assembled gear train shown in Figure 6-2. Enter *Mechanism Design* (by choosing *Applications > Mechanism*), choose *Analysis > Playbacks* to show the gear motion. You should see that the pinion gear *Pinion 1* rotates a complete circle, and the other three gears rotate accordingly. This is what we want to accomplish in this lesson.

Take a look at the model tree; there are four major components in this assembly: *gbox_housing.prt*, *gear_input.asm*, *gear_middle.asm*, and *gear_output.asm*. There are 22 distinct parts in this assembly.

One important thing for the animation to "look right" is to mesh the gear teeth properly. You may want to use the *FRONT* view and zoom in to the tooth mesh areas to check if the two pairs of gears mesh well (see Figure 6-4). Note that this is accomplished by properly orienting the three subassemblies with respect to the root assembly through datum plane alignment. Note that the tooth profile is represented by straight lines, instead of more popular ones such as involutes curves, just for simplicity.

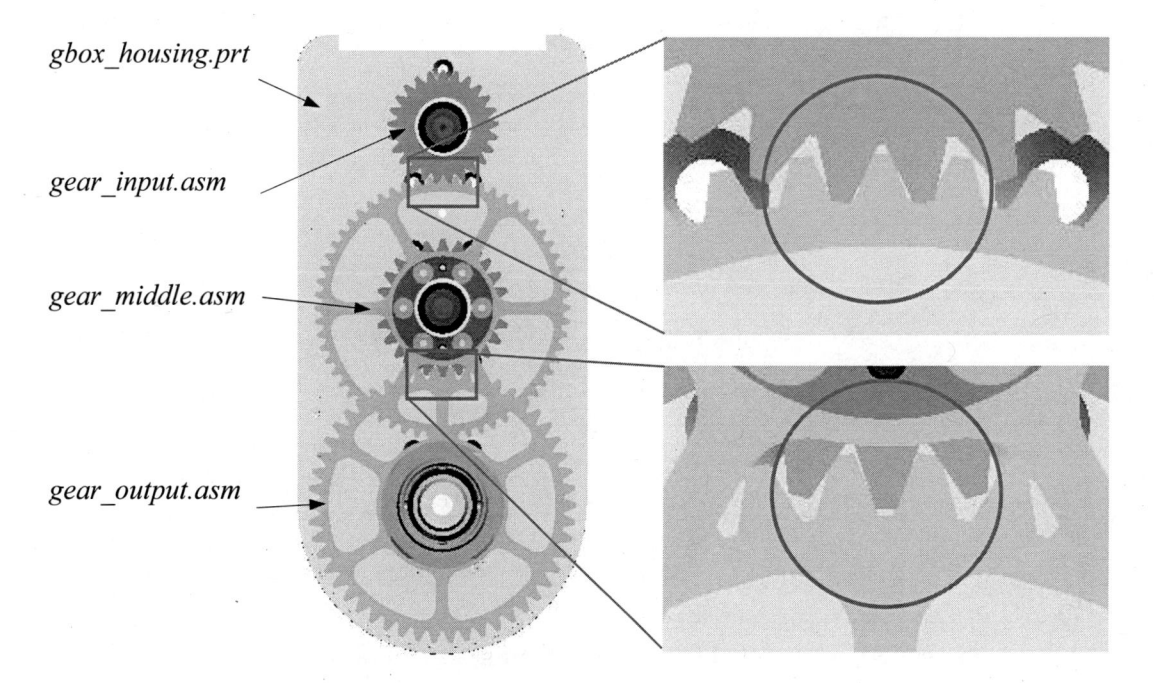

Figure 6-4 Gear Teeth Properly Meshed

Simulation Model

In *Mechanism Design*, gear pairs are created by connecting two gears (or rack or pinion) and their carrier, as discussed earlier (see Figure 6-1). A pin joint must be created first between the gear and its carrier when you assemble the gear part. In this example, gear housing part serves as the carrier for all gears. There are three pin joints to be created for the input, middle, and output gear assemblies. A motor will be added to drive the pin joint between the input gear subassembly and its carrier (the housing part). We will conduct a kinematic analysis for this example.

6.3 Using *Mechanism Design*

Creating an Assembly

In the *lesson6* folder, you should see a total of 22 distinct parts and 3 assemblies. The assemblies and associated parts are listed in Table 6.1.

Table 6.1 List of Parts and Assemblies in Lesson 6 Folder

Part/Subassemblies	Part Names	Remarks
gbox_housing.prt		
gear_input.asm	*wheel_gbox_shaft_input.prt*	
	wheel_gbox_pinion_1s.prt	Pinion 1
	spacer_12×18×5mm.prt	
	spacer_12×20×1mm.prt	
	bearing_12×18×8mm.prt (2)	
	spacer_10×18×014mm.prt	
	wheel_gbox_sft_mid_washer.prt	
	screw_tapper_head_5×15.prt	
	screw_set_tip_6×6.prt (2)	
gear_middle.asm	*wheel_gbox_pinion_2s.prt*	Pinion 2
	wheel_gbox_gear_1s.prt	Gear 1
	wheel_gbox_shaft_mid_pinion.prt	
	wheel_gbox_shaft_mid_gear.prt	
	bearing_12×18×8mm.prt (2)	
	screw_tapper_head_5×28.prt (6)	
	wheel_gbox_sft_mid_washer.prt (2)	
	screw_tapper_head_5×15.prt (2)	
	align_pin_4×27mm.prt (2)	
gear_output.asm	*wheel_gbox_gear_2s.prt*	Gear 2
	wheel_gbox_connect_wheel.prt	
	bear_tap_roller25×47×15mm.prt	
	screw_straight_head_4×15.prt (10)	
	align_pin_4×20mm.prt (2)	
	wheel_gbox_connect_wh_setscrew.prt (4)	

Start *Pro/ENGINEER*, change the working directory, and create a new assembly: *gear_train* (or a different name you prefer). You should see three datum planes and one datum coordinate system in the *Graphics* window. The first thing to do in this new assembly is to set unit system. From the pull-down menu, choose

File > Properties.

Lesson 6: A Compound Spur Gear Train 6-5

In the *Model Properties* dialog box, *Inch lbm Second (Pro/E Default)* is listed, as shown in Figure 6-5. Click *change* to bring up the *Units Manager* dialog box (Figure 6-6).

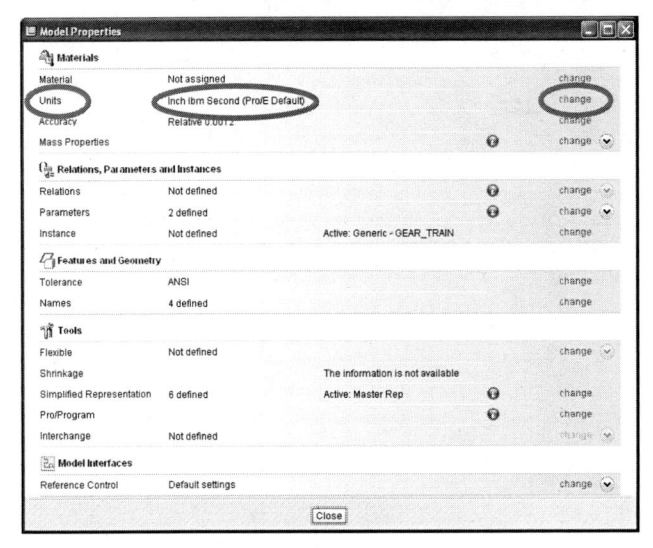

Figure 6-5

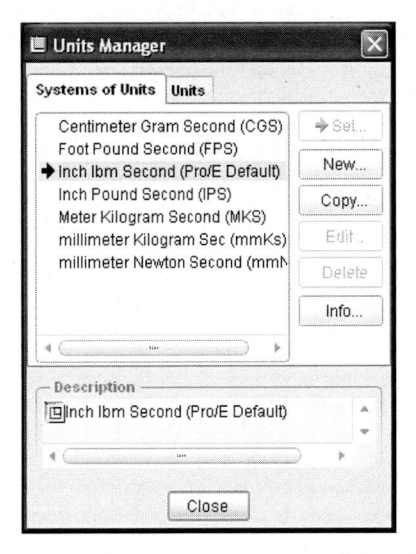

Figure 6-6 The *Units Manager* Dialog Box

In the *Units Manager* dialog box, choose *millimeter Newton second (mmNs)*, then click the *Set* pushbutton.

In the *Changing Model Units* dialog box, click *Interpret dimension (for example 1" becomes 1mm)*. In fact, it does not matter which option you choose since no component has been brought in yet. Click *OK* to accept the option (Figure 6-7) and click *Close* in the *Units Manager* dialog box to accept the unit system (Figure 6-6). Click *Close* again for the *Model Properties* dialog box (Figure 6-5).

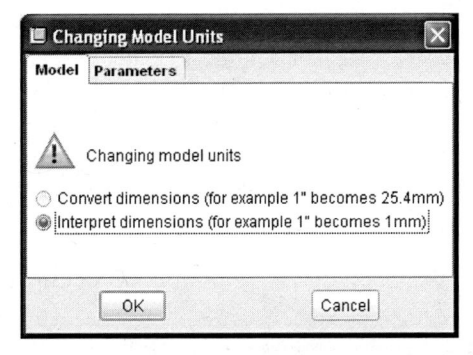

Figure 6-7 The *Changing Model Units* Dialog Box

Now we are ready to bring in the first part *gear_housing.prt*. The gear housing will be fixed to the assembly by aligning their respectively coordinate systems.

Click the *Add component* shortcut button and choose *gear_housing.prt*. In the *Component Placement* dashboard choose *Coord Sys* from the *Constraint Type* list.

From the *Graphics* window, pick *ASM_DEF_CSYS* (assembly) and *PRT_DEF_CSYS* (*gear_housing.prt*), then click the button to accept the definition. You should see that the gear housing is brought into the assembly like that of Figure 6-8.

Note that three datum axes *A_191*, *A_189*, and *A_160* of the three features *Cut id 10858*, *Cut id 10788*, and *Protrusion id 10035*, respectively, will be used to align with those of gears for creating pin joints. Note that there are many axes in this part. In order to see these three datum axes, you may want to use the layer option to turn off some other axes.

The layer option can be accessed from the *Set layers* button on top of the *Graphics* window. As shown in Figure 6-8, the *Model Tree* area will now display default layers created by *Pro/ENGINEER*. Expand *02__PRT_ALL_AXES*, and then click *in GBOX_HUISONG.PRT*, a number of solid features that contain datum axes will be listed.

Click the solid features *F13(PROTRUSION)*, *F12(CUT)*, and *F11(CUT)* to locate them in the *Graphics* window. We will use the axes embedded in these three solid features.

Use the right mouse button to hide all the other items. You should see a cleaner view of the datum axes with the part. Click the *Set layers* button again to bring back the standard *Model Tree*.

Figure 6-8 The Gear Housing Brought into Assembly

Next, we will bring in the first gear assembly, *gbox_input.asm*. Click the *Add component* button and choose *gbox_input.asm*. In the *Component Placement* dashboard from the *User Defined* list choose the *Pin* joint. Pick *A_191* (housing) and *A_21* (*gbox_input.asm*), as shown in Figure 6-9a. Now turn off the datum axis display. Rotate the view (similar to Figure 6-8b) to pick the back face of the housing and the groove face of the *gbox_input.asm* (*Bearing_12×28×8MM: Surf:F5(PRUTRUSION)*), as shown in Figure 6-9b. The *gbox_input.asm* should be properly assembled to the housing with a pin joint, as shown in Figure 6-9c. Click the ✓ button to accept the definition.

Pick A_191 (*gear_housing.prt*) and A_21 (*gbox_input.asm*)

(a) Pick Two Datum Axes

Pick these two faces

(b) Pick Two Faces

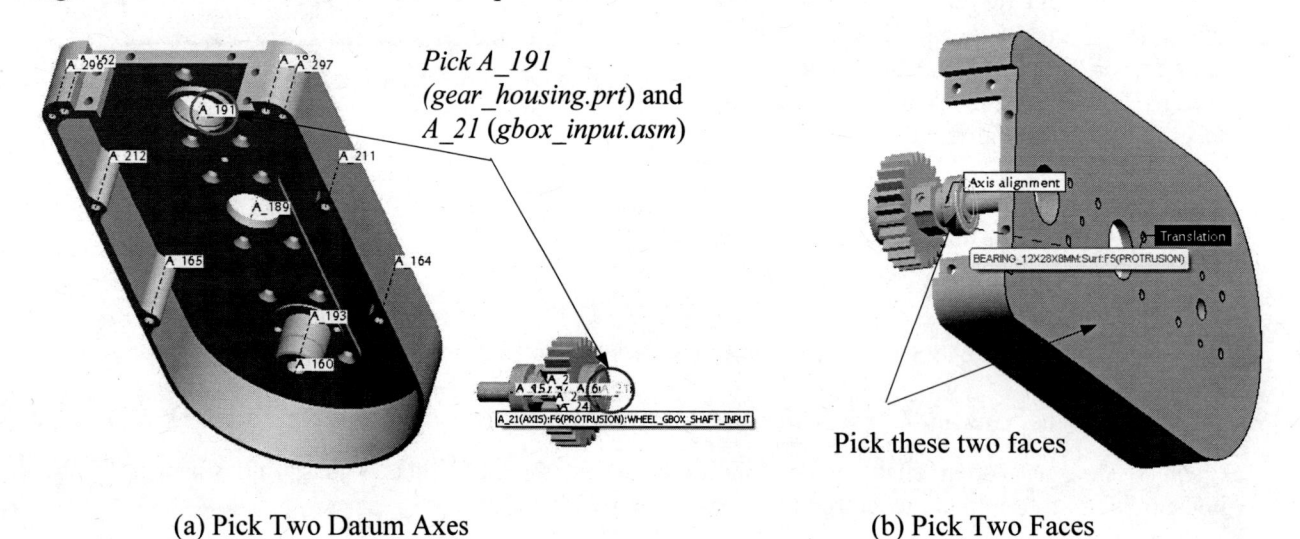

Figure 6-9 Assembling *gbox_input.asm* to Housing

Lesson 6: A Compound Spur Gear Train

The next assembly we will bring in is *gbox_middle.asm*. Click the *Add component* button and choose *gbox_middle.asm*. Choose the *Pin* joint, turn on datum axis display, and pick *A_189* (*gear_housing.prt*) and *A_66* of *gbox_middle.asm* (*A_66(AXIS):F5(PROTRUSION): WHEEL_GBOX_SFT_MID_WASHER*), as shown in Figure 6-9a. Now turn off the datum axis display, pick the back face of the housing and the groove face of *gbox_middle.asm* (*F5* of *Bearing 12×28×8*), as shown in Figure 6-9b. The *gbox_middle.asm* should be properly assembled to the housing with a pin joint, as shown in Figure 6-9c. Click the ✓ button to accept the definition.

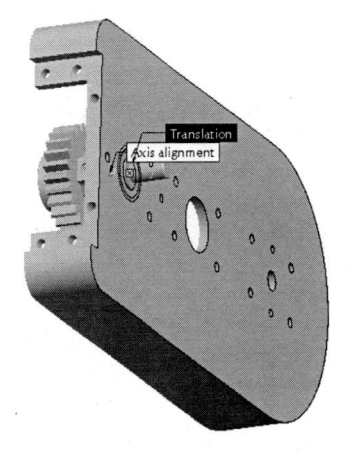

(c) *gbox_input.asm* Assembled

Figure 6-9 Assembling *gbox_input.asm* to Housing (cont'd)

(a) Pick Two Datum Axes

(b) Pick Two Faces

(c) *gbox_input.asm* Assembled

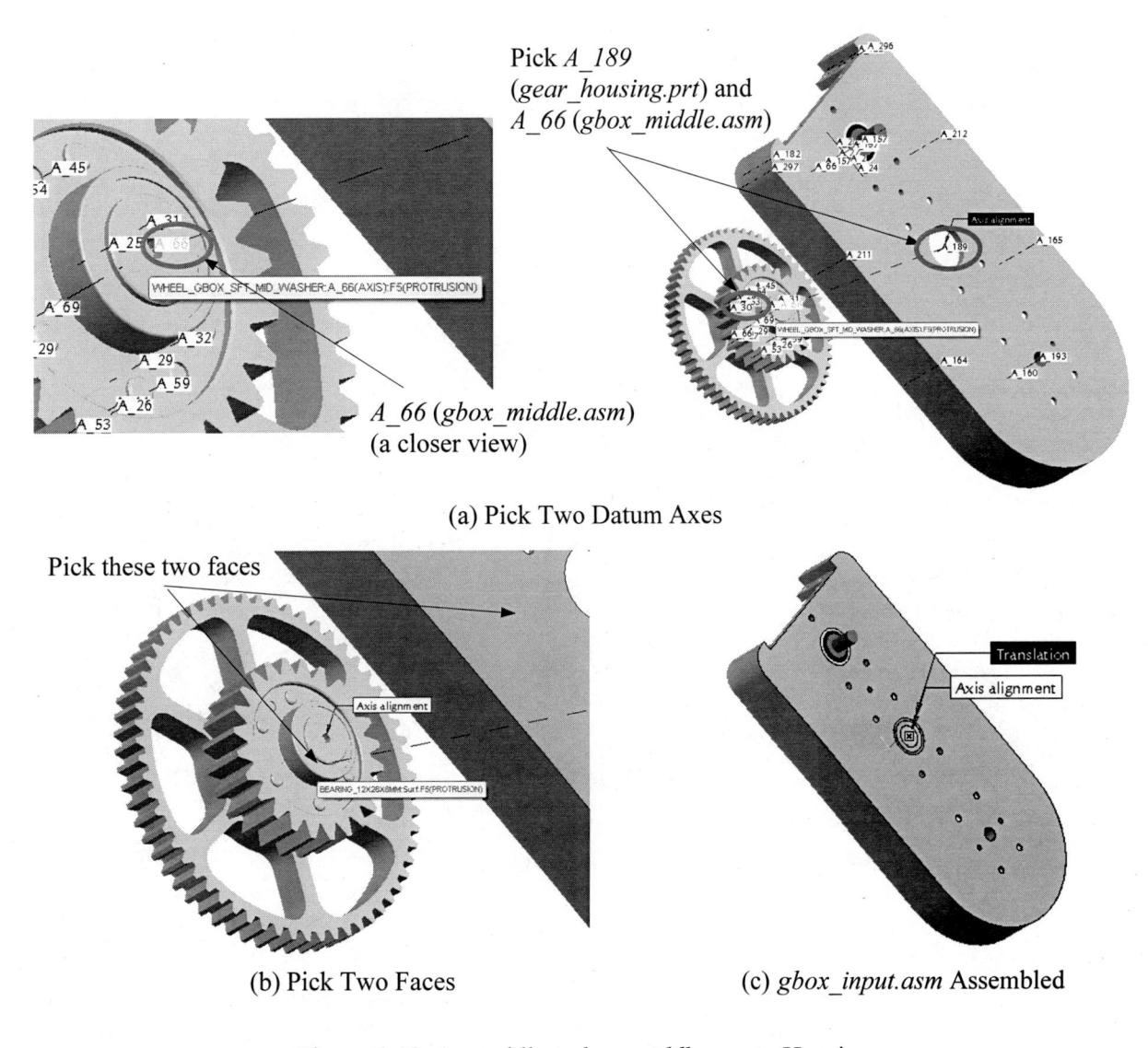

Figure 6-10 Assembling *gbox_middle.asm* to Housing

The third and final assembly we will bring in is *gbox_output.asm*. Following the same procedure to choose a pin joint type, pick *A_193* (*gear_housing.prt*) and *A_66* of *gbox_output.asm* (*WHEEL_GBOX_CONNECT_WHEEL:A_66(AXIS):F5 (PRUTRUSION)*), as shown in Figure 6-11a. Now turn off the datum axis display, pick the back face of *gbox_output.asm* (*F71* of *wheel_gbox_gear_25*), as shown in Figure 6-11b. Then, turn the view around so you can pick the inner face of the housing. Pick the inner face of the housing, as shown in Figure 6-11b. The *gbox_output.asm* is assembled to the housing. If *gbox_output.asm* is not properly assembled (like that of Figure 6-11c), click the *Change orientation of constraint* button on top of the *Graphics* window (see Figure 6-11c). The *gbox_output.asm* should now be properly assembled with a pin joint, as shown in Figure 6-11d. Click the ✓ button to accept the definition.

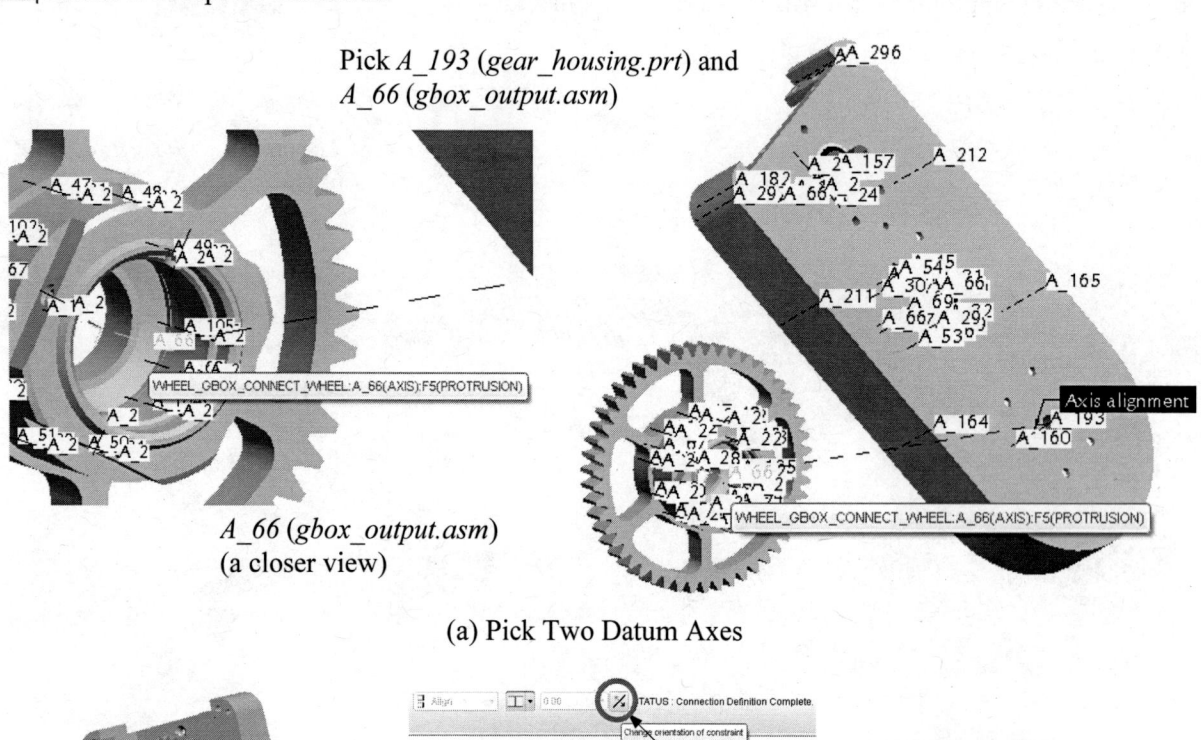

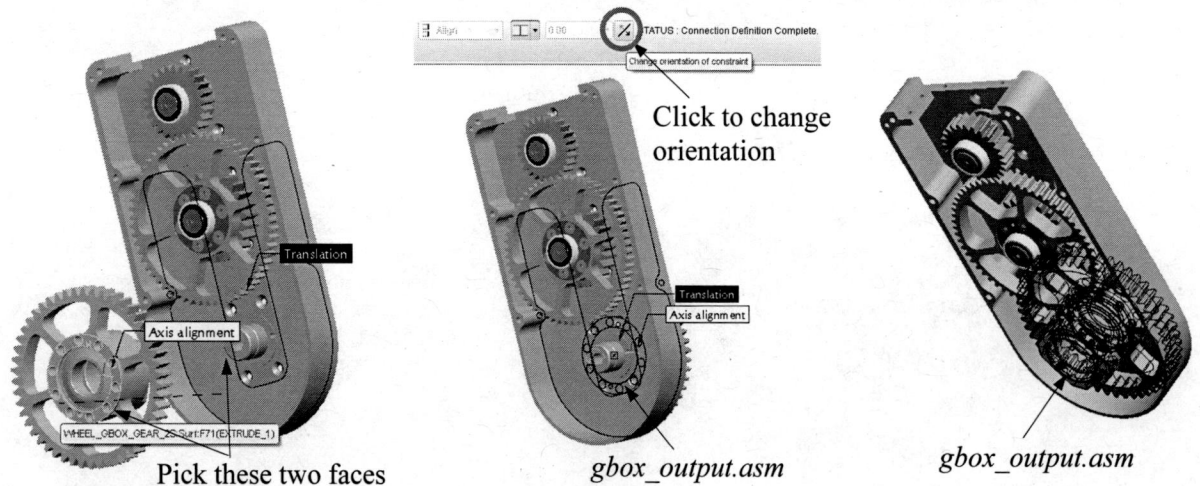

(a) Pick Two Datum Axes

(b) Pick Two Faces   (c) *gbox_output.asm* incorrectly assembled   (d) *gbox_output.asm* Assembled

Figure 6-11 Assembling *gbox_output.asm* to Housing

Lesson 6: A Compound Spur Gear Train

Now we have completed the assembly of the gear train. You may want to hide the housing and rotate the view to see more closely how these gears are assembled (Figure 6-12). Note that the gear teeth between *Pinion 1* and *Gear 1* are meshed well, but not those between *Pinion 2* and *Gear 2*. We will use the *Drag* option to align datum planes of the gears so that their teeth would mesh properly. Before that we will have to hide some of the datum planes and only keep those we need to use for aligning the gear teeth.

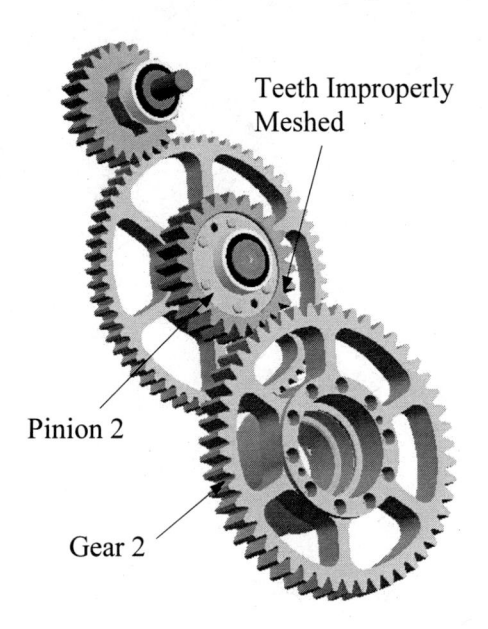

Figure 6-12 The Gear Train

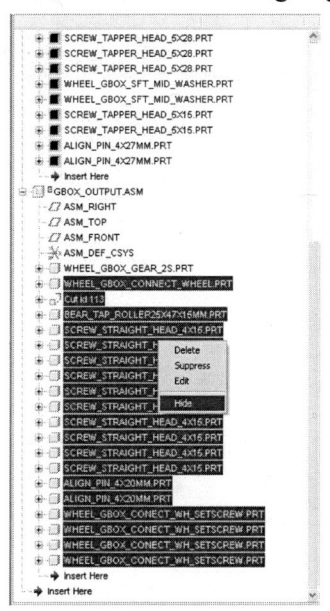

Figure 6-13 The Model Tree

First turn on datum planes display, you will see a huge number of datum planes appear. Now go to the *Model Tree* window. Expand all three subassemblies, and hide all parts, except *wheel_gbox_pinion_1s.prt* (in *gbox_input.asm*), *wheel_gbox_gear_1s.prt* (in *gbox_middle.asm*), and *wheel_gbox_gear_2s.prt* (in *gbox_output.asm*). The best way to do that is to select all parts you want to hide (press *Shift* key to select multiple items), press the right mouse key, and select *Hide*, as shown in Figure 6-13.

Use the same approach to hide datum planes of the three subassemblies. In order to display datum features in the *Model Tree*, you may click *Settings* (on top of the *Model Tree* shown in Figure 6-14), and choose *Tree Filters*. In the *Model Tree Filters* dialog box (Figure 6-15), click *Features* and then *OK*. All features, including datum planes, will now appear in the *Model Tree*.

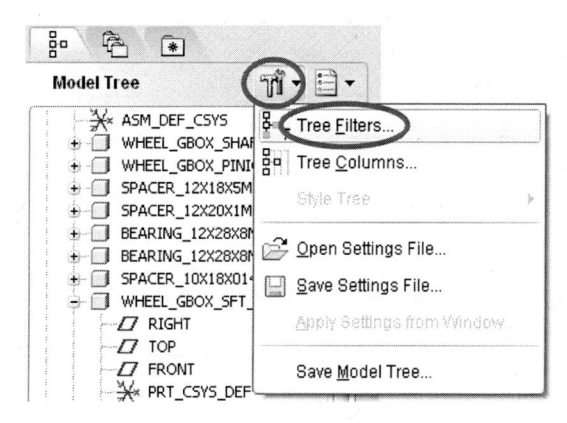

Figure 6-14 Choose the Tree Filters

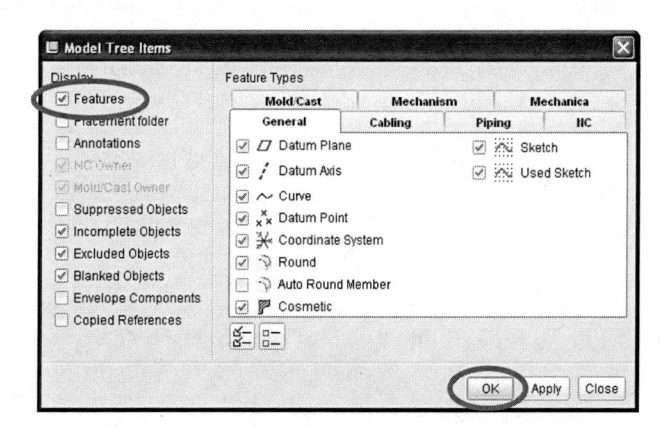

Figure 6-15 The *Model Tree Filters* dialog box

Also, hide *ASM_TOP* and *ASM_FRONT* of the root assembly. You should see a cleaner view like that of Figure 6-16a. Since the first two gears align properly, we will keep their orientations by aligning coincident datum planes. We will only need to adjust the orientation of *Gear 2*.

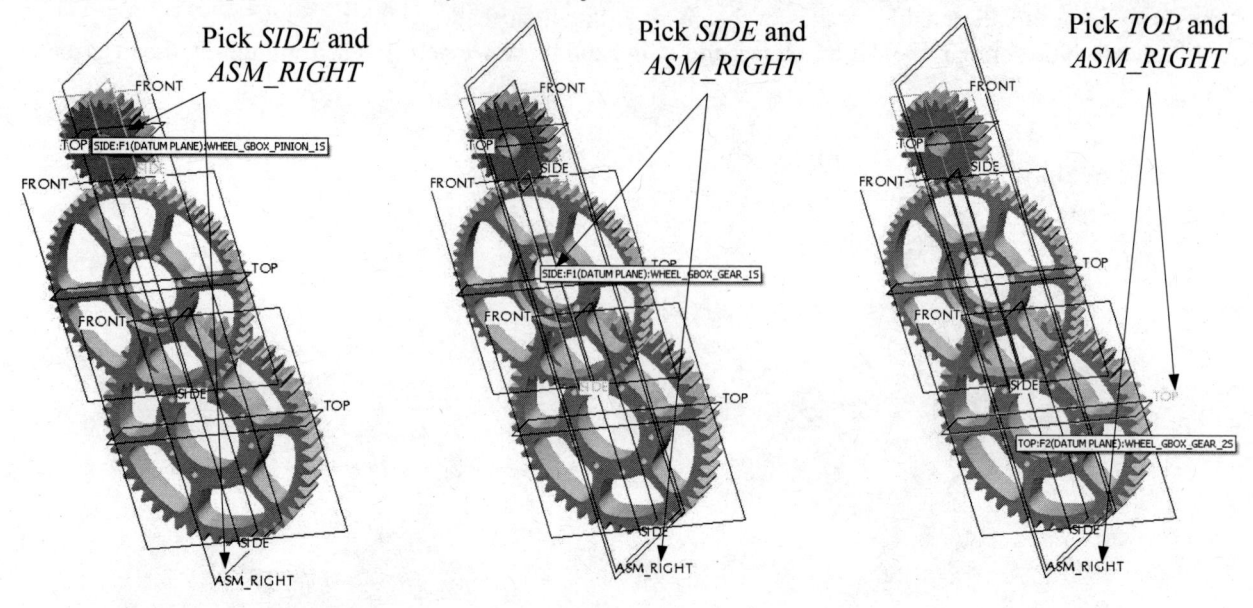

(a) Align *SIDE* and *ASM_RIGHT*   (b) Align *SIDE* and *ASM_RIGHT*   (c) Align *TOP* and *ASM_RIGHT*

Figure 6-16 Aligning Datum Planes for Meshing Gear Teeth

Click the *Drag Packed Components* button on top of the *Graphics* window, the *Drag* dialog box appears. Click the *Constraints* tab, and choose the *Align Two Entities* button (first on the left). Choose datum planes *SIDE* (*wheel_gbox_pinion_1s*) and *ASM_RIGHT* (assembly), as shown in Figure 6-16a. Click the *Align Two Entities* button again, and choose *SIDE* (*wheel_gbox_gear_1s*) and *ASM_RIGHT* (assembly), as shown in Figure 6-16b. Click the *Align Two Entities* button again, and choose *TOP* (*wheel_gbox_gear_2s*) and *ASM_RIGHT* (assembly), as shown in Figure 6-16c. Unhide *wheel_gbox_pinion_2s* of the *gear_middle.asm* by pressing the right mouse button and choosing *Unhide*. Change to the *FRONT* view and zoom in to check the tooth meshing areas. All teeth should now be properly meshed.

Click the *Current Snapshot* button on top, a default name *Snapshot1* will appear. Click *Close*. The snapshot *Snapshot1* has been saved for future use. Now the gear train is completely assembled. Save your model before we enter *Mechanism Design*.

Creating a Simulation Model

From the pull-down menu, choose

Applications > Mechanism.

Turn off the datum plane display; you should see three pin joints shown in the *Graphics* window (see Figure 6-17). Note the third pin joint is in the opposite direction of the first two.

We will define two gear pairs and a servo motor for a motion model.

Lesson 6: A Compound Spur Gear Train

From the shortcut buttons on the right, click *Define Gear-Pair connections* (3rd from the top), or choose from the pull-down menu

Insert > Gears.

The *Gear Pair Definition* dialog box will appear (Figure 6-18). Use the default name (*GearPair1*), choose *Spur* for *Type*, then pick the first pin joint *Pin 1*. Note that you may want to turn off all datum features in order to see the pin joint. After picking the pin joint, *gbox_input.asm* and *gbox_housing.prt* will be highlighted. Enter *50* for *Pitch Circle Diameter*.

Click the *Gear 2* tab to define the second gear in the pair. Pick *Pin 2* and enter *120* for *Pitch Circle Diameter* (should have been determined). Click *OK*. A pair of gear symbols will appear next to the two pin joints chosen (*Pin 1* and *Pin 2*), as shown in Figure 6-19.

Repeat the same procedure to define the second pair. Pick *Pin 2* and *Pin 3* and enter diameters *60* and *125* for *Gear1* and *Gear2*, respectively.

Click the *Drag* button and click *Pinion 1*. Move the mouse around, you should see that *Pinion 1* starts turning, and the gears in the gear train move.

Now we will create a driver at pin joint *Pin 1* to drive *Pinion 1*; therefore, the gear train.

From the shortcut buttons on the right, click *Define Servo Motors* (4th from the top), or choose from the pull-down menu

Insert > Servo Motors.

The *Servo Motor Definition* dialog box will appear (Figure 6-20). Enter *Motor1* for *Name*, leave *Motion Axis* (default) for *Driven Entity* (under *Type* tab), then pick *Pin 1*. Note that you may want to turn off all datum features in order to see the pin joint. After picking the pin joint, a larger arrow appears to confirm your selection.

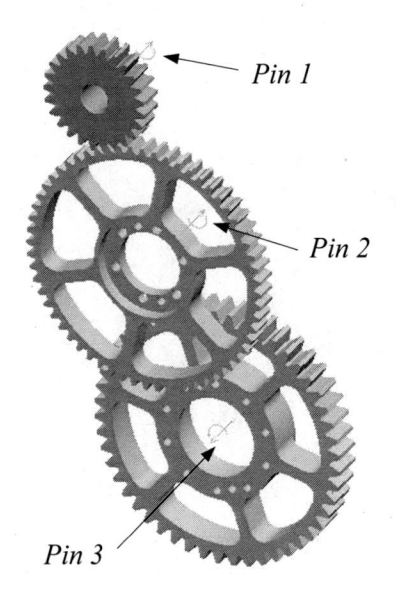

Figure 6-17 Pin Joints Defined in the Assembly

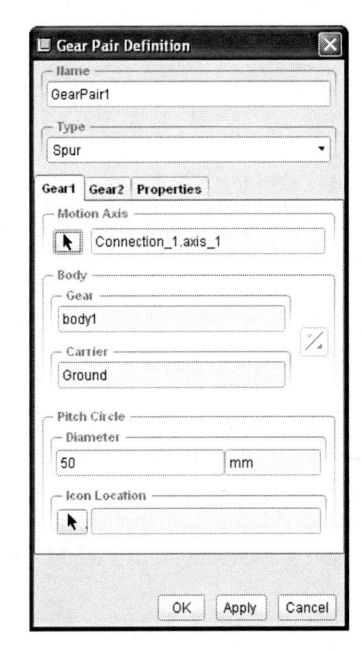

Figure 6-18 The *Gear Pair Definition* Dialog Box

The next step is to specify the profile of the motor. From the *Servo Motor Definition* dialog box pick the *Profile* tab, choose *Velocity* and *deg* (default) in *Specification*, and leave *Constant* (default) in *Magnitude*. Enter *360* for the constant *A*, and click *OK*. A driver symbol should appear at the pin joint in the *Graphics* window (Figure 6-21). Use the saved snapshot (*Snapshot1*) for initial configuration before defining and running the analysis.

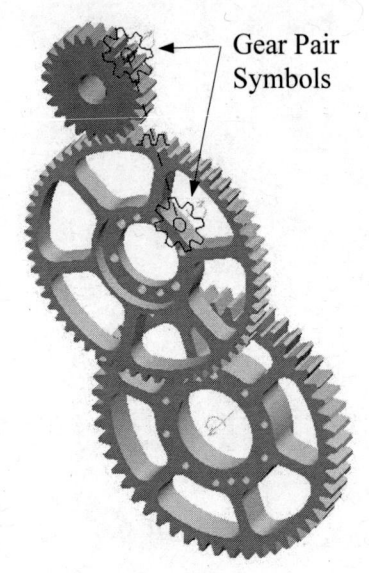

Figure 6-19 The *Gear Pair* Symbols

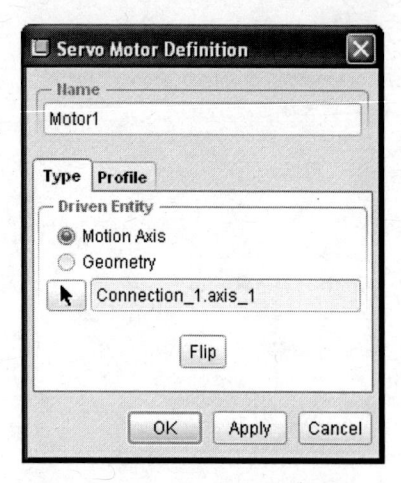

Figure 6-20 The *Servo Motor Definition* Dialog Box

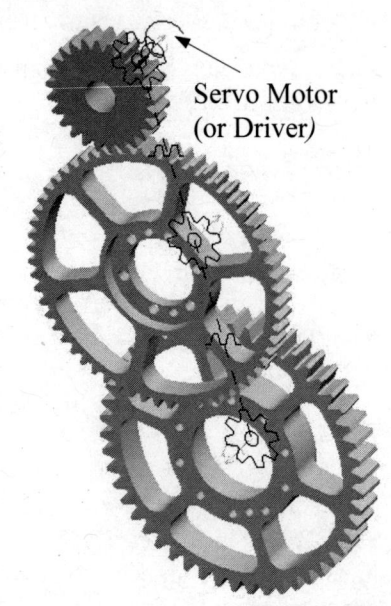

Figure 6-21 *Servo Motor* Symbol

Creating and Running a Kinematic Analysis

From the shortcut button list on the right, click the *Mechanism Analysis* shortcut button to define an analysis. In the *Analysis Definition* dialog box appearing, leave the default name, *AnalysisDefinition1*, and enter:

Type: *Kinematic*
Start Time: *0*
End Time: *1*
Frame Rate: *100*
Minimum Interval: *0.01*
Initial Configuration: *Current*

Make sure the servo motor is included. Run the analysis. In the *Graphics* window, the mechanism starts moving. You should see *Pinion 1* rotates 360 degrees as expected. Click *OK* to close the dialog box.

Saving and Reviewing Results

Click the *Playbacks* button on the right to bring up the *Playbacks* dialog box and repeat the motion animation. On the *Playbacks* dialog box, click *Save* button to save the results as a *.pbk* file.

Note that we want to create a measure to monitor the output angular velocity of the gear train. We will choose the pin joint *Pin 3* and the angular velocity of it rotational axis for the measure. To do so, click the *Generate Measure Results of Analyses* button . In the *Measure Results* dialog box appearing (Figure 6-22), click the *Create New Measure* button . The *Measure Definition* dialog box opens. Enter *Angular_Velocity_Output* for *Name*. Under *Type*, select *Velocity*. Pick *Pin 3* in the *Graphics* window. Under *Evaluation Method*, leave *Each Time Step*. Click *OK* to accept the definition.

In the *Measure Results* dialog box, choose *AnalysisDefinition1* in the *Result Set* and click the *Graph* button on the top left corner to graph the measure. The graph should be similar to that of Figure 6-23, which shows that the output velocity is a constant of −72 degrees/sec. Note that this magnitude is one fifth of the input velocity since the gear ratio is 1:5. The negative sign is simply due to the direction of the joint *Pin 3*. Physically, both the input (*Pinion 1*) and output gears (*Gear 2*) rotate in the same direction.

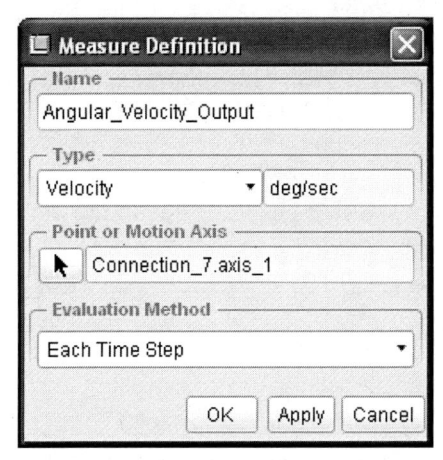

Figure 6-22 The *Measure Definition* Dialog Box

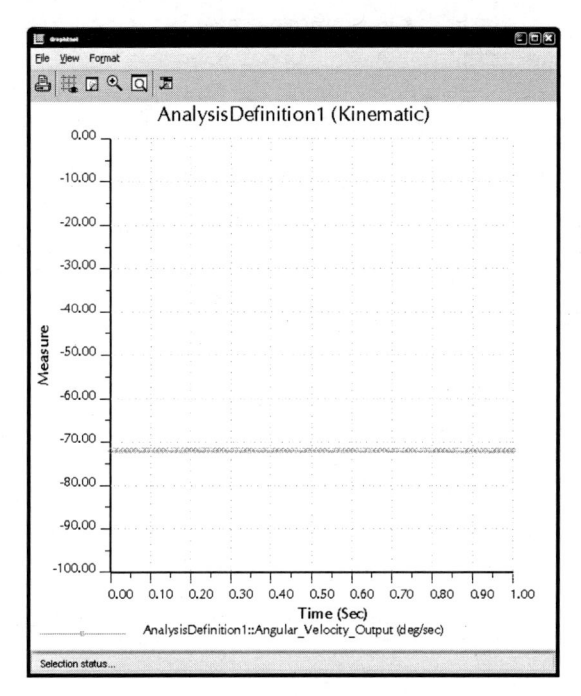

Figure 6-23 Output Angular Velocity

Exercises:

1. The same spur gear train will be used for this exercise. Create a constant torque for the input gear (*gbox_input.asm*) along the Z-direction of the *WCS*. Define and run a 2-second dynamic simulation for the gear train.

   (a) What is the minimum torque that is required to rotate the input gear, and therefore, the entire gear train?
   (b) If the torque applied to the input gear is 100 mm N, what will be the maximum output angular velocity of the gear train at the end of the 2-second simulation? Verify the simulation result using your own calculation. Note that you may check mass properties of the bodies from *Model Tree*. Click the body name and use right mouse button to choose *Info > Details*.
   (c) Create a graph for the reaction moment between gears of the first gear pair due to the 100 mm N torque. What is the reaction moment obtained from simulation?

Lesson 7: Planetary Gear Train Systems

7.1 Overview of the Lesson

In this lesson we will discuss planetary gear train systems. Planetary gearing is a gear system that consists of one or more outer gears, or *planet* gears, rotating about a central, or *sun* gear, as shown in Figure 7-1. Typically, the planet gears are mounted on a movable arm or *carrier* which may rotate relatively to the sun gear. A planetary gear system may also incorporate the use of an outer ring gear or *annulus*, which meshes with the planet gears.

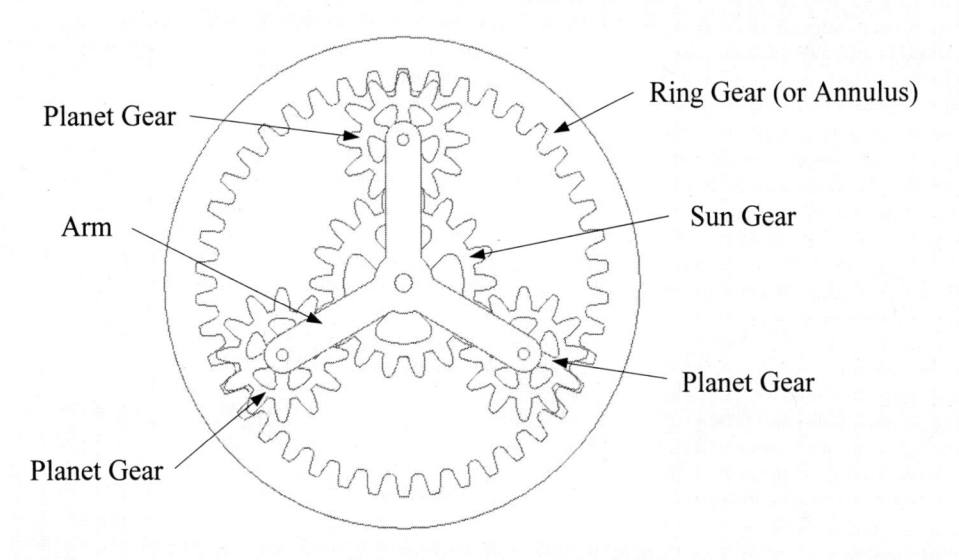

Figure 7-1 Planetary Gear Train

In many planetary gearing systems, one of these three basic components (that is, sun gear, planet gears, and arm) is held stationary (in addition to the ring gear); one of the two remaining components is an *input*, receiving power to the gear train system, while the last component is an *output*, disseminating power from the system. The ratio of input rotation to output rotation is dependent upon the number of teeth in each gear, and upon which component is held stationary. One situation is when the ring gear is held stationary, and the sun gear is used as input. In this case, the planet gears rotate around the sun gear at a rate determined by the number of teeth in meshed gear pairs; i.e., sun/planet and planet/ring gears.

Planetary gear trains are very commonly employed in mechanical systems. They are primarily designed for large gear reductions; hence, building up sufficient torque to drive mechanism system. One of the common places to find the planetary gear trains is in the power screwdriver (Figure 7-2), where a large gear reduction is necessary for a large torque output in a small package. Series of planetary gear trains are very often packaged to receive a maximum gear reduction.

In general, one of the most important tasks in designing planetary gear train systems is to achieve a required gear reduction, usually in a small given space. In this lesson, we will learn how to simulate motion of planetary gear trains and calculate the gear ratios. Note that some simulation results obtained from *Mechanism Design* for the planetary gear trains are not reliable. They are wrong. Therefore, we will discuss the theory to make correct calculations. It is very important that you understand the theory and are able to compute the gear ratio accurately.

Figure 7-2 Planetary Gear Trains Found in Power Screw Driver

7.2 The Planetary Gear Train Examples

Physical Model

There are two examples we will discuss. The first example is a single planetary gear train, as shown in Figure 7-3. This gear train consists of only one planet gear mounted on the arm. The planet gear is meshed with a stationary ring gear. In this system, there is only one pair of meshed gears: the planet and the ring gears. The pitch circle diameters of the planet and ring gears are $d_p = 2.333$ and $d_r = 8.167$ in., respectively. There are 12 and 42 teeth on the planet and ring gears, respectively. Therefore, the circular pitch P_c and diametral pitch P_d of the gears are, respectively,

$$p_c = \frac{\pi d_p}{N_p} = \frac{\pi d_r}{N_r} = \frac{\pi(2.333)}{12} = \frac{\pi(8.167)}{42} = 0.6108 \text{ in.} \tag{7.1a}$$

$$p_d = \frac{N_p}{d_p} = \frac{N_r}{d_r} = \frac{12}{2.333} = \frac{42}{8.167} = 5.143 \tag{7.1b}$$

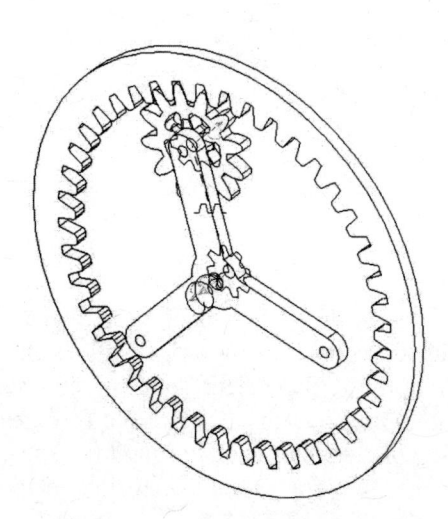

Figure 7-3 The Single Planetary Gear Train System

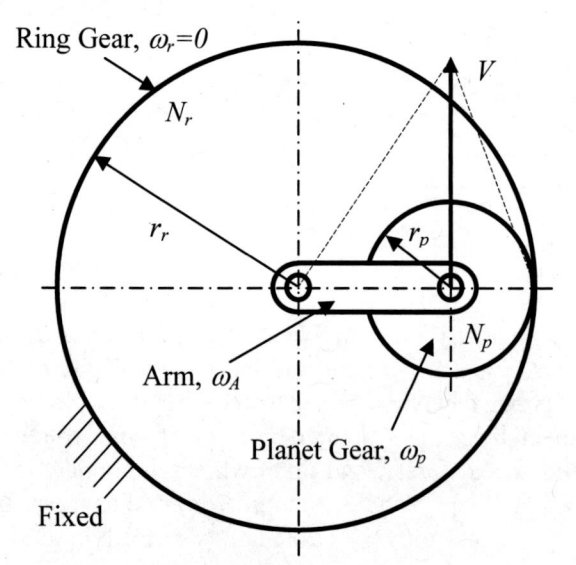

Figure 7-4 Velocity Analysis for the Single Planetary Gear Train System

Note that every one counterclockwise turn of the arm produces $(1-N_r/N_p)$ clockwise turns of the planet gear. This can be easily figured out from velocity analysis. For example, as shown in Figure 7-4, the linear velocity at the end of the arm where it connects to the center of the planet gear is $V = (r_r - r_p)\omega_A$.

Lesson 7: Planetary Gear Train Systems

Since the planet gear is "rolling" along the ring gear, the linear velocity at it center, which is the same as V, is $V = r_r \omega_p$. Therefore,

$$V = (r_r - r_p)\omega_A = r_p \omega_p \tag{7.2a}$$

$$\omega_p = \left(1 - \frac{r_r}{r_p}\right)\omega_A = \left(1 - \frac{N_r}{N_p}\right)\omega_A \tag{7.2b}$$

The gear ratio g_r of the gear train is:

$$g_r = \frac{\omega_{out}}{\omega_{int}} = \frac{\omega_p}{\omega_A} = \left(1 - \frac{N_r}{N_p}\right) = \left(1 - \frac{42}{12}\right) = -2.5 \tag{7.3}$$

That is, every one counterclockwise turn of the arm produces 2.5 clockwise turns on the planet gear. If the arm is rotating at 360 degrees/sec counterclockwise, the planet gear will rotate at –900 (that is, –2.5×360) degrees/sec (clockwise).

The second example, as shown in Figure 7.5, consists of an additional sun gear and two additional planet gears. Again, the ring gear is stationary and the sun gear is driven by a constant motor. The pitch circle diameter of the sun gear is d_s = 3.5 and the number of teeth is 18. Therefore, the circular pitch P_c and diametral pitch P_d of the sun gear are 0.6108 and 5.143 in., respectively, which are identical to the remaining gears in the system, as expected.

Note that for a general planetary gear train system, the arm is usually not directly driven by the power source (such as a motor). The general equation for calculating the gear ratio is the following:

$$g_r = \frac{\omega_{out} - \omega_A}{\omega_{in} - \omega_A} = \Pi\left(\pm \frac{N_{driving}}{N_{driven}}\right) \tag{7.4}$$

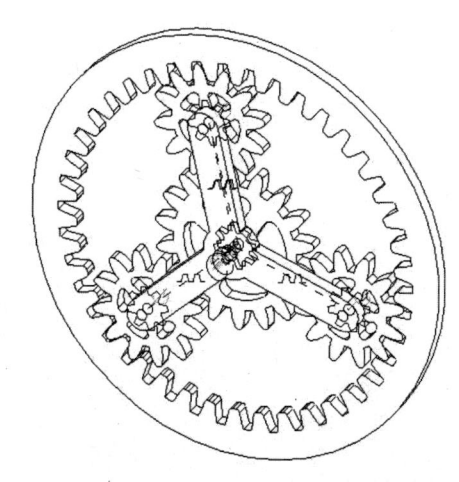

Figure 7-5 The Multiple Planetary Gear Train System

where $N_{driving}$ and N_{driven} are the number of teeth on the driving and driven gears, respectively; and Π is an operator that creates a product for the terms enclosed in the parenthesis. Note that the driving and driven gears can be identified by power input and output within each gear pairs. For example, for the gear system shown in Figure 7-5, if the sun gear is directly connected to a motor, then the sun gear will be the driving gear and the planet gear (any one of the three) is the driven gear. In the second gear pair; i.e., the planet and the ring gears, the planet gear will be the driving gear and the ring gear will be the driven gear. The sign on the right hand side of Eq. 7.4 will be determined by the gear pairs. For a gear pair consisting of two regular spur gears, such as the one discussed in *Lesson 6*, the sign is negative since the two spur gears rotate in the opposite directions. For a gear pair including a ring gear, the sign will be positive since, in this case, the planet and the ring gears rotate in the same direction. Therefore, for the second example, if the sun gear is driven by a motor with a constant angular velocity of 360 degrees/sec counterclockwise, what will be the gear ratio of the system? Well, we know the output gear; i.e., the ring gear, is stationary; therefore, $\omega_{out} = 0$. In order to calculate the gear ratio, we will have to figure out the angular velocity of the arm first. This can be accomplished by using Eq. 7.4.

$$\frac{\omega_{out} - \omega_A}{\omega_{in} - \omega_A} = \frac{0 - \omega_A}{360 - \omega_A} = \left(\frac{N_s}{N_p}\right)\left(-\frac{N_p}{N_r}\right) = \left(\frac{18}{12}\right)\left(-\frac{12}{42}\right) = -0.4286 \tag{7.5}$$

Therefore, ω_A = *108.0* degree/sec counterclockwise, and the gear ratio is *–0.4286* if the input and output gears of the system are the sun and ring gears, respectively.

If the sun gear is the input gear and the planet gear is the output gear, then the angular velocity of the planet gear can be calculated by using Eq. 7.4; i.e.,

$$\frac{\omega_{out} - \omega_A}{\omega_{in} - \omega_A} = \frac{\omega_p - 108}{360 - 108} = \left(\frac{N_s}{N_p}\right) = \left(-\frac{18}{12}\right) = -1.5 \tag{7.6}$$

Therefore, ω_p = *–270.0* degrees/sec (clockwise), and the gear ratio is *–1.5*.

Note that the angular velocity of the planet gear in the single planetary gear train example can also be calculated using Eq. 7.4, in which the planet gear is the input gear and the ring gear is the output gear. Therefore,

$$\frac{\omega_{out} - \omega_A}{\omega_{in} - \omega_A} = \frac{0 - 360}{\omega_p - 360} = \frac{N_p}{N_r} = \frac{12}{42} = 0.2857 \tag{7.7}$$

and ω_p = *–900* degrees/sec; i.e., the planet gear will make a 2.5 clockwise turn for every counterclockwise turn of the arm. This is identical to what we obtained from velocity analysis.

Pro/ENGINEER Parts and Assembly

The single planetary gear train consists of three parts *arm.prt*, *plant.prt*, and *ring.prt*. You may want to open the final assembly, *single_gear_train_final.asm*, to check the assembled gear train shown in Figure 7-3. Enter *Mechanism Design* (by choosing *Applications > Mechanism*), choose *Analysis > Playbacks* to show the gear motion. You should see that the arm rotates and drives the planet gear to rotate around the inner side of the ring gear. This is the first example we want to accomplish in this lesson.

The multiple planetary gear train consists of *sun.prt*, *arm.prt*, *plant.prt (3)*, and *ring.prt*. You may want to open the final assembly, *multiple_gear_train_final.asm*, to check the assembled gear train shown in Figure 7-5. Again, choose *Analysis > Playbacks* to show the gear motion.

Similar to what was discussed in *Lesson 6*, one important thing for the animation to "look right" is that the gear pairs must mesh correctly. You may want to use the *BACK* view and zoom in to the tooth mesh areas to check if the two pairs of gears mesh well (see Figure 7-6). They are properly meshed. This is accomplished by properly orienting the individual gear parts with respect to the assembly through datum plane alignment.

Note that the example files you downloaded from the publisher's web site should consist of two subfolders, *single* and *multiple*. The files enclosed in the folders are, respectively:

lesson7/final/single/single_gear_train_final.asm
lesson7/final/single/arm.prt
lesson7/final/single/planet.prt
lesson7/final/single/ring.prt

and

lesson7/final/multiple/multiple_gear_train_final.asm
lesson7/final/multiple/sun.prt
lesson7/final/multiple/arm.prt
lesson7/final/multiple/planet.prt
lesson7/final/multiple/ring.prt

Note that in this lesson, we will use the default unit system; i.e., in-lb_m-sec.

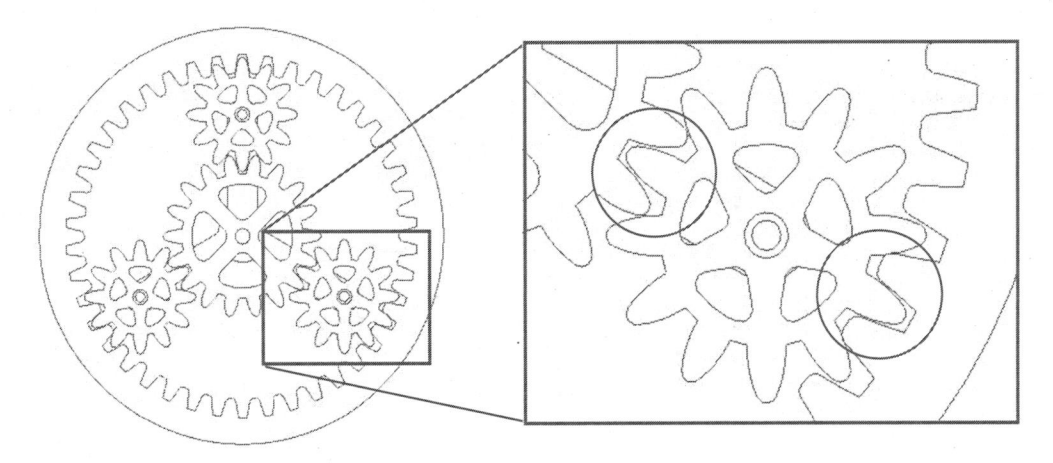

Figure 7-6 Gear Teeth Properly Meshed

Simulation Model

As discussed in *Lesson 6*, in *Mechanism Design*, gear pairs are created by selecting two gears and their carriers. A pin joint must be created first between the gear and its carrier when you assemble the gear. In both examples, the datum axis (*AA_1*, to be created in assembly) will be the carrier for both the sun and ring gears. In addition, *AA_1* will be chosen to define a pin joint for the arm. Only one pair of gears will be defined for the single planetary gear train example, the planet and ring gears. There are multiple gear pairs defined for the multiple planetary gear train example, the sun and planet gears, and planet and ring gears.

Two motors will be created for both examples. One motor will be used to drive the arm and the sun gear for the single and multiple planetary gear train examples, respectively, at a constant angular velocity. The second motor will be connected to the ring gear, in which the angular velocity will be set to zero since the ring gear is assumed stationary.

7.3 Using *Mechanism Design*

Creating an Assembly

Start *Pro/ENGINEER*, change the working directory, and create a new assembly: *example_1* (or any name you prefer). You should see three datum planes and one datum coordinate system in the *Graphics* window. We will first create a datum axis that is normal to the datum plane *ASM_FRONT*, and lies on both *ASM_TOP* and *ASM_RIGHT*. To create a datum axis, click the datum axis button on the right of the *Graphics* window (3rd from the top) or choose from the pull-down menu

Insert > Model Datum > Axis.

In the *Datum Axis* dialog box appearing (Figure 7-7), the *References* field is active (filled with yellow color) and is ready for you to pick a reference entity from the *Graphics* window. Pick *ASM_FRONT*, a temporary axis that is normal to *ASM_FRONT* will appear with two handles (small square), as shown in Figure 7-8. Drag one handle to touch *ASM_TOP*. When the *ASM_TOP* is highlighted, release the mouse button. In the *Graphics* window, you should see a dimension appears, defining the distance between the axis and *ASM_TOP*. In the *Datum Axis* dialog box, *ASM_TOP* is listed in the *Offset references* with an offset value. Enter *0* for the offset. Repeat the same to drag the other handle to lie on the datum plane *ASM_RIGHT*. Set the offset value to *0*, and click *OK*. You should see a datum axis *AA_1* created in the *Graphics* window. Note that datum axis *AA_1* will be the carrier for the ring gear, as well as one of the axes for the pin joint between the arm and the assembly.

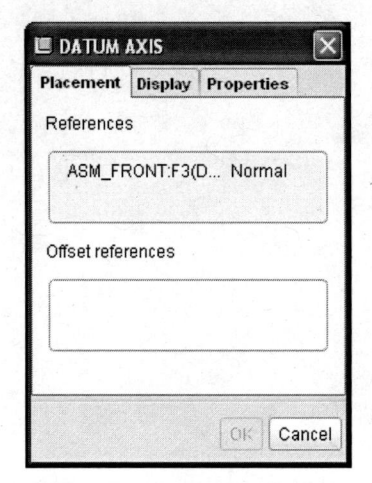

Figure 7-7 The *Datum Axis* Dialog Box

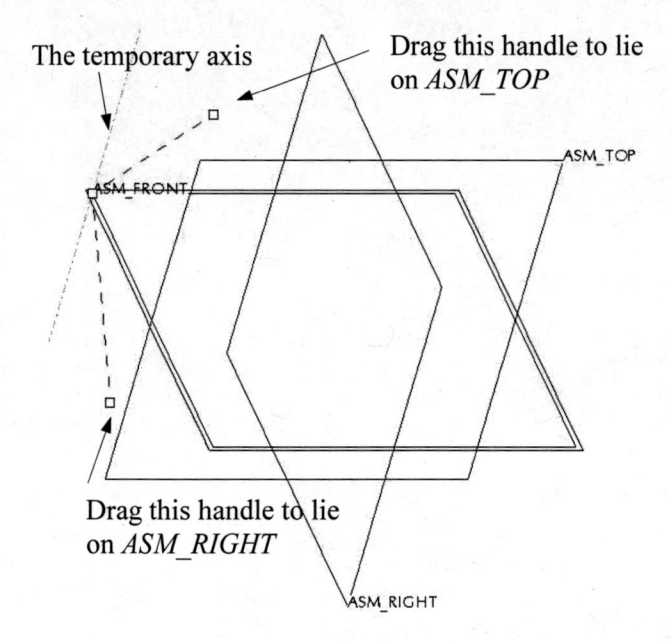

Figure 7-8 Creating a *Datum Axis*

Next, we will bring in the first part, *arm.prt*. Click the *Add component* shortcut button and choose *arm.prt*. In the *Component Placement* dashboard from the *User Defined* list choose the *Pin* joint, and pick *AA_1* (assembly) and *A_3* (*arm.prt*), as shown in Figure 7-9a. Now turn off datum axis display and turn on datum plane display. Pick two datum planes, *ASM_FRONT* (assembly) and *FRONT* (*arm.prt*), as shown in Figure 7-9b. The *arm.prt* should be properly assembled to the assembly through a pin joint. The default name of the pin joint is *Connection_1*. In order to minimize possible confusion (*Mechanism Design* may give the same name to two different joints), we will name this joint *Pin1*. This can be done by clicking the *Placement* button, clicking the joint name *Connection_1*, and entering *Pin1* in the *Set Name* text field, as shown in Figure 7-10. Press the *Enter* key to accept the joint name. Click the button to accept the joint definition.

The next part we will bring in is the planet gear. Click the *Add component* button and choose *planet.prt*. Choose the *Pin* joint, turn on datum axis display, and pick *A_2* (*planet.prt*) and *A_5* (*arm.prt*),

Lesson 7: Planetary Gear Train Systems

as shown in Figure 7-11a. Pick the front face of the planet gear, *F5(REVOLVE_1):PLANET*, and rotate the view to pick the back face of the arm, *F5(REVOLVE_1):ARM*, as shown in Figure 7-11b. The *planet.prt* should be properly assembled to the arm with a pin joint. Change the joint name to *Pin2*. Click the ✓ button to accept the definition.

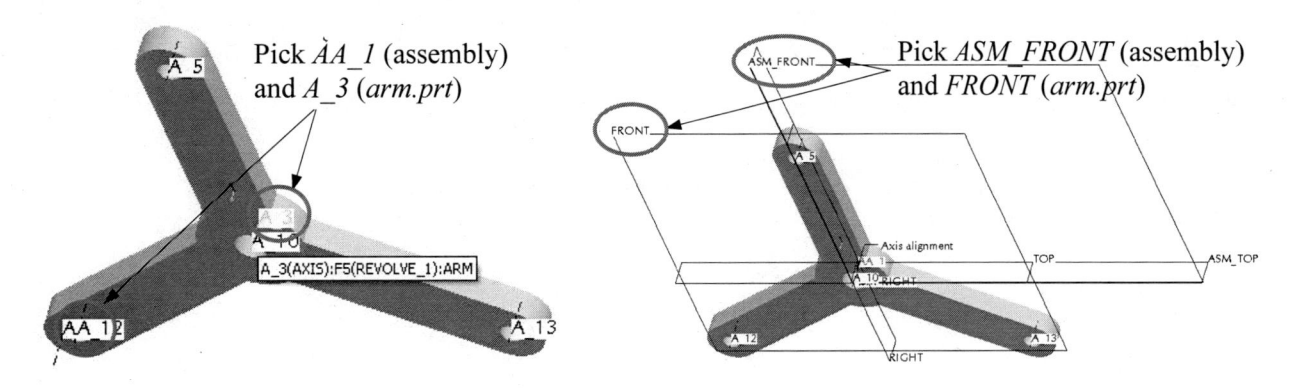

(a) Align Datum Axes (b) Align Datum Planes

Figure 7-9 Assembling *arm.prt*

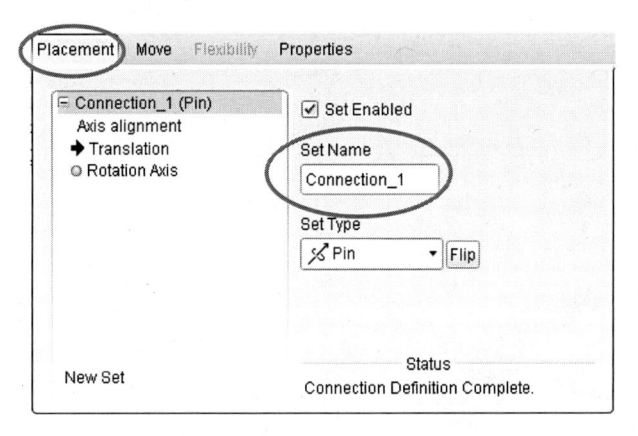

Figure 7-10 Changing the Joint Name to *Pin1*

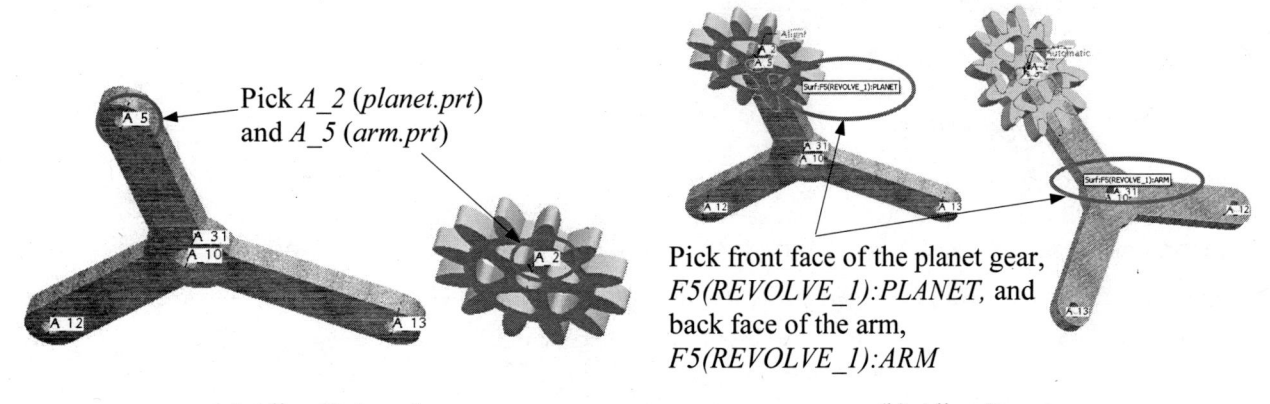

(a) Align Datum Axes (b) Align Faces

Figure 7-11 Assembling *planet.prt*

The third and final part we will bring in is *ring.prt*. Following the same procedure to choose a pin joint type, pick *AA_1* (assembly) and *A_3* (*ring.prt*), as shown in Figure 7-12a. Now turn off the datum axis display, turn on datum plane display, and pick *ASM_FRONT* (assembly) and *FRONT* (*ring.prt*), as shown in Figure 7-12b. The ring is not properly aligned with the planet gear yet. Click the *Placement* button, select *Translation* (should be selected already) and select *Offset* (see Figure 7-12c), and enter −0.3125 for offset. Note that this value is the thickness of the arm. With this offset, the ring gear will be properly aligned with the planet gear. Enter *Pin3* for name. The *ring.prt* should now be properly assembled to the assembly with a pin joint. Again, click the ✓ button to accept the definition.

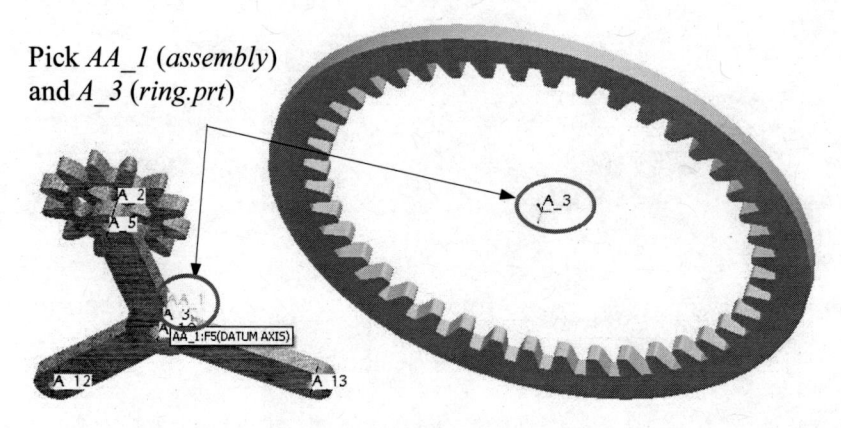

(a) Align Datum Axes

(b) Align Datum Planes

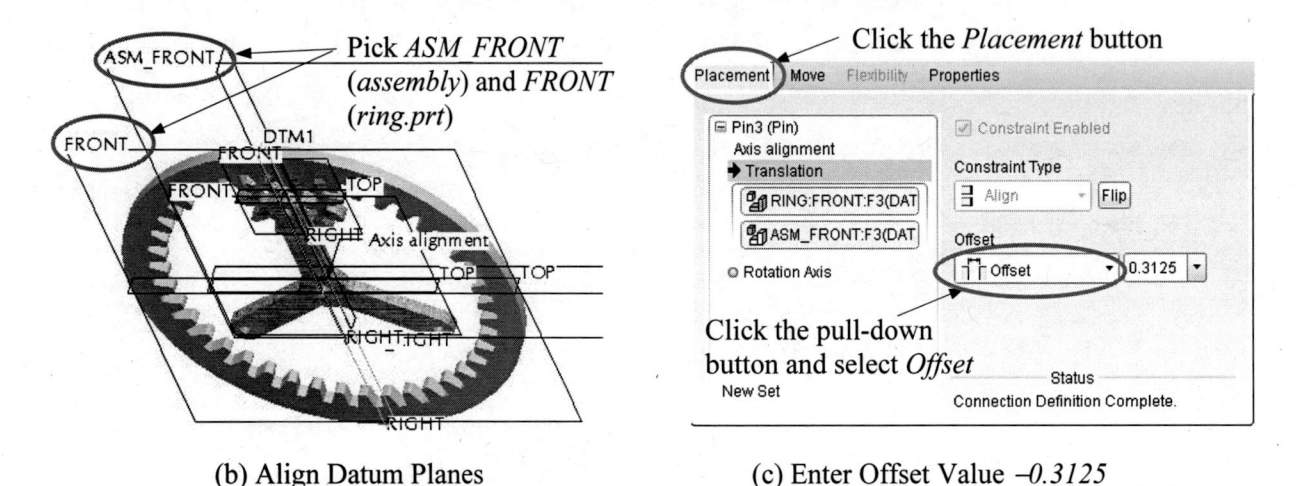

(c) Enter Offset Value −0.3125

Figure 7-12 Assembling *ring.prt*

The assembly is now complete. You may want to rotate the view to see if these gears are meshed properly. Note that the gear teeth between planet and ring gears should mesh well. We will capture this configuration, save it as a snapshot, and use the snapshot as the initial condition for motion analysis. You may use the *Drag Packed Components* button at the top of the *Graphics* window to save the current configuration as a snapshot. In the *Drag* dialog box appearing, click the *Current Snapshots* button at the top, a default name *Snapshot1* will appear. Click *Close*. The snapshot *Snapshot1* is saved for future use. Now we are ready to carry out a simulation for the gear train system. Save your model before we move into *Mechanism Design*.

Lesson 7: Planetary Gear Train Systems

Creating a Simulation Model

From the pull-down menu, choose

Applications > Mechanism.

There are three pin joints appeared, as shown in Figure 7-13. Note that there are two pin joints *Pin1* and *Pin3* overlap at the center of the gear train system. Click the *Connections* branch in the *Mechanism Model Tree* (lower half) to expand its contents, and then *Joints*. There should be three connections listed: *Pin1*, *Pin2*, and *Pin3* (Figure 7-14). Click *Pin1* and *Pin3*, and then see the joint symbols highlighted in the *Graphics* window.

Expand the joint *Pin1*, you should see that *Pin1* is defined between Ground and *body1* (that is, *arm.prt*), and so on. Since there are two joints overlap, we have to be very carefully in picking the right joints for defining the motion model.

We will define one gear pair and two motors for a motion model. The gear pair consists of the planet and ring gears. The motor defined at joint *Pin1* will have a constant angular velocity driving the arm. The second motor will be defined at *Pin3* and is stationary (since the ring gear is stationary).

From the shortcut buttons on the right, click *Define Gear-Pair connections* (3rd from the top), or choose from the pull-down menu

Insert > Gears.

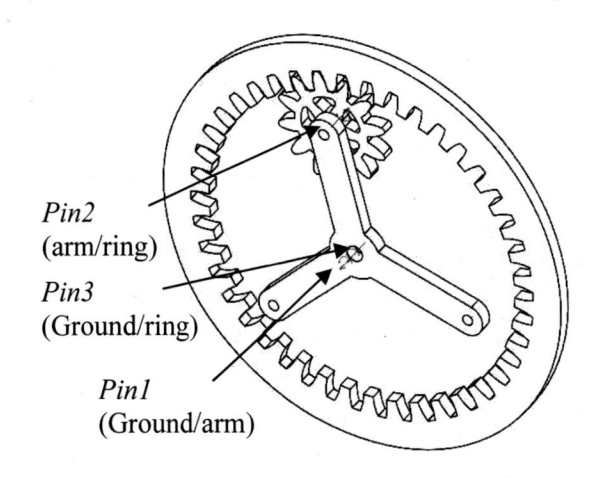

Figure 7-13 The Three Pin Joints Defined

Figure 7-14 Motion Entities in the *Model Tree*

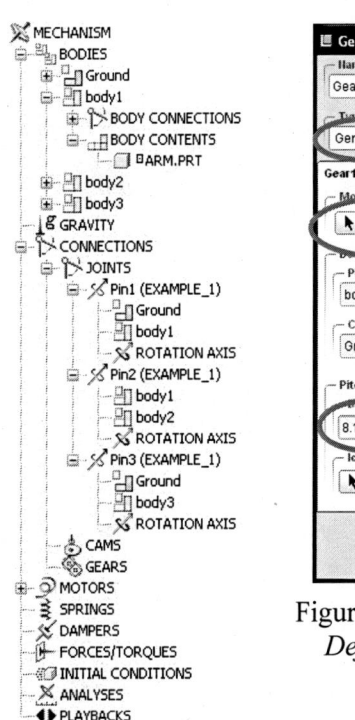

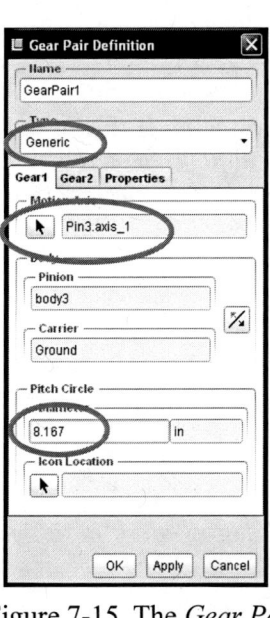

Figure 7-15 The *Gear Pair Definition* Dialog Box

The *Gear Pair Definition* dialog box will appear. Use the default name (*GearPair1*), leave *Generic* (default) for *Type*, then pick the joint *Pin3* (between the ring gear and the ground) from the *Graphics* window. Note that you may want to turn off all datum features in order to see the pin joint. If you picked a wrong joint, simply click the arrow button under the *Motion Axis* in the *Gear Pair Definition* dialog box (Figure 7-15), and pick again. The best way to pick the right joint is to move the mouse close to the joints, and wait for a few seconds until a label showing the joint to appear. If the label indicates the correct joint, then click to pick the joint. If not, click the right mouse button to shuffle the joints until a label indicating the correct joint appears, then click.

After picking the pin joint the ring gear will be highlighted. Enter 8.167 for *Pitch Circle Diameter*.

Click the *Gear 2* tab to define the second gear in the pair. Pick the pin joint *Pin2* (between the planet gear and the arm), and enter 2.333 for *Pitch Circle Diameter*. Click *OK*. A gear symbol will appear between the two pin joints chosen (Figure 7-16).

Now we will create a driver at joint *Pin1* to drive the arm; therefore, the gear train system.

From the shortcut buttons on the right, click *Define Servo Motors* (4th from the top), or choose from the pull-down menu

Insert > Servo Motors.

The *Servo Motor Definition* dialog box will appear. Enter *Motor1_arm* for *Name*, leave *Motion Axis* (default) for *Driven Entity* (under *Type* tab), then pick *Pin1*. After picking the pin joint, a larger arrow appears to confirm your selection. The next step is to specify the profile of the motor. From the *Servo Motor Definition* dialog box pick the *Profile* tab, choose *Velocity* in *Specification*, and leave *Constant* (default) in *Magnitude*. Enter *360* for the constant *A*, and click *OK*. A driver symbol should appear at the pin joint in the *Graphics* window.

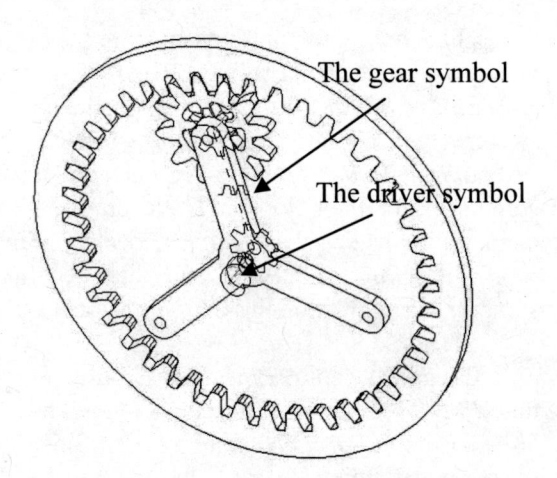

Figure 7-16 The Gear and Driver Symbols

Repeat the process to define the second motor. Enter *Motor2_ring_gear* for *Name*, leave *Motion Axis* (default) for *Driven Entity* (under *Type* tab), then pick *Pin3*. Click the *Profile* tab, leave *Position* and *deg* (default) in *Specification*, leave *Constant* (default) in *Magnitude*. Leave *0* for the constant *A*, and click *OK*. Again, a driver symbol should appear at the pin joint in the *Graphics* window.

Creating and Running a Kinematic Analysis

From the shortcut button list on the right, click the *Mechanism Analysis* shortcut button to define an analysis. In the *Analysis Definition* dialog box appearing, leave the default name, *AnalysisDefinition1*, and enter:

Type: *Kinematic*
Start Time: *0* (to drive the crank for a full cycle)
End Time: *1* (to drive the crank for a full cycle)
Frame Rate: *100*
Minimum Interval: *0.01*
Initial Configuration: *Current*

Make sure that both motors are included. Run the analysis, in the *Graphics* window, the gears should start turning. The arm rotates 360 degrees counterclockwise as expected.

Saving and Reviewing Results

Click the *Playbacks* button on the right to bring up the *Playbacks* dialog box and repeat the motion animation. On the *Playbacks* dialog box, click *Save* button to save the results as a *.pbk* file.

Note that we want to create a measure to monitor the output angular velocity of the planet gear. We will choose joint *Pin2* and the angular velocity of its rotational axis for the measure. To do so, click the *Generate Measure Results of Analyses* button. In the *Measure Results* dialog box appearing, click the *Create New Measure* button. The *Measure Definition* dialog box opens. Enter *Planet_Gear_Velocity* for *Name*. Under *Type*, select *Velocity*. Pick *Pin2* in the *Graphics* window. Under *Evaluation Method*, leave *Each Time Step*. Click *OK* to accept the definition.

In the *Measure Results* dialog box, choose *AnalysisDefinition1* in the *Result Set* and click the *Graph* button at the top left corner to graph the measure. The graph should be similar to that of Figure 7-17, which shows that the angular velocity of the planet is a constant of −1,260 degrees/sec. Note that this value is different from what we calculated in page 7-3; i.e., −900 degrees/sec. Unfortunately, in this case, *Mechanism Design* gave wrong results. Basically, *Mechanism Design* considers this gear train as a simple spur gear train, and calculated the velocity using equations discussed in *Lesson 6*; i.e.,

$$\omega_{out} = \frac{N_r}{N_p}\omega_{in} = \frac{42}{12}360 = 1,260 \qquad (7.4)$$

Note that this is why the gears are not properly meshed while in motion due to the inaccurate rotation speed of the planet gear. Save your model before we move to the next example.

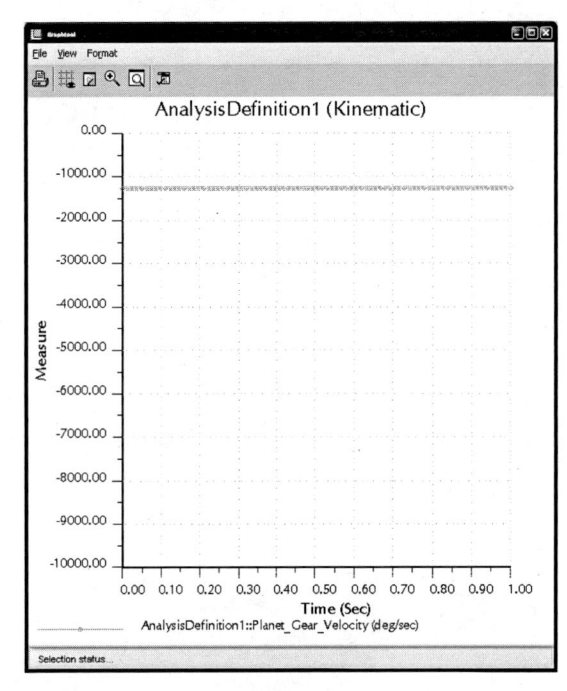

Figure 7-17 Angular Velocity of the Planet Gear

Example 2: Multiple Planetary Gear Train

We will add a sun gear and two planet gears to the current model for the second example. The sun gear will be assembled to the ground using a pin joint and will be driven by a motor. Note that in this example, the motor that drives the arm will be removed. The two planet gears will be carried by the arm, similar to that of Example 1.

Use *Applications > Standard* to go back to *Pro/ENGINEER Standard* mode. Save the current model as *Example_2* (use *File > Save a Copy*). In the *Assembly Save A Copy* dialog box, click *Save Copy*. Close the current model (using *File > Erase*) and open *Example_2*.

We will bring in the sun gear, *sun.prt*. Click the *Add component* button and choose *sun.prt*. In the *Component Placement* dashboard from the *User Defined* list choose the *Pin* joint, and pick *AA_1* (assembly) and *A_2* (*sun.prt*), as shown in Figure 7-18a. Now turn off datum axis display and turn on datum plane display. Pick two datum planes, *ASM_FRONT* (assembly) and *FRONT* (*sun.prt*), as shown in Figure 7-18b. The sun gear is not properly aligned with the planet gear yet. Similar to the steps in bringing the ring gear discussed earlier, click the *Placement* button, click the pull-down button and select *Offset* (see Figure 7-12c), and enter *−0.3125* for offset. With this offset, the sun gear will be properly aligned with the planet gear. Change the joint name to *Pin4* and click the ✓ button to accept the definition.

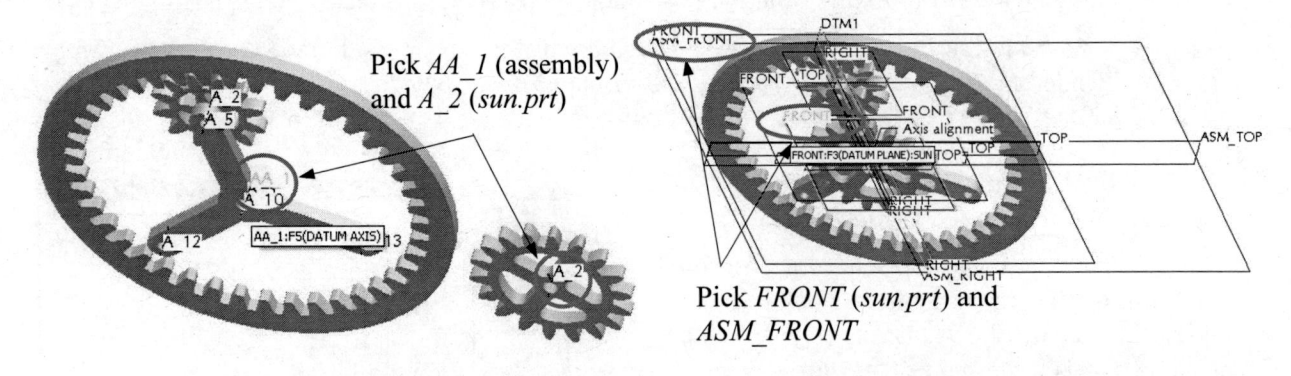

Pick *AA_1* (assembly) and *A_2* (*sun.prt*)

Pick *FRONT* (*sun.prt*) and *ASM_FRONT*

(a) Align Datum Axes　　　　　　　　　　(b) Align Datum Planes

Figure 7-18 Assembling *sun.prt*

Now we will repeat the same steps as we discussed earlier to assemble two additional planet gears to the arm. Basically, we define the pin joint between the planet gear and the arm by aligning axis *A_2* of the planet gear with *A_12* and *A_13* of the arm (see Figure 7-19), and aligning the front face of the planet gear to the back face of the arm. Change the joint names to *Pin5* and *Pin6*, respectively. The complete assembly should be like the one shown in Figure 7-20.

Axes for alignment

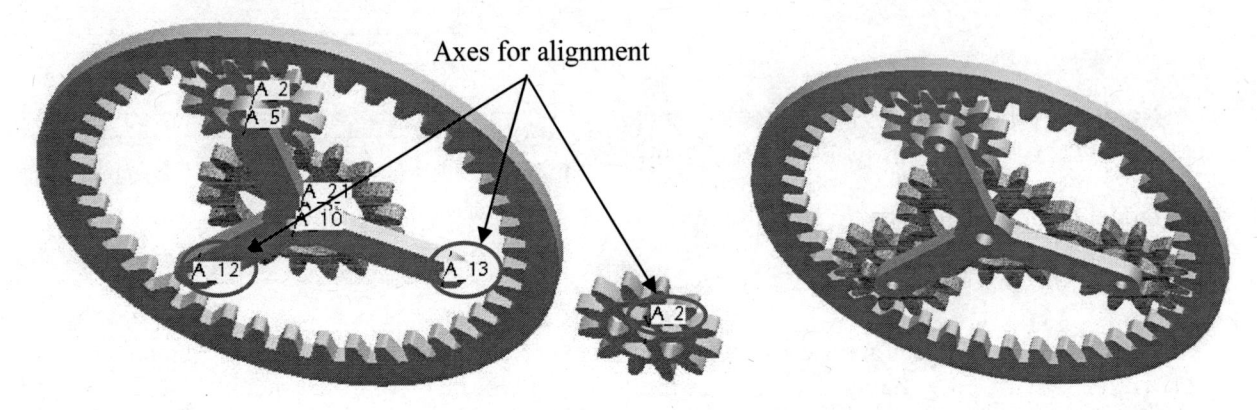

Figure 7-19 Axes for Alignment　　　　　　　　　　Figure 7-20 The Complete Assembly

Now we must see if all gears mesh properly. Hide the arm (click *ARM.PRT* from the *Model Tree*, and press the right mouse button to choose *Hide*). Use the *FRONT* view to see the four gears, such as in Figure 7-21. The gear teeth are not properly meshed. It is not too difficult to fix the problem. The only part that needs to be adjusted is the sun gear. The adjustment is to rotate the sun gear 90 degrees counterclockwise. This can be accomplished by aligning datum planes of the sun and the assembly using the *Drag* option. Before we rotate the sun gear, we will hide all other parts. Select all three planet gears and the ring gear from the *Model Tree* to hide them. You should see only the sun gear and six datum planes are displayed (three datum planes for sun gear and three for the assembly), as shown in Figure 7-22.

Now, click the *Drag Packed Components* button at the top of the *Graphics* window. In the *Drag* dialog box, click the *Constraints* tab, and choose the *Align Two Entities* button (first on the left). Choose

Lesson 7: Planetary Gear Train Systems

two datum planes *TOP* (*sun.prt*) and *ASM_RIGHT* (assembly), as shown in Figure 7-22. The sun gear is immediately rotated with these two datum planes aligned, and the gears should now mesh properly. Click the *Current Snapshot* button on top, a default name *Snapshot2* will appear. Click *Close*. The snapshot *Snapshot2* has been saved for future use. Now the gear train is properly assembled.

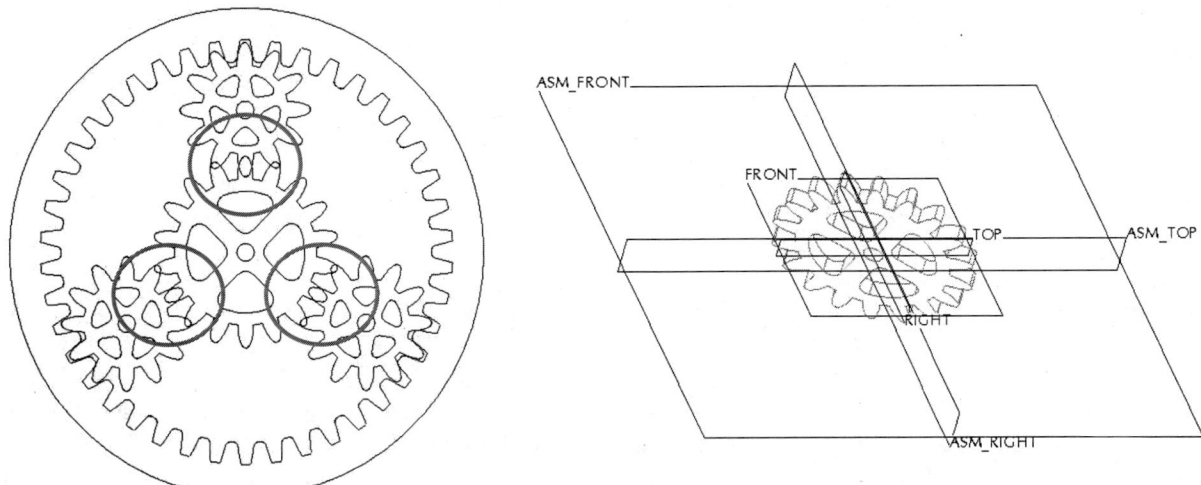

Figure 7-21 Gears Meshed Incorrectly

Figure 7-22 Sun Gear and Six Datum Planes

Unhide all gears (by choosing the three planet gears and the ring gear in the *Model Tree* and right mouse click to choose *Unhide*). Choose the *FRONT* view, you should see the gears are properly meshed, as shown in Figure 7-23. Now you can unhide the arm. Save your model before we move into *Mechanism Design*.

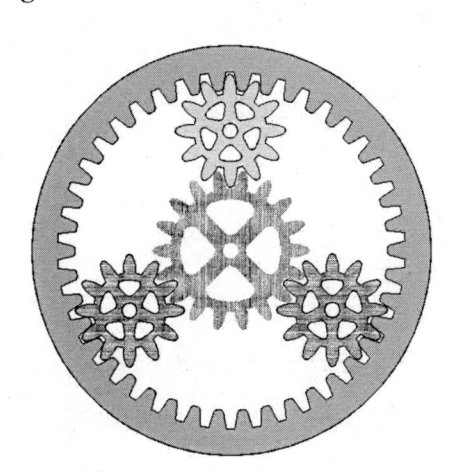

Figure 7-23 The Gears Properly Meshed

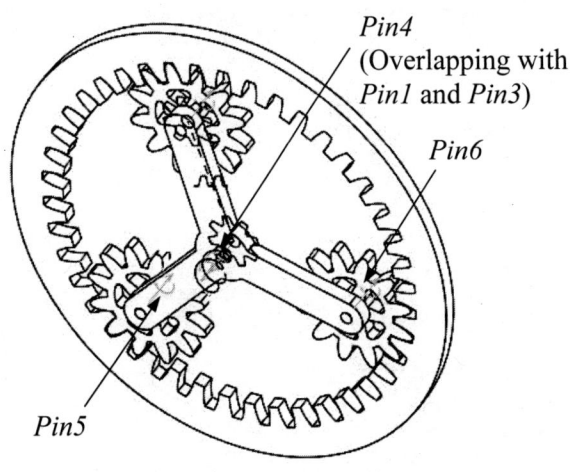

Figure 7-24 Three Pin Joints Added

Enter *Mechanism Design*. There are additional three pin joints appearing, as shown in Figure 7-24. Note that *Pin4* overlaps with the other two pin joints *Pin1* and *Pin3* at the center of the gear train system. Note that we will define a driver at *Pin4* (the joint between the sun gear and the ground).

First, we will define additional three gear pairs: sun gear and the three planet gears, respectively. Follow the same steps as discussed earlier. One thing to pay attention to is the fact that you must pick the right joint for the sun gear since there are now three joints that overlap at the center. Note that the joint to pick is *Pin4*. The pitch circle diameter of the sun gear is 3.5. Recall that the pitch circle diameter of the planet gear is 2.333.

Next, we will add two gear pairs between the two newly added planet gears and the ring gear. Recall that the pitch circle diameter of the ring gear is 8.167. The pin joint between the ring gear and the ground is *Pin3*.

Follow the same process as before to define the third motor. Enter *Motor3_sun_gear* for *Name*, pick *Pin4*. Click the *Profile* tab to define constant angular velocity of 360 degrees/sec, and click *OK*. Again, a driver symbol should appear at the pin joint in the *Graphics* window.

Now that the motion model is completed, we are ready to create and run a kinematic analysis. Note that we will turn off the first motor (*Motor1_arm*) and include both *Motor2_ring_gear* (to keep the ring gear stationary) and *Motor3_sun_gear*.

Expand the *ANALYSES* entity in the lower half of the *Model Tree* (which list entities related to *Mechanism Design*). Right mouse click *AnalysisDefinition1*, and choose *Edit Definition*. The *Analysis Definition* dialog box will be brought back. We will keep the same *Preferences* for the time being. Click the *Motors* tab, two motors should be listed (*Motor1_arm* and *Motor2_ring_gear*). Click the *Add All Motors* button (3rd on the right) to include all three motors. Click the first motor (*Motor1_arm*) and click the *Delete Highlighted Row(s)* button to delete the motor (2nd on the right). The second and third motors should be listed as shown in Figure 7-25.

Click the *Run* button to run the analysis. In the *Graphics* window, the mechanism should start moving. The sun gear rotates counterclockwise, which drives the arm and planet gears, both rotate in the clockwise direction.

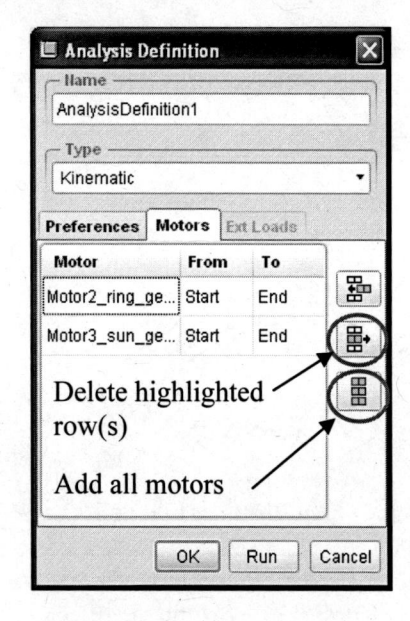

Figure 7-25 The *Analysis Definition* Dialog Box

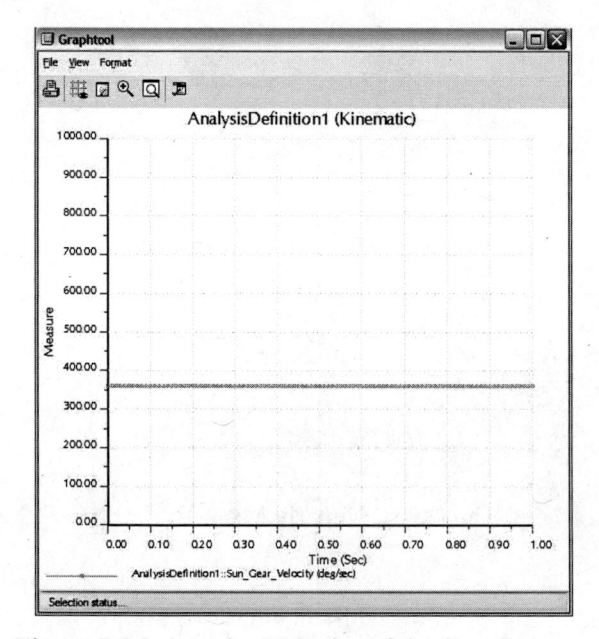

Figure 7-26 Angular Velocity of the Sun Gear

Define measures for the angular velocities of the sun gear (*Pin4*), the arm (*Pin1*), and the planet gear (any one of the three). Graph all three measures. You should see these graphs as shown in Figures 7-26 to

Lesson 7: Planetary Gear Train Systems   7-15

7-28. As shown in Figure 7-26, the angular velocity of the sun gear is 360 degrees/sec as expected (driven by *Motor3*. The angular velocities of the planet gear and arm are 945.1 degrees/sec and −269.9 degrees/sec, respectively, as shown in Figures 7-27 and 7-28.

Note that our calculations indicate that the arm will rotate only 108 degrees in the same direction as that of the sun gear; i.e., counterclockwise. Also, the planet gears should turn 270 degrees per revolution of the sun gear in the clockwise direction. *Mechanism Design* does not produce accurate simulations. As shown in this lesson, it is extremely important that you verify the simulation results before accepting them for any purposes.

Figure 7-27 Angular Velocity of the Planet Gear

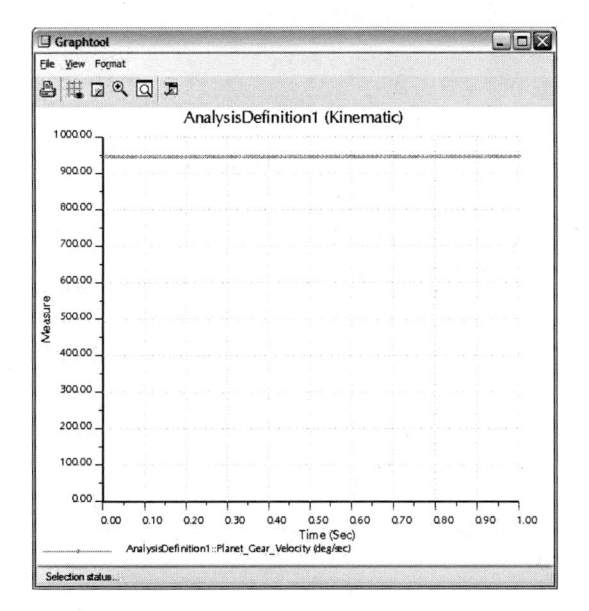

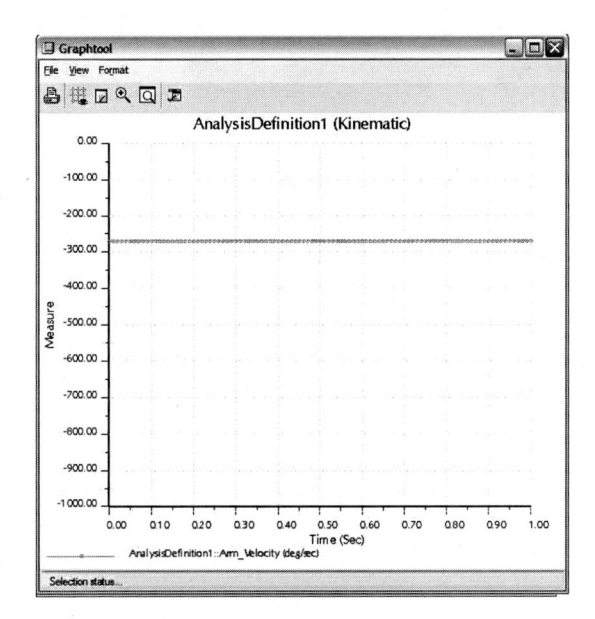

Figure 7-28 Angular Velocity of the Arm

Exercises:

1. Modify *Example_1* (single planetary gear train) by removing the arm, allowing the ring gear to rotate, and keeping the planet gear stationary. Create a driver to rotate the planet gear at 360 degrees/sec counterclockwise, what is the angular velocity of the ring gear? Does *Mechanism Design* provide correct answer?

2. From *Example_2* (multiple planetary gear train), change the rotation speed of the sun gear from 360 to −360 degrees/sec. Edit the kinematic analysis by removing *Motor2_ring_gear* and including *Motor1_arm*. The arm will be driven by the motor at 360 degrees/sec. Run the kinematic analysis. What is the angular velocity of the ring gear obtained from *Mechanism Design*? Is the result Correct? Verify it using analytical calculation discussed in Section 7.2.

Lesson 8: Cam and Follower

8.1 Overview of the Lesson

In this lesson, we will learn cam and follower, or cam-follower connection. A cam-follower is a device for converting rotary motion into linear motion. The simplest form of a cam is a rotating disc with a variable radius, so that its profile is not circular but oval or egg-shaped. When the disc rotates, its edge pushes against a follower (or cam follower), which may be a small wheel at the end of a lever or the end of the rod itself. The follower will thus rise and fall at exactly the same amount as the variation in cam radius. By profiling a cam appropriately, a desired cyclic pattern of linear or straight-line motion, in terms of position, velocity, and acceleration, can be produced.

We will learn to create a motion model to simulate the control of opening and closing of inlet or exhaustive valves, usually found in internal combustion engines, using cam-follower connections. In a design such as that of Figure 8-1, the drive for the camshaft is taken from the crankshaft through a timing chain, which keeps the cams synchronized with the movement of the positions so that the valves are opened or closed at a precise instant. The mechanism we will be working with consists of a camshaft, pushrod, rocker, valve, and spring, as shown in Figure 8-1. There are three pairs of cam-followers; connecting the camshaft and the pushrod, the pushrod and the rocker, and the rocker and the valve. When the cam on the camshaft pushes the pushrod up, the rocker rotates and pushes the valve on the other side downward. The spring surrounding the valve gets compressed, and opens up the inlet for air to flow into the combustion chamber.

8.2 The Cam and Follower Example

Figure 8-1 The Mechanism of Engine Inlet or Outlet Valve

Physical Model

The camshaft and the rocker will rotate along their respective pin joints connecting them to the ground body. The camshaft is driven by a motor of constant velocity of 600 rpm. The profile of the cam consists of two circular arcs of 0.25 and 0.5 in. radii, respectively, as shown in Figure 8-2. The lower arc is concentric with the shaft, and the center of the upper arc is 0.52 in. above the center of the shaft. When the camshaft rotates, the cam mounted on the shaft pushes the pushrod up by up to 0.27 in. (that is, 0.52+0.25−0.5 = 0.27). As a result, the rocker will rotate and push the valve at the other end downward at a frequency of 10 times/sec. When the camshaft rotates where the larger circular arc (0.5 in. radius) of the cam is in contact with the follower (the pushrod), the pushrod has room to move downward. The rocker will rotate since the spring is being uncompressed. As a result, the valve will move up, and therefore, close the inlet. The valve will be open for about 120 degree per cycle. Note that this cam-follower connecting the camshaft and the pushrod is the only true cam-follower among the three.

The unit system chosen for this example is in-lb$_f$-sec and all parts are made up of steel.

Pro/ENGINEER Parts and Assembly

The cam and follower example consists of one assembly and four parts *partial_cam_follower.asm*, *cam_shaft.prt*, *rocker.prt*, *pushrod.prt*, and *valve.prt*. You may want to open the final assembly, *cam_follower.asm*, to check the assembled cam and follower example shown in Figure 8-1 before going through this lesson. Enter *Mechanism Design* (by choosing *Applications > Mechanism*). Choose *Analysis > Playbacks* to show the motion. This is what we want to accomplish in this lesson.

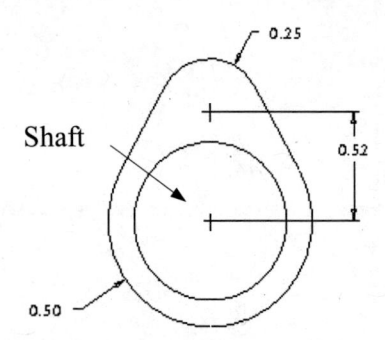

Figure 8-2 The Cam Profile

The *partial_cam_follower.asm* is where we will start this lesson. This partial assembly consists of three datum planes and a datum coordinate system by default. In addition, there are four datum axes (*AA_1* to *AA_4*) and one datum point *APNT0* for assembling components, as shown in Figure 8-3.

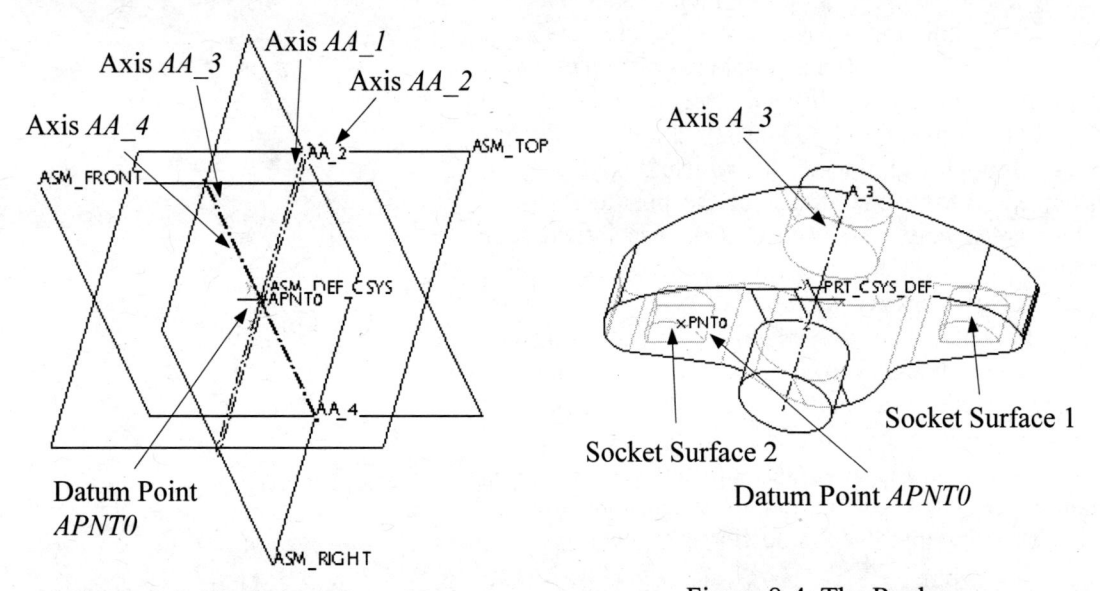

Figure 8-3 The Partial Assembly

Figure 8-4 The Rocker

The datum axis *A_3* in the rocker shown in Figure 8-4 will be used to create a pin joint between the rocker and the ground body (axis *AA_1* in assembly). The datum point *PNT0* is on the bottom face of the rocker, which will be used for creating a spring (with datum point *APNT0*) that wraps around the valve once it is assembled. The two socket surfaces, which are semi-circular cylindrical surfaces, will be used to assemble the pushrod (with *Socket Surface 1*) and the valve (with *Socket Surface 2*), respectively, using cam-follower connections.

The datum axis *A_14* in the pushrod (Figure 8-5) will be used to align with assembly datum axis *AA_4*. In addition, the datum plane *FRONT* of the pushrod will be aligned with assembly datum plane *ASM_FRONT* for proper orientation. The circular cylindrical surface *Cylindrical Surface 1* will be

Lesson 8: Cam and Follower   8-3

assembled to the camshaft (with *Cam Surface* of the camshaft shown in Figure 8-6) using a cam-follower connection. The second cylindrical surface *Cylindrical Surface 2* at the top will be assembled to the rocker (with *Socket Surface 1* of the rocker shown in Figure 8-4) using a cam-follower connection.

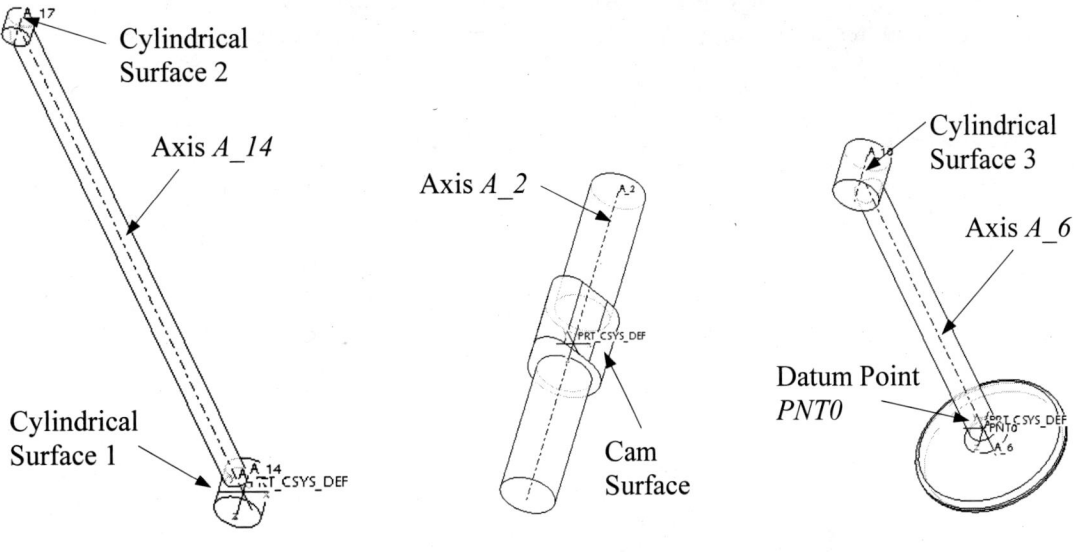

Figure 8-5 The Pushrod   Figure 8-6 The Camshaft   Figure 8-7 The Valve

The datum axis *A_2* in the camshaft shown in Figure 8-6 will be used to create a pin joint between the camshaft and the ground body (with datum axis *AA_2*). The cam surface, with the profile shown in Figure 8-2, will be used to create a cam-follower with *Cylindrical Surface 1* of the pushrod (Figure 8-5).

The datum axis *A_6* in the valve (Figure 8-7) will be used to create a cylinder joint with assembly datum axis *AA_3*. The circular cylindrical surface *Cylindrical Surface 3* at the top will be assembled to the rocker (with *Socket Surface 2* of the rocker shown in Figure 8-4) using a cam-follower connection. The datum point *PNT0* is for creating measures that monitor the valve motion.

Simulation Model

The simulation model shown in Figure 8-8 consists of two pin joints, one cylinder joint, three cam-followers, a spring, and a servo motor. The servo motor rotates 600 rpm (3,600 degrees/sec) that drives the mechanism. The spring surrounding the valve has a spring constant of 10 lb$_f$/in and an unstretched length of 1.45 in., which is the vertical distance (along the *Y*-direction of ASM_DEF_CSYS) between the two datum points, *APNT0* of the assembly and *PNT0* of the rocker. Note that cam-followers 1 and 3 simply connect pushrod to rocker and rocker to the valve, respectively. The connecting surfaces are circular cylindrical surfaces of constant radii. Therefore, they are not converting circular motion to linear motion, not like that of cam-follower 2.

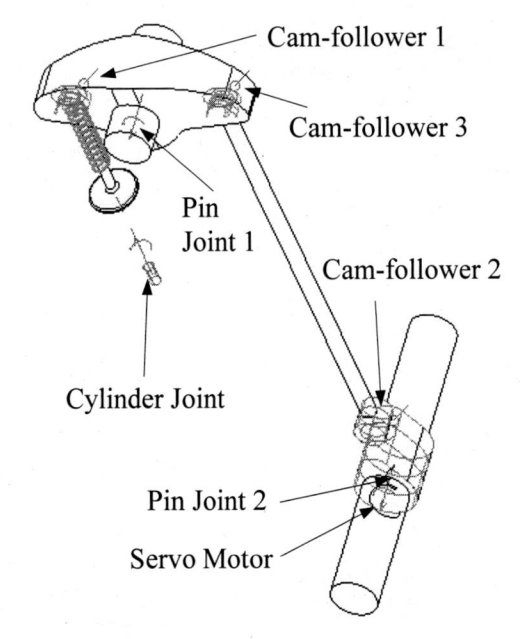

Figure 8-8 The Simulation Model

8.3 Using *Mechanism Design*

Creating an Assembly

Start *Pro/ENGINEER*, change the working directory, and open *partial_cam_follower.asm*. You should see datum features in the *Graphics* window. You may want to save the assembly to a different name.

First, we will bring in *rocker.prt*. Click the *Add component* shortcut button and choose *rocker.prt*. In the *Component Placement* dashboard from the *User Defined* list, choose *Pin* joint, turn on datum axis display and pick *AA_1* (*partial_cam_follower.asm*) and *A_3* (*rocker.prt*), as shown in Figure 8-9a. Now turn off datum axis display and turn on datum plane display. Pick two datum planes, *ASM_FRONT* (*partial_cam_follower.asm*) and *FRONT* (*rocker.prt*), as shown in Figure 8-9b. The *rocker.prt* should be properly assembled through a pin joint. Click the button to accept the definition.

Pick *AA_1* (*assembly*) and *A_3* (*camshaft.prt*)

Pick *ASM_FRONT* (*assembly*) and *FRONT* (*rocker.prt*)

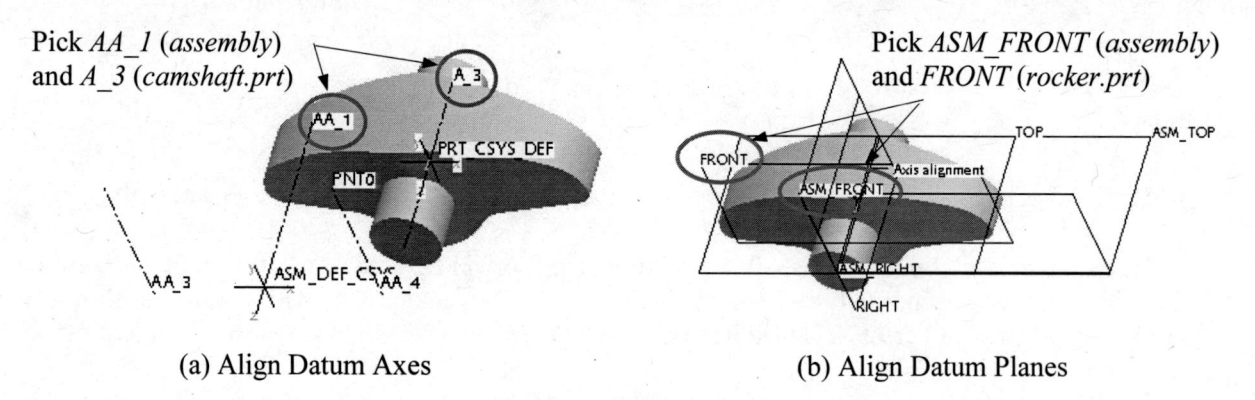

(a) Align Datum Axes   (b) Align Datum Planes

Figure 8-9 Assembling *rocker.prt*

Pick *A_2* (*camshaft.prt*) and *AA_2* (*assembly*)

ASM_FRONT (*assembly*) and *FRONT* (*camshaft.prt*)

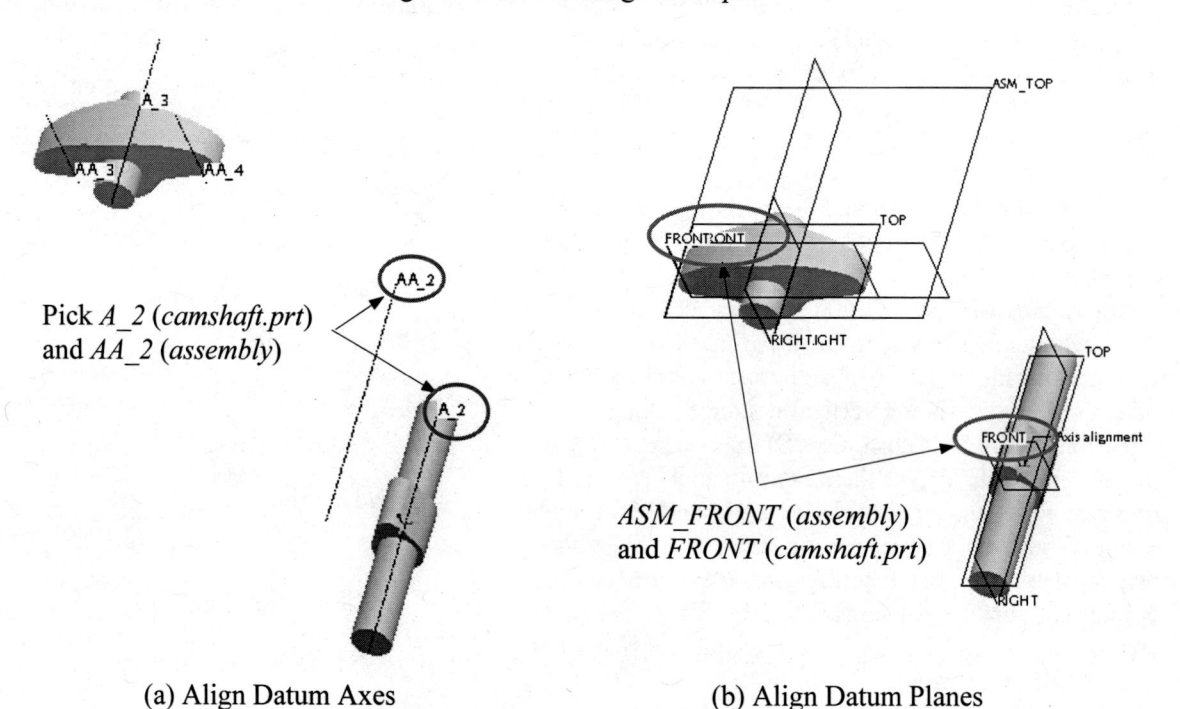

(a) Align Datum Axes   (b) Align Datum Planes

Figure 8-10 Assembling *camshaft.prt*

Lesson 8: Cam and Follower

The next part we will bring in is the camshaft. Click the *Add component* button and choose *camshaft.prt*. Choose the *Pin* joint, turn on datum axis display, and pick *A_2* (*camshaft.prt*) and *AA_2* (*partial_cam_follower.asm*), as shown in Figure 8-10a. Now turn off datum axis display and turn on datum plane display. Pick two datum planes, *ASM_FRONT* (*partial_cam_follower.asm*) and *FRONT* (*camshaft.prt*), as shown in Figure 8-10b. The *camshaft.prt* should be properly assembled to the ground body with a pin joint. Click the ✓ button to accept the definition.

The third part we will bring in is *valve.prt*. Choose the *Cylinder* joint (from the *User Defined* list), turn on datum axis display, and pick *AA_3* (*partial_cam_follower.asm*) and *A_6* (*valve.prt*), as shown in Figure 8-11. The valve is free to move along the axis. We will leave it as it is for the time being. We will later define a cam-follower in *Mechanism Design* to properly position the valve to the rocker. For the time being, click the ✓ button to accept the definition.

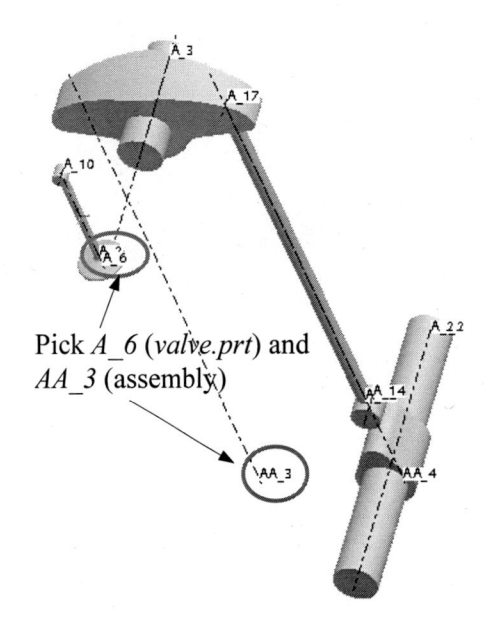

Pick *A_6* (*valve.prt*) and *AA_3* (assembly)

Figure 8-11 Assembling *valve.prt*

Pick *AA_4* (assembly) and *A_12* (*pushrod.prt*)

Pick *ASM_FRONT* (assembly) and *FRONT* (*pushrod.prt*)

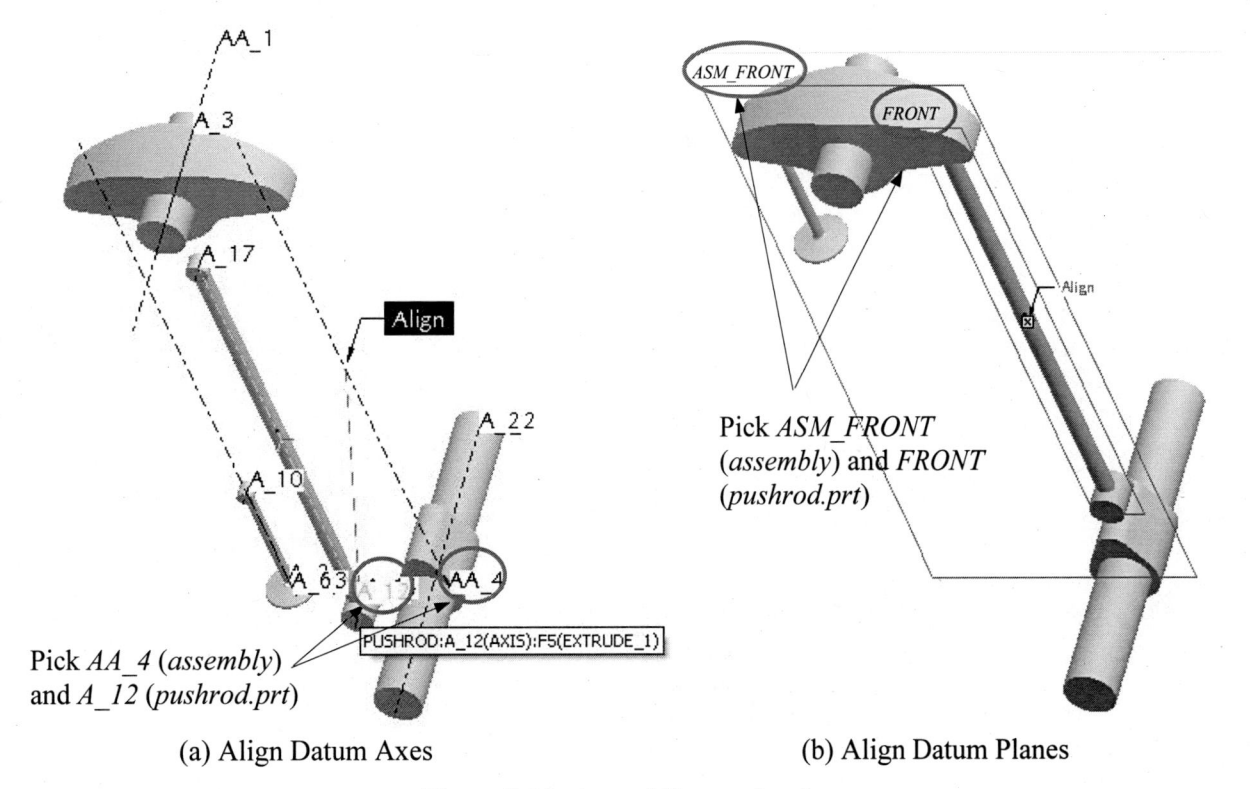

(a) Align Datum Axes   (b) Align Datum Planes

Figure 8-12 Assembling *pushrod.prt*

The fourth and final part we will bring in is *pushrod.prt*. Choose *Align* (from the *Automatic* list), turn on datum axis display, and pick *AA_4* (*partial_cam_follower.asm*) and *A_12* (*pushrod.prt*), as shown in Figure 8-12a. Choose *Align* again (note that you will have to choose *Placement*, click *New Constraint*, and then choose *Align*), and pick *ASM_FRONT* (*partial_cam_follower.asm*) and *FRONT* (*pushrod.prt*), as shown in Figure 8-12b. Similar to the valve, we will later define a cam-follower in *Mechanism Design* to properly position the pushrod between the rocker and the camshaft. Now the pushrod is partially constrained. It is fine since we will create cam-follower connections later. Click the ✓ button to accept the definition.

The model is now mostly assembled. Save your model and move to *Mechanism Design*.

Creating a Simulation Model

From the pull-down menu, choose

Applications > Mechanism.

There are three connection symbols appearing: two pin joints and one cylinder joint, as shown in Figure 8-13. We will choose three pairs of surfaces to define three cam-followers.

From the shortcut buttons on the right, click *Define Cam-Follower connections* (2nd from the top), or choose from the pull-down menu

Insert > Cams.

The *Cam-Follower Connection Definition* dialog box appears (Figure 8-14). Use the default name (*CamFollower1*), click *Autoselect* (to select all surfaces surrounding the cam or follower), and click ▶ (the *Select* button). Pick the cylindrical surface of the roller on top of the valve, all the surfaces surrounding the roller will be selected, as shown in Figure 8-15a. Click the *OK* button in the *Select* dialog box (right underneath the *Cam-Follower Connection Definition* dialog box). The surface selected will appear in the *Surfaces/Curves* text area (see Figure 8-14). An arrow will also appear on the surfaces selected showing their normal. Make sure the normal vector is pointing outward.

Click the *Cam2* tab, and repeat the same process but select the inner cylindrical surface of the rocker (*Socket Surface 2*), as shown in Figure 8-15a. Make sure the normal vector is pointing outward. Click the *Flip* button (Figure 8-14) to reverse the normal vector if necessary. Click *OK* in the *Cam-Follower Connection Definition* dialog box. A cam-follower symbol will appear between the two surfaces selected.

Repeat the same process and pick the two surfaces shown in Figure 8-15b for the second cam-follower between the pushrod and the camshaft. Finally, pick the two surfaces to create the third cam-follower connection between the rocker and the pushrod (Figure 8-15c).

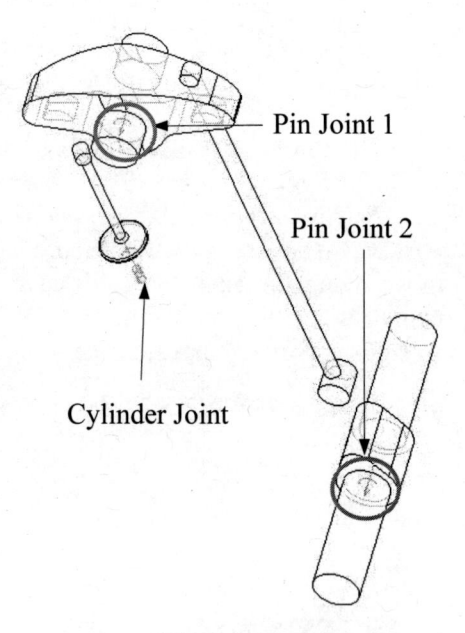

Figure 8-13 The Assembly Ready for Entering *Mechanism Design*

Figure 8-14

Lesson 8: Cam and Follower 8-7

(a) Cam-Follower 1 (b) Cam-Follower 2 (c) Cam-Follower 3

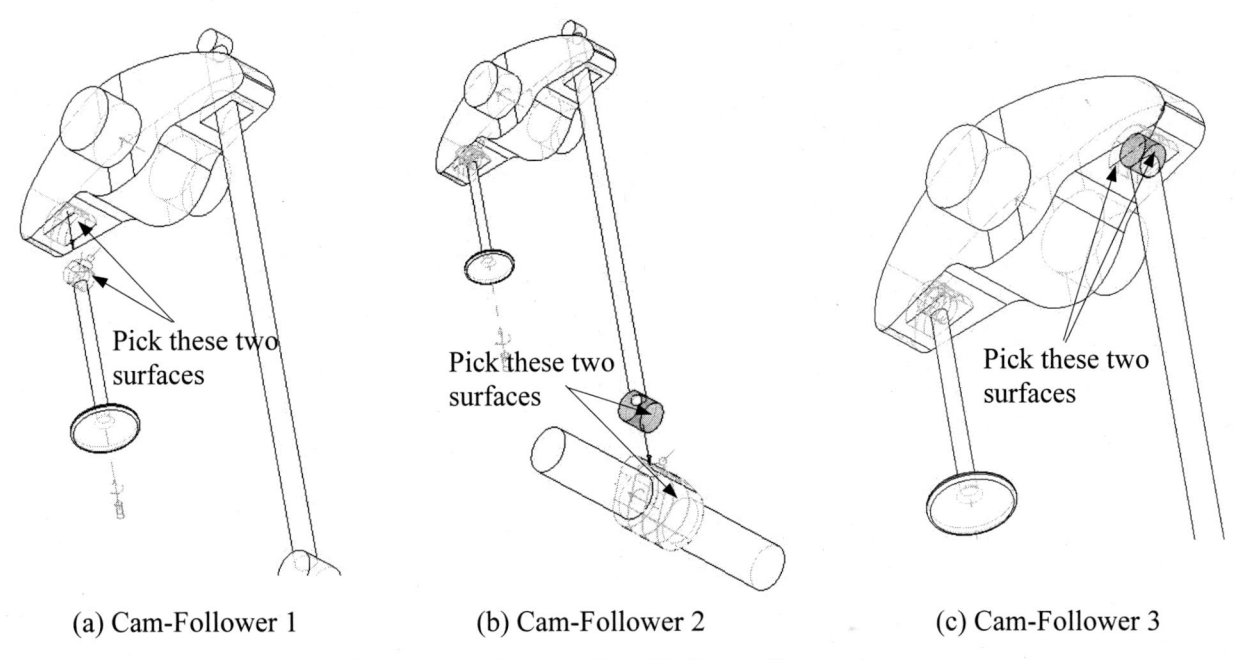

Figure 8-15 Creating Cam-Follower Connections

Now we will create a servo motor at pin joint 2 (between the camshaft and the ground body). The servo motor will drive the camshaft at an angular velocity of 3,600 degrees/sec; therefore, the whole system.

From the shortcut buttons on the right, click *Define Servo Motors* (4th from the top), or choose from the pull-down menu

Insert > Servo Motors.

The *Servo Motor Definition* dialog box will appear (Figure 8-16). Leave the default name *ServoMotor1*, select *Motion Axis* (default) for *Driven Entity* (under *Type* tab), then pick the pin joint of the camshaft. Note that you may want to turn off all datum features in order to see the pin joint. After picking the pin joint, a larger arrow appears to confirm your selection. The next step is to specify the profile of the motor. From the *Servo Motor Definition* dialog box, pick the *Profile* tab (Figure 8-17), choose *Velocity* in *Specification*, and leave *Constant* (default) in *Magnitude*. Enter *3600* for the constant *A* (3,600 degrees/sec; i.e., 600 rpm) and click *OK*. A driver symbol should appear at the pin joint in the *Graphics* window (Figure 8-18).

Next we will create a spring surrounding the valve. The spring will be created by connecting two datum points: *PNT0* (*rocker*) and *APNT0* (assembly), as shown in Figure 8-18. Note that *APNT0* is located at (−1.25, −1.75, 0) from the assembly coordinate system *ASM_DEF_CSYS*. *PNT0* is located at the bottom face of the rocker. It is 1.25 in. from the *RIGHT* datum plane and is 0.3 in. below axis *A_3*. (that passes through the origin of *ASM_DEF_CSYS*). Therefore, these two points align vertically and is 1.45 in. apart (along the Y-direction of *ASM_DEF_CSYS*). Note that you may choose from the pull-down menu *Analysis > Measure > Distance* and pick these two points to find out the distance. You may want to turn off all datum features except the datum points in order to see these points. The unstretched length of the spring should be about 1.45 in., assuming that the rocker does not rotate.

Figure 8-16

Figure 8-17

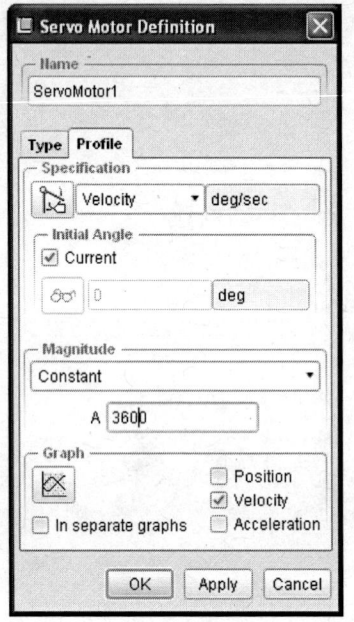

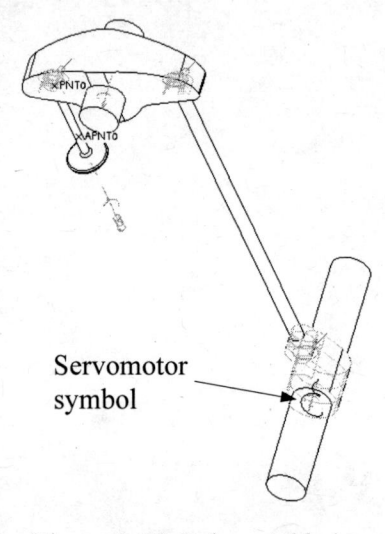

Figure 8-18 Driver Added to Pin Joint 2

From the shortcut buttons on the right, click *Define Springs* (5th from the bottom), or choose from the pull-down menu

Insert > Springs.

A new set of selections appear at the top of the *Graphics* window for defining the spring (Figure 8-19). Choose *Extension or compression spring* button (the first button from the left, should have been selected by default). Activate the *Select items* field by clicking it. Turn on the datum point display. Then, pick *PNT0* of the rocker. Drag the handle appeared in the *Graphics* window (Figure 8-20) and overlap it with *APNT0* (release the mouse button when *APNT0* is highlighted). A spring will appear, connecting *PNT0* (*rocker*) and *APNT0* (*ground*).

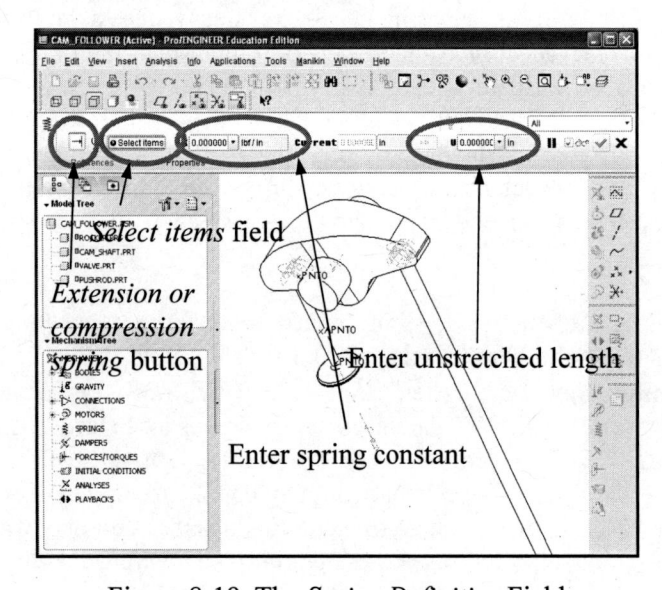

Figure 8-19 The *Spring Definition* Field

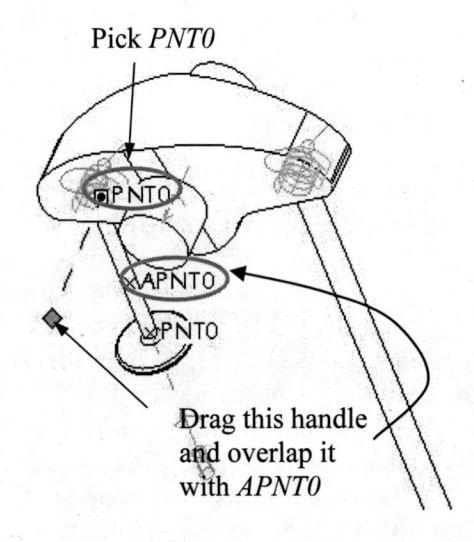

Figure 8-20 Defining the Spring

Lesson 8: Cam and Follower   8-9

Next, enter *10 (lb$_f$/in)* for spring constant (**K**) and *1.45 (in)* for the unstretched spring length (**U**) from the text fields at the top of the *Graphics* window. Note that the spring constant we enter is in lb$_f$/in. Click the ✓ button at right to accept the definition. A spring symbol should appear in the *Graphics* window.

Now the mechanism is completely defined. You may click the *Drag Packed Components* button at the top of the *Graphics* window, and click the camshaft. You should be able to move (rotate) the camshaft along the pin joint, and therefore, drive the whole mechanism. The rocker will rotate and push the valve and compress the spring. You may want to save the model before defining motion analysis.

Creating and Running a Static Analysis

We would like to start with an equilibrium configuration for dynamic analysis. An equilibrium configuration can be obtained by conducting a static analysis. From the shortcut button list on the right, click the *Mechanism Analysis* shortcut button to define an analysis. In the *Analysis Definition* dialog box appearing (Figure 8-21), enter *Static_Analysis* for *Name*, and choose *Static* for *Type*. Click *Run*. The static analysis will start and a *Graphtool* window similar to Figure 8-22 will appear showing the progress of the analysis. Note that the graph you have may be different from that of Figure 8-22, depending on the configuration of the mechanism you currently have. In the *Graphics* window, the mechanism will situate to an equilibrium configuration where the rocker stays leveled and the spring is in its unstretched length, as shown in Figure 8-23. Choose the *Front* view to see the equilibrium configuration.

Use the *Drag Packed Components* button to create a snapshot of the current configuration. You may want to use the snapshot as an initial condition for the dynamic analysis.

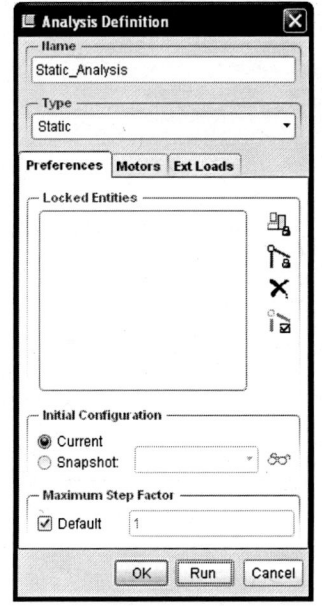

Figure 8-21

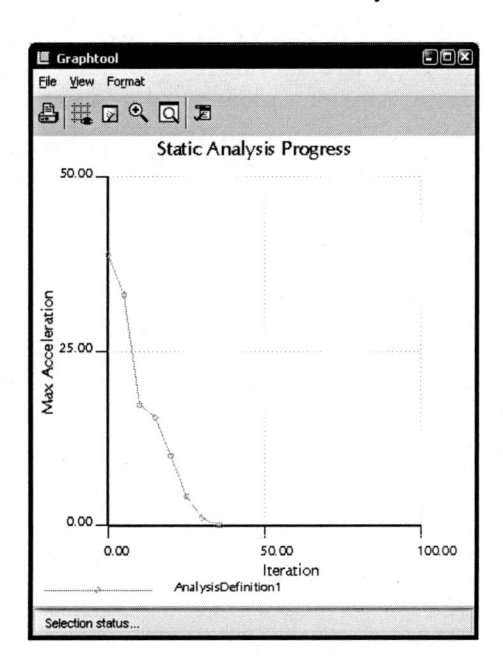

Figure 8-22 *Graphtool* Window

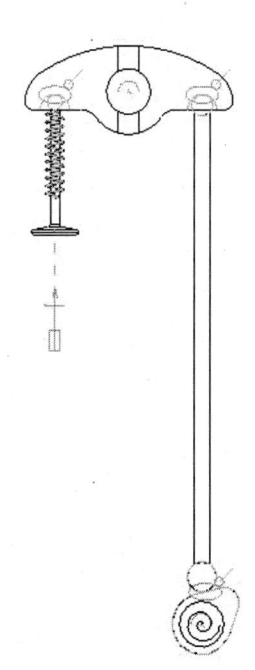

Figure 8-23 An Equilibrium Configuration

Creating and Running a Dynamic Analysis

From the shortcut button list on the right, click the *Mechanism Analysis* shortcut button. In the *Analysis Definition* dialog box appearing (Figure 8-24), enter:

Name: *Dynamic_Analysis*
Type: *Dynamic*
Duration: *0.5* (for the camshaft to rotate 5 full cycles)
Frame Rate: *100*
Minimum Interval: *0.01*
Initial Configuration: *Current*

Make sure that *ServoMotor1* is included. Run the analysis. In the *Graphics* window, the mechanism should start moving. The camshaft rotates 5 complete cycles counterclockwise.

Saving and Reviewing Results

Click the *Playbacks* button on the right to bring up the *Playbacks* dialog box and play the motion animation. On the *Playbacks* dialog box, click on the *Save* button to save the dynamic analysis results as a *.pbk* file.

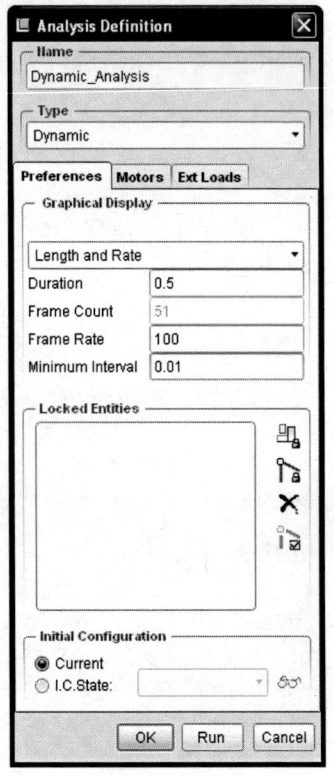

Figure 8-24

Note that we want to create a measure to monitor the position of the valve. We will choose the *Y*-position of the datum point *PNT0* of the valve (see Figure 8-25) for the measure. The graph of the position measure is shown in Figure 8-26, where the valve is moving between –2.45 and –2.15, traveling about 0.3 in.

Pick *PNT0* of the valve for measure

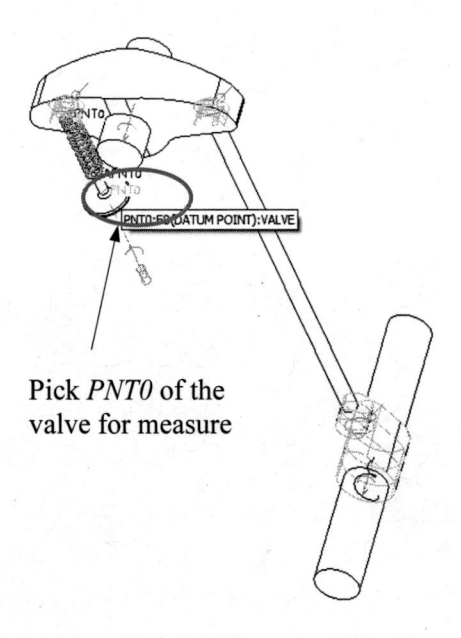

Figure 8-25 Pick Datum Point

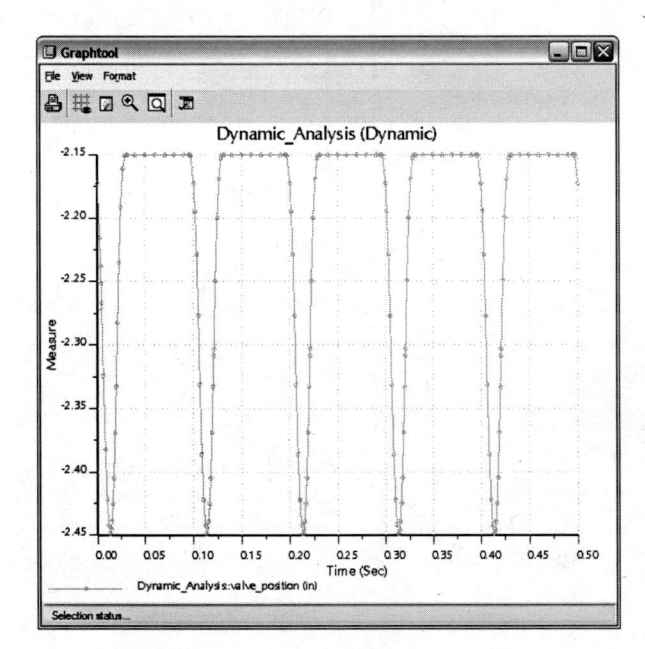

Figure 8-26 Graph of Valve Position

Lesson 8: Cam and Follower

As shown in Figure 8-26, the flat portion at the top indicates that the valve stays completely closed, which spans about 0.066 seconds, approximately 240 degrees of the camshaft rotation in a complete cycle. Therefore, the valve will open for about 0.034 seconds per cycle, roughly 120 degrees.

Create measures to monitor the velocity and acceleration of the valve. We will choose the *Y*-velocity and acceleration of the datum point *PNT0* of the valve for the measures. The graphs of the velocity and acceleration measures are shown in Figures 8-27 and 28, respectively. As shown in Figure 8-27, there are two velocity spikes per cycle, representing the valve being pushed downward (negative velocity) for opening and is being pulled back (positive velocity) for closing, respectively. The valve stays closed with zero velocity.

Figure 8-28 reveals high accelerations when the valve is pushed and pulled. Note that such high acceleration is due to high-speed rotation at the camshaft. However, these high accelerations could produce large inertial force on the valve, yielding high contact force between the top of the valve and the socket in the rocker. The reaction force can be monitored by defining a reaction measure for *Cam-Follower 1* (see Figure 8-8). Choose *Normal Force* under *Component*, as shown in Figure 8-29. The reaction force graph (Figure 8-30) shows that the reaction force between the top of the valve and the socket face of the rocker is about 700 lb_f, which is significant. Note that if the camshaft rotates at a higher speed, e.g., 6,000 rpm, the reaction force would be around 7,000 lb_f, which raises a flag on the durability of the valve. In order to check the structural integrity of the valve under such a large force, a finite element analysis is usually conducted; e.g. using *Pro/MECHANICA Structure*.

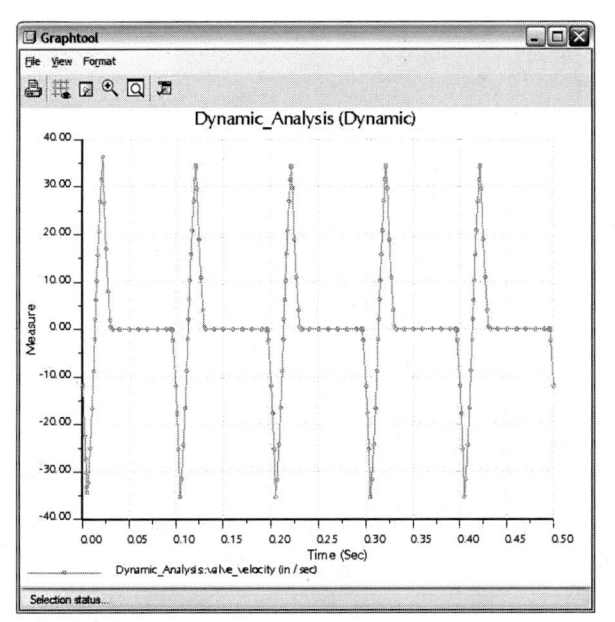

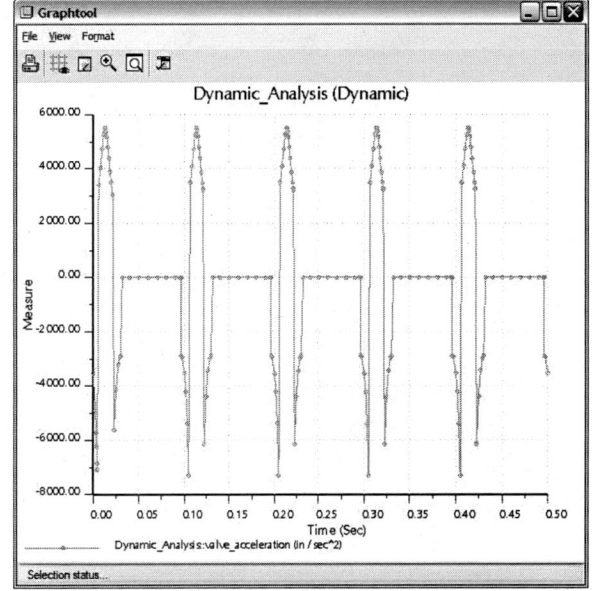

Figure 8-27 Graph of Valve Velocity

Figure 8-28 Graph of Valve Acceleration

The large reaction force looks suspicious. How does this small engine valve produce such a large force? If the force produced by the vavle is indeed this large, the rocker would have been damaged quickly. Before moving to *Pro/MECHANICA Structure*, it is worthwhile to investigate the reaction force further.

It turns out that the problem is that the mass property was not specified properly for the valve. If you open *valve.prt* and choose from the pull-down menu *Analysis > Model > Mass Properties*, you should see a *Mass Properties* dialog box appear, similar to Figure 8-31. Pick the default coordinate system (*PRT_CSYS_DEF*) from the *Graphics* window; mass properties of the valve will appear in the box. It shows that the density is 1.0 $lb_f\ s^2/in^4$ (mass unit in in-lb_f-sec unit system is $lb_f\ s^2/in^4$); hence, a total mass is close to 0.1 $lb_f\ s^2/in$ (0.09397). With acceleration close to 6,000 in/s^2, the inertial force is about 600 lb_f. Note that the mass density is unrealistically large.

If steel is assigned to the valve, the total mass becomes 6.883×10^{-5} $lb_f\ s^2/in$; the inertia (therefore the reaction force) will be in the neighborhood of 0.4 lb_f, which is more manageable and much more realistic.

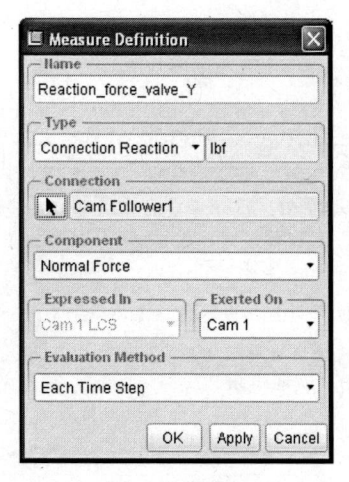

Figure 8-29

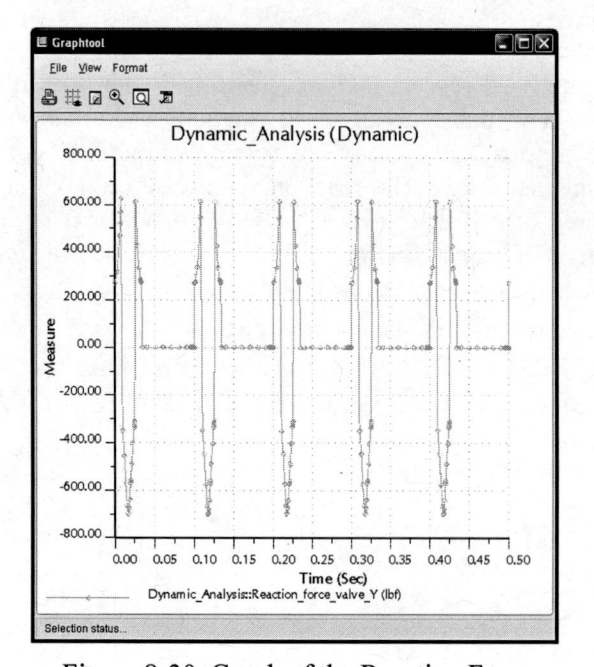

Figure 8-30 Graph of the Reaction Force

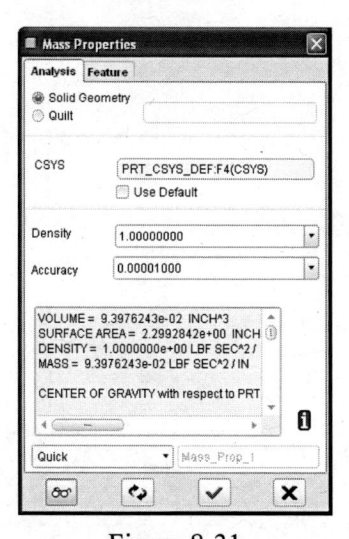

Figure 8-31

Lesson 8: Cam and Follower

Exercises:

1. Redesign the cam by reducing the small arc radius from 0.25 to 0.2 and reducing the center distance of the small arc from 0.52 to 0.40, as shown in Figure E8-1. Repeat the dynamic analysis and check reaction force between the valve and the rocker. Does this redesigned cam alter the reaction force?

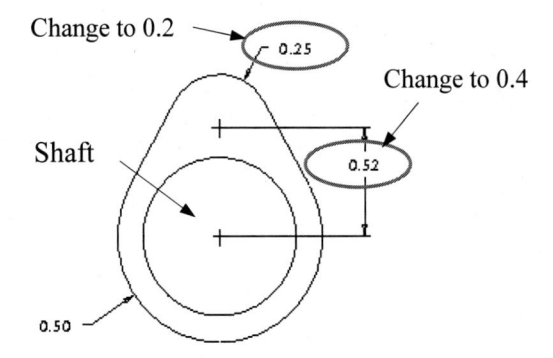

Figure E8-1 The Cam Profile

Notes:

Lesson 9: Assistive Device for Wheelchair Soccer Game

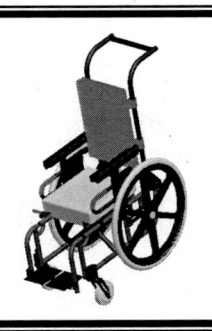

9.1 Overview of the Lesson

This is an application lesson. We will apply what we learned in previous lessons to a real-world application. This application involves designing a special mechanism that can be mounted on a wheelchair to mimic soccer ball-kicking action while being operated by a child sitting on a wheelchair with limited mobility and arm strength. Such a mechanism will provide more incentive and realistic experience for children with physical disabilities to participate in a soccer game. This example was extracted from an undergraduate student design project that was carried out in conjunction with a local children hospital. This device was intended primarily to be used in the summer camp sponsored by the children hospital.

9.2 The Assistive Device

Physical Model

This assistive device for soccer playing consists of five major components: the clamper, handle bar, plate, kicking rod, and spring, as illustrated in Figure 9-1. In reality these five components will be assembled first and clamped to the lower frame of the wheelchair for use.

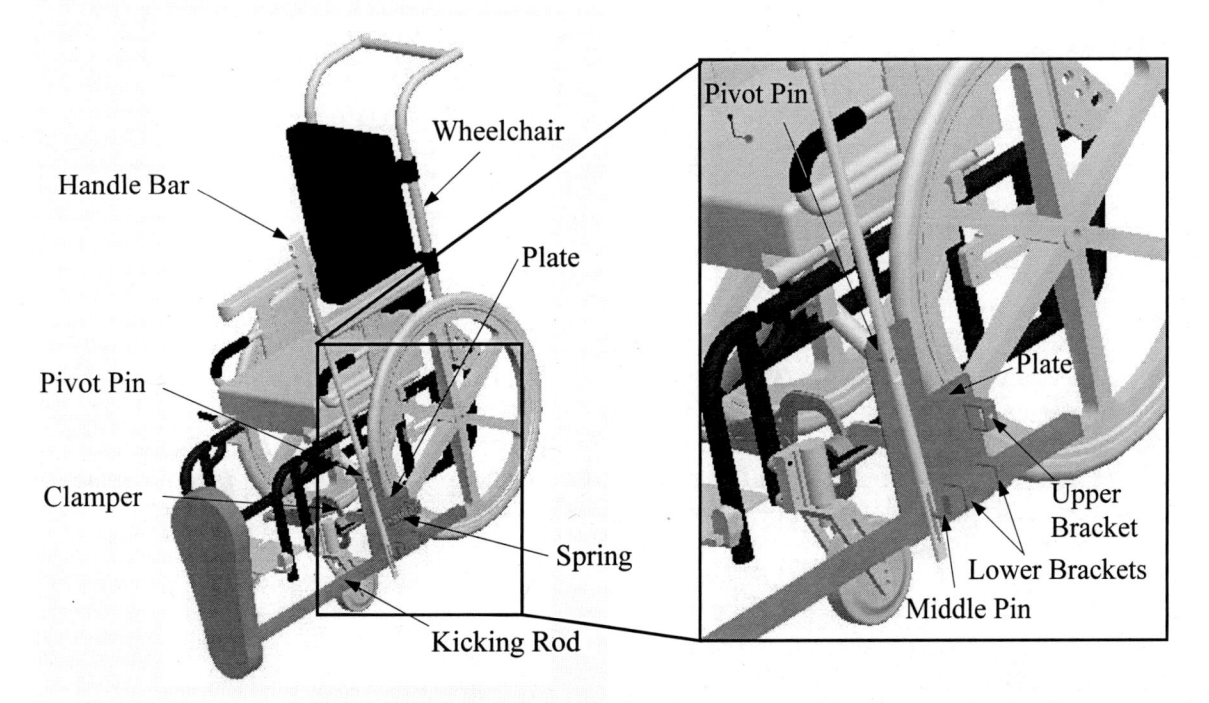

Figure 9-1 Assistive Device for Soccer Game

The handle bar is pinned at the pivot pin of the plate and linked to the middle pin of the kicking rod. The kicking rod is inserted into the two lower brackets mounted on the plate. When the handle bar is pulled backward, the handle bar rotates along the pivot pin; therefore, driving the kicking rod to move forward along the longitudinal direction through the link between the end slot of the handle bar and the middle pin of the kicking rod. The forward movement produces momentum to "kick" the soccer ball. A spring is added between the upper bracket and the handle bar to restore the handle bar to its upright position after pulling.

The goal of this lesson is to use *Mechanism Design* to calculate the position, velocity, and acceleration at the kicking rod for a given force. With the simulation results, the design can be adjusted to ensure that a minimum pulling force will produce a sufficient momentum that drives the kicking rod to realistically mimic the soccer ball kicking. The design adjustment could include the location of the pivot pin on the vertical handle bar, the location of the spring, the spring constant, etc.

Pro/ENGINEER Parts and Assembly

All *Pro/ENGINEER* parts are provided for this lesson. In addition, all parts are assembled, except for the handle bar and the kicking rod. These two components will be assembled with proper joints that allow the mechanism to move as desired. Note that the spring will be added to the system in *Mechanism Design*.

The example files you downloaded from the publisher's web site should consist of five parts and two assemblies, as listed in Table 1. In addition, a completely defined motion model with analysis files (*Static.pbk* and *Dynamic.pbk*) is included for your reference. The in-lb_f-sec unit system has been employed for all parts and assemblies.

Table 9.1 List of Parts and Assemblies in Lesson 9 Folder

Assembly	Parts	Remarks
wheelchair.asm		Partial Assembly to start with
	wheelchair.prt	Wheelchair Part, including Clamper
	plate.prt	Plate with Brackets
handle.prt		To be assembled
kicking_rod.asm	*rod.prt*	To be assembled
	foot.prt	

Note that the *kicking_rod.asm* and *handle.prt* are the only two components to be assembled to the *wheelchair.asm*, which is the assembly we will use to start this lesson. Note that *wheelchair.asm* consists of a wheelchair part and the clamper (*wheelchair.prt*) with a plate (*plate.prt*) attached. In assembling these two components, we will use component placement constraints. The *kicking_rod.asm* will be first assembled to *plate.prt* using axis alignment placement constraint (aligning *A_6* of *plate.prt* and *A_3* of *rod.prt*). The axis alignment constraint will place the rod through the two lower brackets in the plate, as shown in Figure 9-2. The rod will be also oriented with the foot at the end pointing upward, using a plane alignment constraint (with offset). Therefore, the kicking rod will be left with only one degree of freedom enabling it to slide along the longitudinal direction.

The handle bar will be assembled to the kicking rod using an axis alignment and surface tangent constraints. The axis alignment constraint will be defined between the handle bar and the plate by aligning two axes: *A_2* of *plate.prt* and *A_4* of *handle.prt*, as shown in Figure 9-3. The tangent placement

Lesson 9: Assistive Device 9-3

constraint will be created by choosing the outer cylindrical surface of the middle pin of the kicking rod and the inner surface of the end slot of the handle bar, as shown in Figure 9-3. As a result, the handle bar is able to rotate along the pivot pin and drive the kicking rod to move along the longitudinal direction through the surface tangent constraint between the end slot and the middle pin.

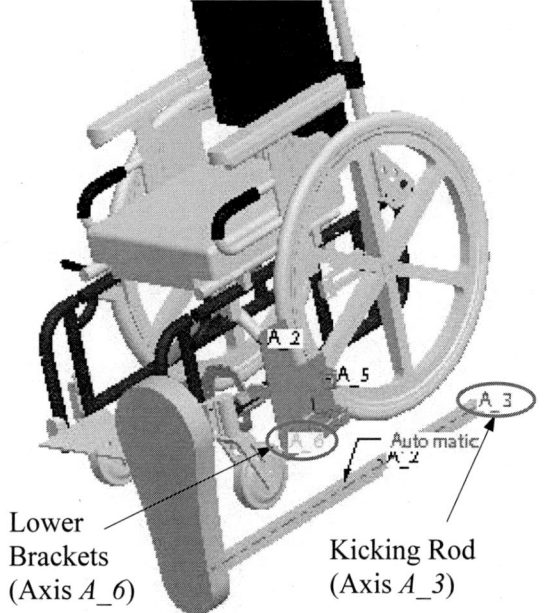

Figure 9-2 Assembling the Kicking Rod

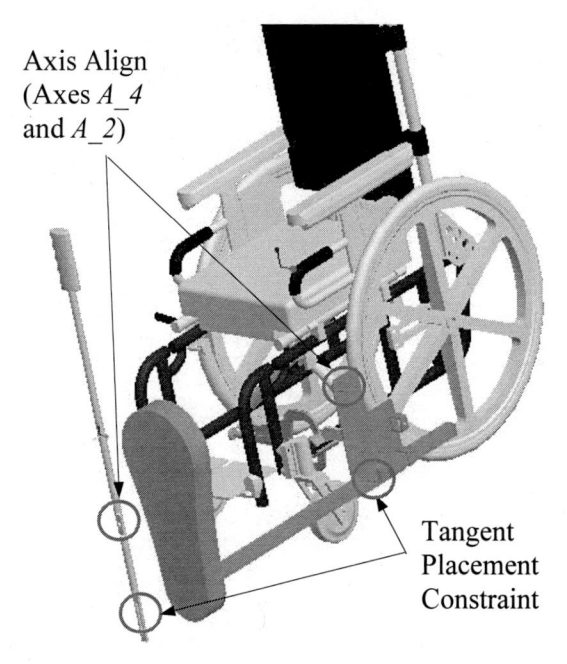

Figure 9-3 Assembling the Handle Bar

Simulation Model

In this example, the partial assembly *wheelchair.asm* will be assigned as the ground body. The pin joint at the pivot pin will allow a rotational motion between the handle bar and the ground body, as shown in Figure 9-3. The kicking rod assembly will slide along a longitudinal direction. A spring will be added to restore the vertical orientation of the handle bar after pulling, as shown in Figure 9-4. Finally, an impulse force of 5 lbs in a time span of 0.5 seconds will be added to the handle bar to simulate the pulling force.

9.3 Using *Mechanism Design*

Assembling the Handle Bar and Kicking Rod

Start *Pro/ENGINEER*, change the working directory, and open the assembly: *wheelchair.asm*. You should see *wheelchair.asm* appear in the *Graphics* window (see Figure 9-5). Note that the partial assembly consists of two components: the wheelchair (with clamper), and the plate (with brackets). They are listed in the *Model Tree* window; i.e., WHEELCHAIR.PRT, and PLATE.PRT.

Make sure the unit system has been set to in-lb_f-sec.

Next, we will bring in the first component, *kicking_rod.asm*. Click the *Add component* shortcut button and choose *kicking_rod.asm*. The kicking rod will be brought in with a default position and orientation similar to that of Figure 9-6. We will define an alignment placement constraint to align axis

A_3 in the rod and A_6 that passes through the center of the two lower brackets in the plate. In addition, we will add another alignment placement constraint to orient the end foot to the upright position.

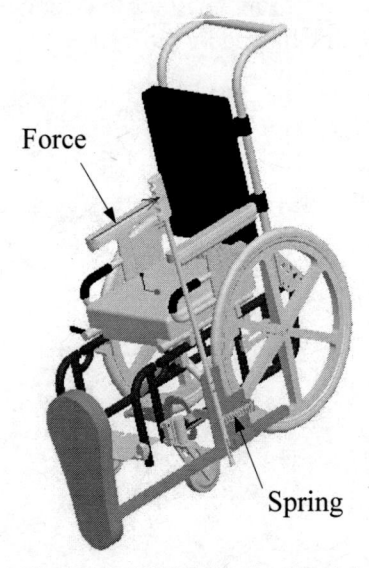

Figure 9-4 Simulation Model

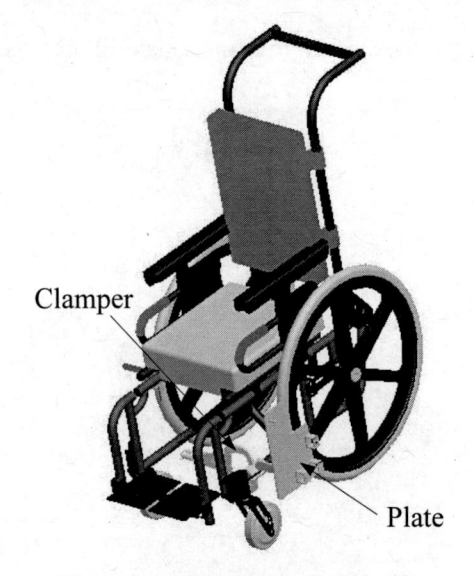

Figure 9-5 The Partial Assembly

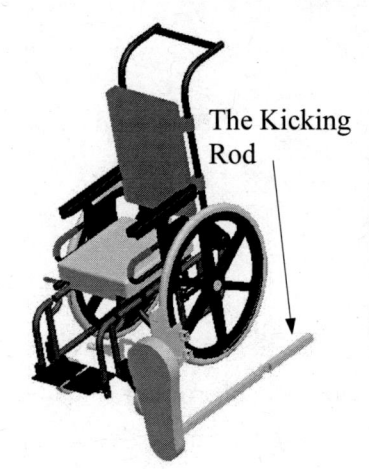

Figure 9-6 The Kicking Rod Being Brought into the Assembly

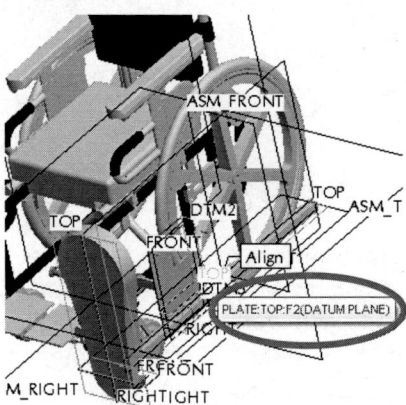

Figure 9-7 *PLATE:TOP: F2(DATUM PLANE)* (Plate)

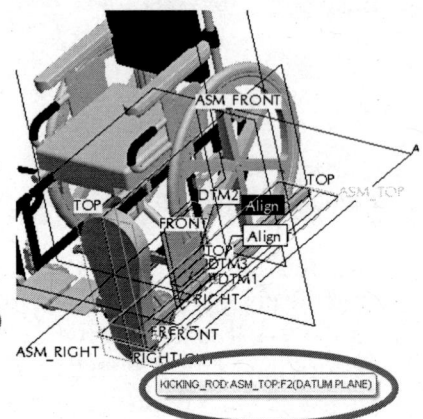

Figure 9-8 *KICKING_ROD: ASM_TOP:F2(DATUM PLANE)* (Kicking Rod)

Turn on the datum axis display. You should see a number of axes appear, including the two axes we need. In the *Component Placement* dashboard, click *Placement*, then choose *Align* from the *Constraint Type* list. Pick A_3 (kicking rod) and A_6 (plate), as shown in Figure 9-2. After defining the axis alignment constraint, turn off the datum axis display.

Next, we will align (with offset) *TOP* of the plate and *ASM_TOP* of the kicking rod to constrain the orientation of the kicking rod. Turn on datum plane display. Click *Placement* and choose *New Constraint*. Choose *Align* (with offset: *Oriented*) from the *Constraint Type* list. Move the pointer closer to the horizontal datum plane of the plate, as shown in Figure 9-7, until you see that the plane is highlighted and the plane label *PLATE:TOP:F2(DATUM PLANE)* appears. Pick the plane. Similarly, move the pointer closer to the vertical datum plane of the kicking rod assembly, as shown in Figure 9-8, until you see that the plane is highlighted and the plane label *KICKING_ROD:ASM_TOP:F2(DATUM PLANE)* appears.

Lesson 9: Assistive Device 9-5

Pick the plane. The constraint status is invalid since the two planes are parallel and separated. Modify the constraint by clicking the *Placement* button, choosing the align constraint, and choosing *Oriented* for *Offset*. The kicking rod should be properly oriented and the constraint status becomes partially constrained, allowing longitudinal movement.

Click the *Drag Packed Components* button at the top of the *Graphics* window, and click the kicking rod. You should be able to move the rod along the longitudinal direction (through the two lower brackets). Click the resume button (left of the button). Click the button to accept the definition.

Next, we will bring in the handle bar. Click the *Add component* button and choose *handle.prt*. The handle bar will be brought in with a default position and orientation similar to those of Figure 9-3. We will create alignment and tangent placement constraints, as discussed earlier.

In the *Placement* window, choose *Align* from the *Constraint Type* list. Pick A_2 of *plate.prt* and A_4 of *handle.prt*, as shown in Figure 9-9 (note that you may need to zoom in to pick A_4). Click *Placement* and choose *New Constraint*. Choose *Tangent* from the *Constraint Type* list, and pick the outer cylindrical surface of the middle pin of the rod and the inner surface of the end slot of the handle bar (*HANDLE:Surf: F14(EXTRUDE_5)*), as shown in Figure 9-10. Click *New Constraint* again, choose *Mate* from the *Constraint Type* list, and pick the front flat face (*ROD:Surf:F8(EXTRUDE_2)* at the root of the middle pin of the kicking rod (see Figure 9-11) and the back flat surface (*HANDLE:Surf: F12(EXTRUDE_4)*) close to the end of the handle bar where the tangent constraint was defined, as shown in Figure 9-11.

Choose *Offset* and enter *0.125* for *Offset*. Click the button to accept the definition. The handle bar should now be partially constrained allowing rotation through the pivot pin.

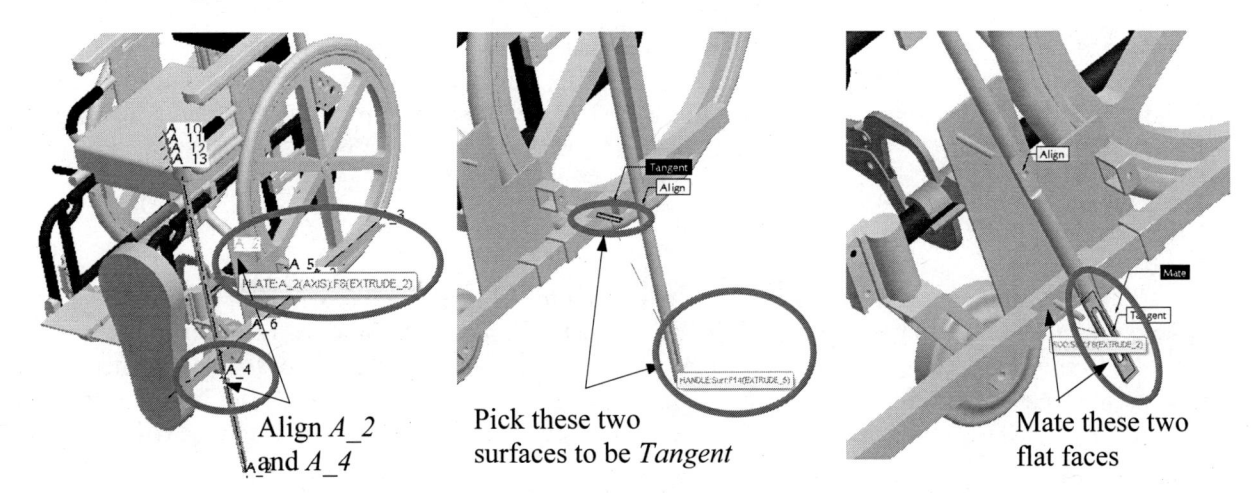

Figure 9-9 Align Two Axes Figure 9-10 Two Tangent Surfaces Figure 9-11 Mate Flat Faces

Click the *Drag Packed Components* button at the top of the *Graphics* window, and click the handle bar. You should be able to move (rotate) the handle bar along the pivot pin and therefore drive the kicking rod back and forth along the longitudinal direction, as shown in Figure 9-12. The whole assembly is now completed.

We will use the *Drag Packed Components* button to create a snapshot for initial condition. Refer to previous lessons for details in creating a snapshot. The snapshot will orient the handle bar vertically. The snapshot can be created by orienting (align with orient option) two faces, e.g., *RIGHT:F1(DATUM PLANE): HANDLE* and *ASM_FRONT* of the wheel chair, as shown in Figure 9-13. Save the snapshot.

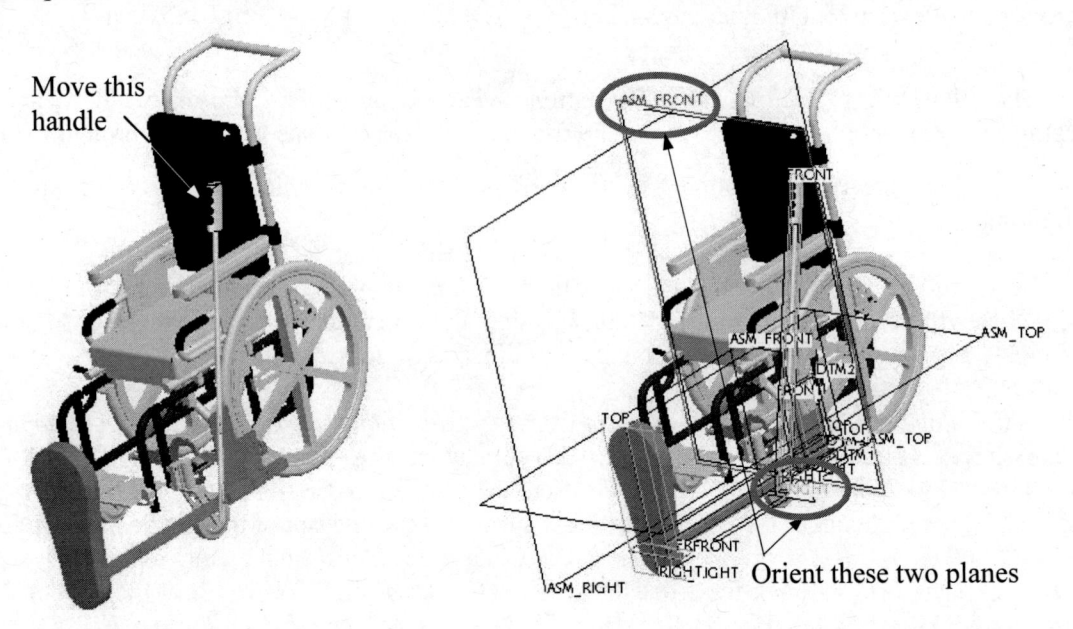

Figure 9-12 Align Two Axes

Figure 9-13 Orient Two Planes

Creating a Simulation Model

As part of the simulation model, we will add a spring to connect the handle bar to the plate in order to restore the handle bar to the upright position after pulling. In addition, we will add a point force on top of the handle bar and define a dynamic simulation. The force will be an impulse force of a triangular shape with a magnitude of 5 lb$_f$ in a 0.5 second period. From the pull-down menu, choose

Applications > Mechanism.

Click the *Define Springs* shortcut button. From the *Graphics* window, pick *PNT0* of the handle bar and drag the handle to overlap with *PNT0* of the plate, as shown in Figure 9-14 (refer to *Lesson 3* or *Lesson 8* for defining spring). In addition, enter *20* for spring constant, and *4.5* for the unstretched spring length. Note that the unstretched distance is smaller than the distance that keeps the handle bar in the upright position. Therefore, the handle bar will lean forward in the equilibrium configuration due the spring. Click the ✓ button at right to accept the definition. A spring symbol should appear in the *Graphics* window, as shown in Figure 9-14.

Next, we will define a force. Click the *Define Force/Torque* button or *Insert > Force/Torque* to access the *Force/Torque Definition* dialog box. In the *Force/Torque Definition* dialog box, enter *Force1* for *Name*, choose *PNT1* of the handle bar from the *Graphics* window. A purple solid arrow will appear pointing in the direction parallel to that of the kicking rod as default (Figure 9-15). Choose *Table* from the *Function* area (see Figure 9-16). Click the *Add rows to table* button (see Figure 9-17) three times to create three empty rows. Enter three pairs of data *0, 0*; *0.25, 5*; and *0.5, 0* for the force magnitude, as shown in Figure 9-17. Choose the *Direction* tab, and enter *–1* for Z-direction to reverse the direction of the force (see Figure 9-18). Click *OK*.

Lesson 9: Assistive Device 9-7

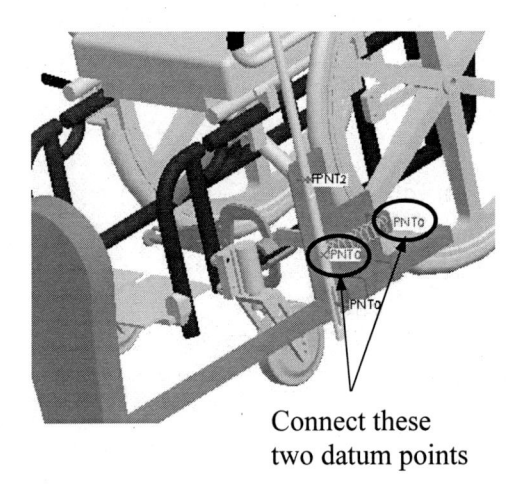

Figure 9-14 Connecting Two Datum Points for Defining a Spring

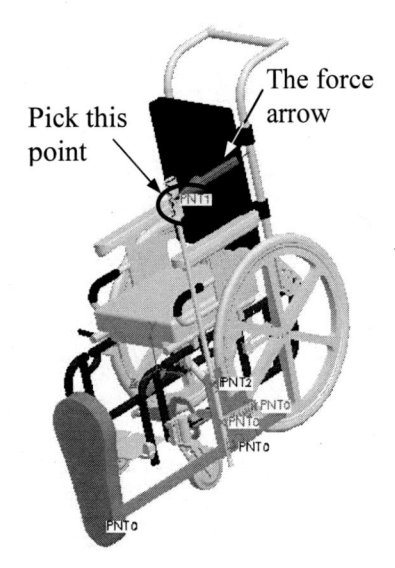

Figure 9-15 Defining Force

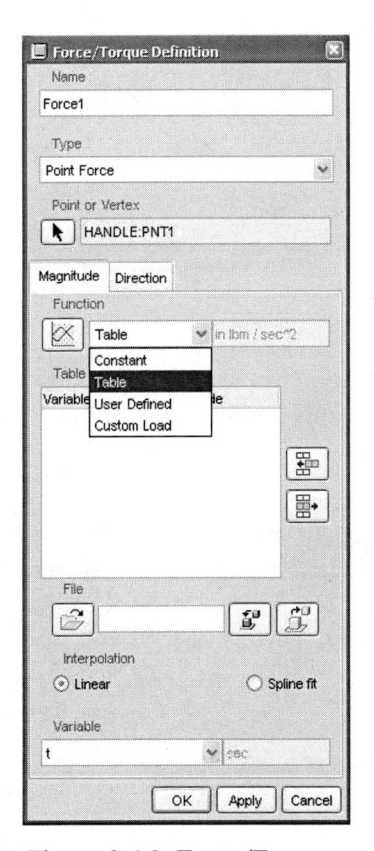

Figure 9-16 *Force/Torque Definition* Dialog Box

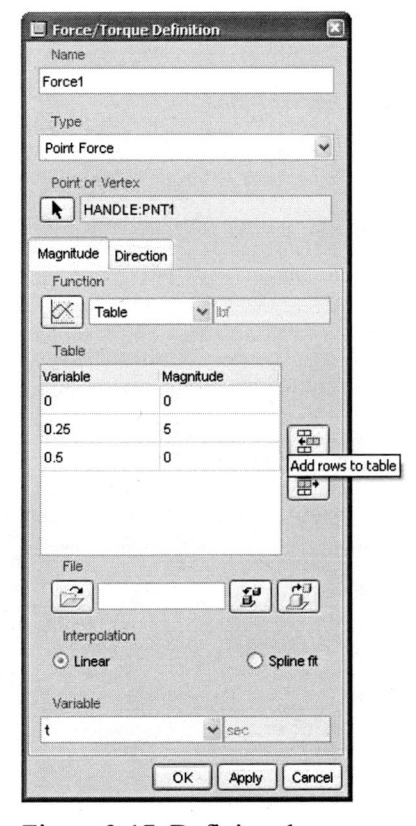

Figure 9-17 Defining the Impulse Force

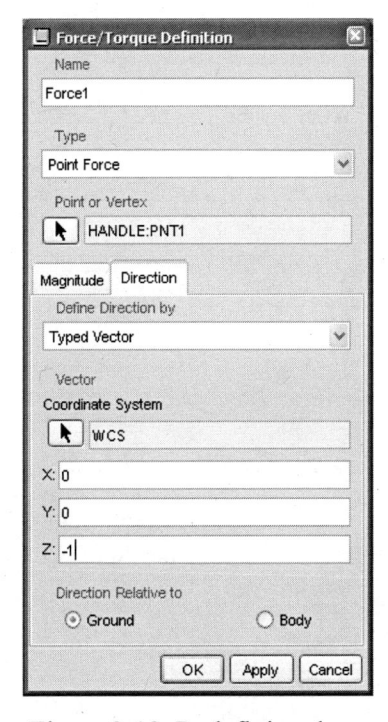

Figure 9-18 Redefining the Force Direction

Creating and Running a Static Analysis

We will first run a static analysis to determine the equilibrium configuration of the mechanism. This equilibrium configuration will be used as the initiation configuration for the following dynamic simulation. From the shortcut button list on the right, click the *Mechanism Analysis* button to define an analysis. In the *Analysis Definition* dialog box appearing, enter *Static_Analysis* for *Name* and choose *Static* for *Type*. Click the *Ext Loads* tab and remove *Force1* by clicking on the data cell and click the remove button (middle one on the right), as shown in Figure 9-19. Click *Run*. The static analysis will start and a *Graphtool* window similar to Figure 9-20 will appear showing the progress of the analysis. In the *Graphics* window, the handle bar will lean forward, as shown in Figure 9-21, due to the fact that the unstretched spring length is 4.5 in.

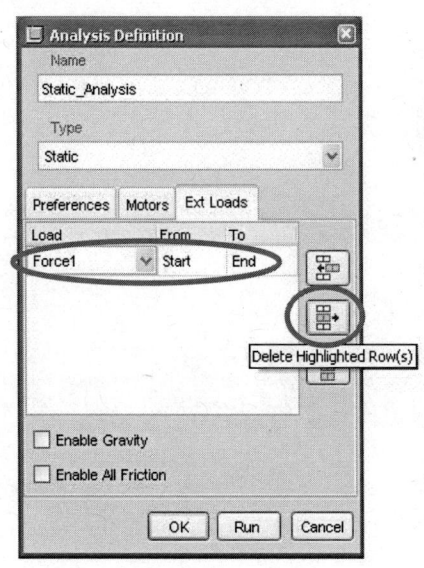

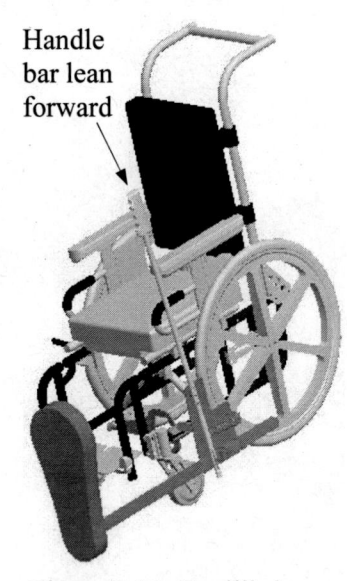

Figure 9-19 *Analysis Definition* Dialog Box

Figure 9-20 *Graphtool* Window

Figure 9-21 Equilibrium Configuration

Again, we will use the *Drag Packed Components* button to create a snapshot for the current configuration, which will be used as the initial condition for dynamic simulation.

Creating and Running a Dynamic Analysis

From the shortcut button list on the right, click the *Mechanism Analysis* button to define an analysis. In the *Analysis Definition* dialog box appearing, enter *DynamicAnalysis* for the name, and enter the following:

Type: *Dynamic*
Duration: *3*
Frame Rate: *100*
Minimum Interval: *0.01*
Initial Configuration: *Current*

Make sure that the external force is included this time (click the *Ext Loads* tab of the *Analysis Definition* dialog box to check). Run the analysis. In the *Graphics* window, the handle bar should pull back and the kicking rod should start moving forward. After a short period (about 0.5 seconds), the motion is reversed, then back and forth until the end of the 3-second simulation period.

Saving and Reviewing Results

Click the *Playbacks* button on the right to bring up the *Playbacks* dialog box and repeat the motion animation. On the *Playbacks* dialog box, click *Save* button to save the results as a *.pbk* file.

We will create measures to monitor the position, velocity, and acceleration of the kicking rod along the longitudinal direction (Z-direction). All three measures will be defined at datum point *PNT0* of the foot, as shown in Figure 9-22.

Click . In the *Measure Definition* dialog box, enter *Position_Rod* for *Name*. Under *Type*, select *Position*. Pick *PNT0* in the *Graphics* the *Generate Measure Results of Analyses* button . In the *Measure Results* dialog box appearing, click the *Create New Measure* button window. Choose *Z-component*. Under *Evaluation Method*, leave *Each Time Step*. Click *OK* to accept the definition.

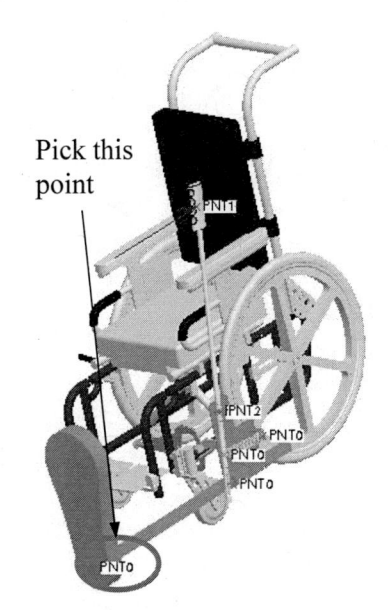

Pick this point

Figure 9-22 Defining Measures

In the *Measure Results* dialog box, choose *AnalysisDefinition1* in the *Result Set* and click the *Graph* button on the top left corner to graph the measure. The graph should be similar to that of Figure 9-23, which shows that the kicking rod travels to about 31 in. forward due to the pulling force applied at the handle bar and about 25.5 in. backward due to the spring. The overall distance that the kicking rod travels is about 5.5 in., which probably will not produce enough momentum to kick the ball. On the other hand, the middle pin of the rod (therefore the handle bar) will collide with the two lower brackets during the backward movement. The collision is also evidenced during the motion animation. Note that the rod is moving back and forth because that no friction is being applied to any of the connections.

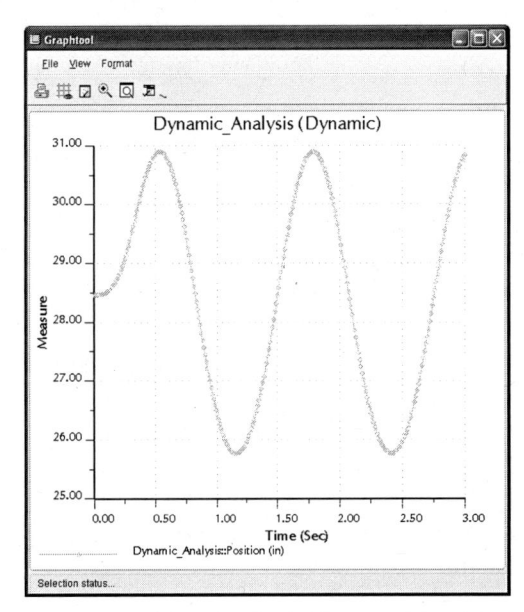

Figure 9-23 Graph of Kicking Rod Position

Similarly, create measures for velocity and acceleration for the kicking rod at the same datum points along the longitudinal direction (Z-direction). Make sure you choose *Z-component* when you define these two measures. The graphs should look like those of Figures 9-24 and 9-25, respectively. Figure 9-24 shows that the velocity of the kicking rod is about 10 in/sec when the force is first applied. The velocity is increased to 15 in/sec when the rod is pulled back by the spring. In Figure 9-25, a maximum acceleration of 50 in/sec^2 is reached when the handle bar is released. The acceleration is increased to 80 in/sec^2 due to the stretch of the spring.

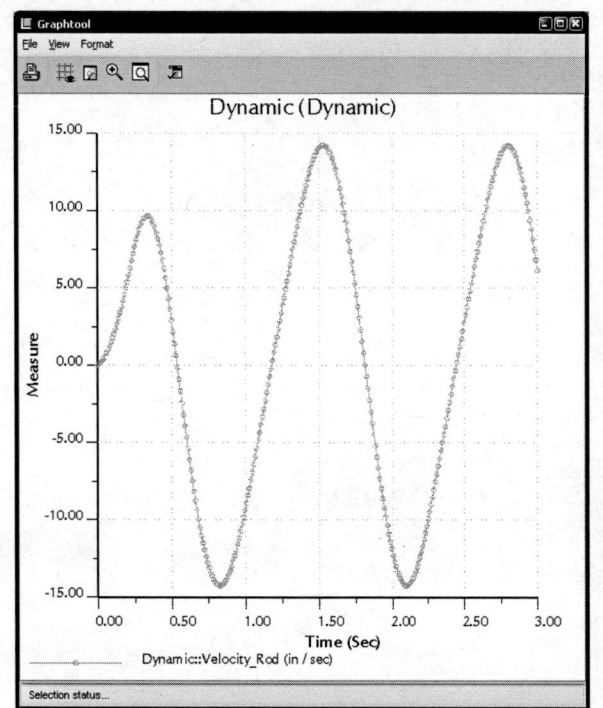

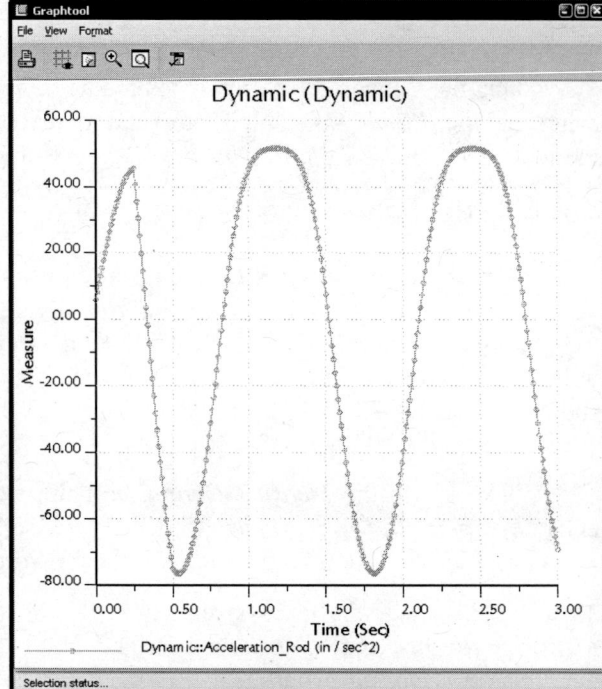

Figure 9-24 Graph of Kicking Rod Velocity

Figure 9-25 Graph of Kicking Rod Acceleration

Define position of the handle bar in the Z-direction as measure at *PNT1* of the handle bar. Display the result in graph. You should see a graph similar to that of Figure 9-26. As shown in Figure 9-26, the handle bar travels between 2 and 17 in., about 15 in. overall, which is about right for users to handle.

9.4 Result Discussion

Looking at the results shown in the graphs, there are at least three problems revealed in the current design. First, the collision appears between the kicking rod (and the handle bar) and the lower brackets on the plate. These two brackets must move backward to provide adequate room for the rod to travel along the longitudinal direction.

Second, the spring exerts a fairly large force on the handle bar, pushing the handle bar with a larger velocity and acceleration. Since the sole purpose of the spring is to restore the handle bar to its equilibrium upward position, a large exerting force is less desirable. In order to reduce the spring force, the spring must move upward, closer to the pivot pin in order to reduce the spring deflection.

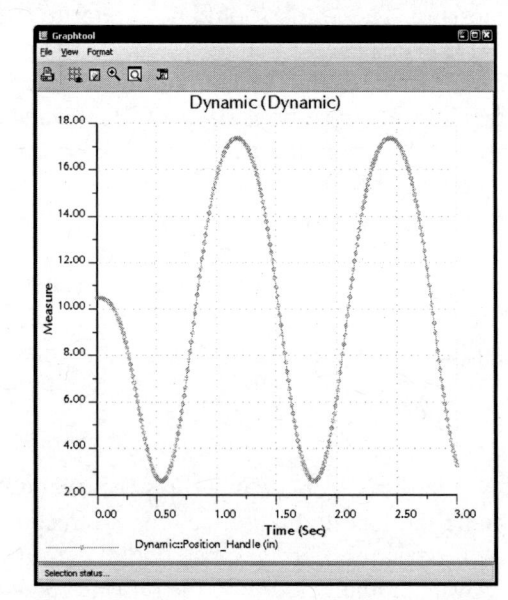

Figure 9-26 Graph of Handle Bar Position

Third, the kicking rod only travels about 5.5 in., while the handle bar travels 17 in. This is due to the current position of the pivot pin. It would be more desirable to have the kicking rod travel more than the handle bar. This can be achieved by moving the pivot pin upward. However, by doing so, users will have to pull the handle bar with a greater force since the moment arm is reduced. There is a trade-off between the amount of the applied force and the effectiveness of the whole mechanism in terms of the kicking action. Design alternatives are to be explored, which is left as an exercise.

The design was revised. A physical device, as shown in Figure 9-27, was built by students. The physical device confirms that the contact between the kicking rod and the two brackets produces a large friction force, resulting in a large operating force to operate the device. For children with limited physical strength, such a device is unattractive.

In order to reduce the friction, four bearings are added to the device, as shown in Figure 9-28. Two are added to the top surface of the kicking rod, and two are underneath the kicking rod. With the bearings, the friction is significantly reduced. Therefore, a smaller force is needed to operate the device. The actual operating force is less than *20* lb$_f$.

Figure 9-27 Device Assembled to the Wheelchair

Figure 9-28 Bearings Added (Top View)

Notes:

Mechanism Design with Pro/ENGINEER   **10-1**

Lesson 10: Kinematic Analysis for Racecar Suspension

10.1 Overview of the Lesson

This is the second application and the final lesson of this book. In this lesson, we will take a quarter of a racecar suspension and create a motion model for kinametic analyses. The racecar model employed, as shown in Figure 10-1, is a Formula SAE (Society of Automotive Engineers) style racecar designed and built by engineering students at the University of Oklahoma (OU) during 2005-2006. Each year engineering students throughout the world design and build formula-style racecars and participate in the annual Formula SAE competitions (students.sae.org/competitions/formulaseries). The result is a great experience for young engineers as a meaningful engineering project as well as an opportunity to work in a dedicated team environment.

(a) Manufactured Racecar on Displayed   (b) Racecar Designed in *Pro/ENGINEER*

Figure 10-1 Formula SAE Racecar Designed and Built by OU Engineering Students

The suspension of the entire racecar was modeled for both kinematic and dynamic analyses during 2005-2007. These analysis results were validated using experimental data. The experimental data were acquired by mounting a data acquisition system on the racecar and driving the racecar on the test track following specific driving scenarios that are consistent with those of the simulations. These results were used to aid the suspension design for handling and cornering. Assembling an entire vehicle suspension for motion analysis is non-trivial and is beyond the scope of this book. Therefore, only the right front quarter of the racecar suspension, as shown in Figure 10-2, will be employed in this lesson. The purpose of this lesson is mainly to show you that *Mechanism Design* is capable of supporting design of kinematic characteristics of vehicle suspension, instead of repeating the detailed process of constructing the motion model in *Mechanism Design*. Therefore, in this lesson, we will start with an assembled motion model. The only component we will add to the motion model is the road profile. The road profile is characterized by the geometric shape of a profile cam, which will be assembled to the tire using a cam-follower connection.

Figure 10-2 The Right Front Quarter of the Racecar Suspension (View A)

10.2 The Quarter Suspension

Physical Model

The quarter suspension consists of major components that essentially define the kinematic and dynamic characteristics of the racecar. These components include upper and lower control arms, upright, rocker, shock, push rod, tie rod, and wheel and tire, as shown in Figure 10-3. The dangling end of the shock, both control arms, rocker, and tie rod are connected to the chassis frame using numerous joints. The chassis frame is assumed fixed and the tire is pushed and pulled by the profile cam (not shown) mimicking the road profile. Two views, *View A* and *View B,* shown in Figure 10-3, are created in the assembled model and will be used for illustrations throughout this lesson.

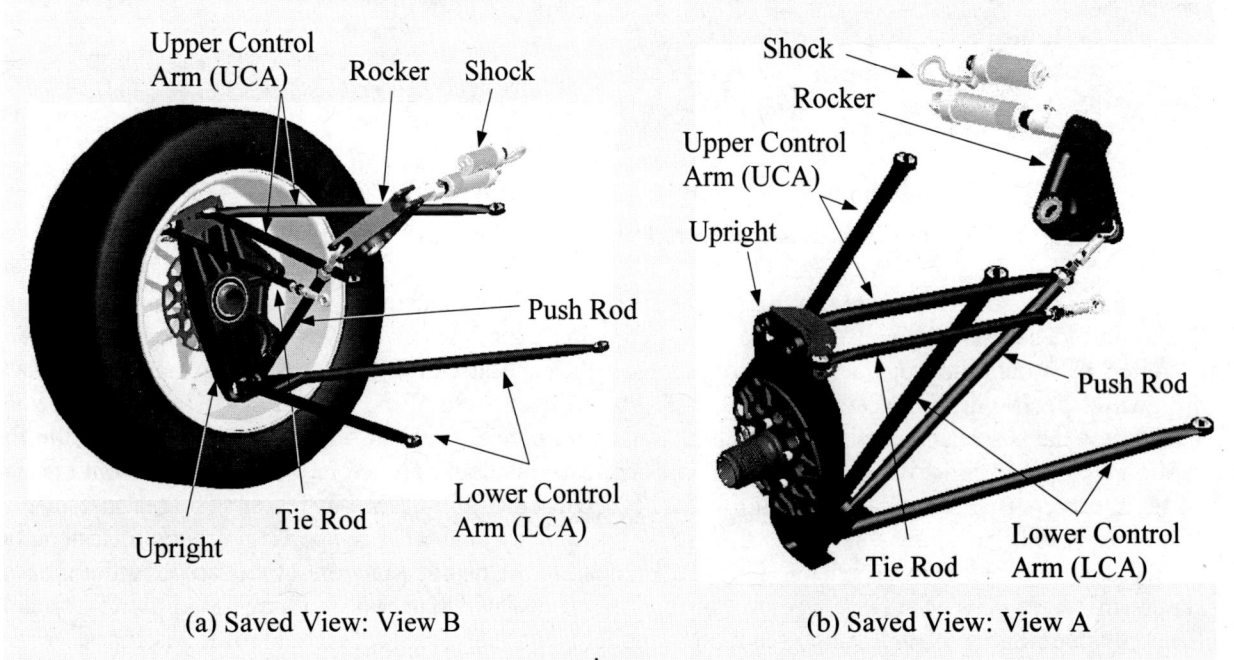

(a) Saved View: View B

(b) Saved View: View A

Figure 10-3 Major Components of the Quarter Suspension

Lesson 10: Kinematic Analysis for Racecar Suspension

The tire of the quarter suspension will be in contact with the profile cam that characterizes the road profile. As shown in Figure 10-4, the geometry of the cam consists of two circular arcs of radius 6.65 in. (AB and FG), which are concentric with the cam center. Therefore, when the cam rotates, these two circular arcs do not push or pull the tire, resulting in two flat segments of the road profile, as shown in Figure 10-5. In addition, the circular arc CDE is centered 4 in. above the cam center with a radius of 4 in. Therefore, when the cam rotates, arc CDE pushes the tire up, mimicking a hump of 1.35 in. (that is 8−6.65, peak at point D). A ditch is characterized by an 8 in. arc (HIJ) centered at 3 in. above the cam center. As the cam rotates, arc HIJ creates a ditch of 1.65 in. deep (that is 6.65−(8−3)). The remaining straight lines and arcs provide smooth transitions among flats, humps, and ditches in the road profile.

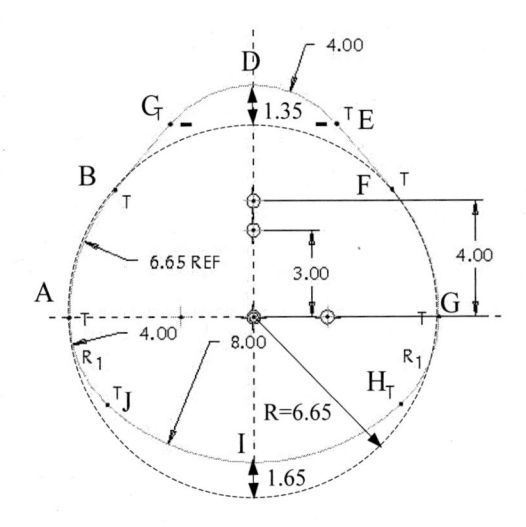

Figure 10-4 Geometry of the Profile Cam

Based on the geometry of the profile cam, this quarter suspension will go over a 1.35 in. hump and a 1.65 in. ditch in one complete rotation of the profile cam. Note that since the radius of arc AB is 6.65 in., the cam will cause the quarter suspension to travel roughly 41.8 in. (3.48 ft.) in one complete rotation. Since the profile cam will rotate a complete cycle in one second, the suspension travels about 3.48 ft/sec; i.e., 2.37 MPH, a very slow motion.

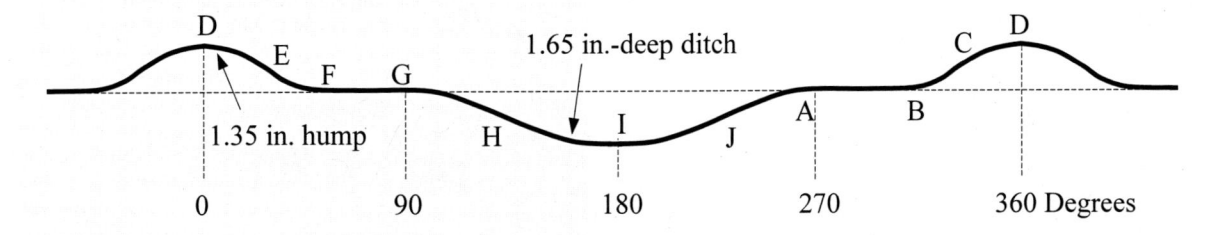

Figure 10-5 Road Profile Generated by the Profile Cam

Pro/ENGINEER Parts and Assembly

All *Pro/ENGINEER* parts and assemblies are provided for this lesson. In addition, all parts and subassemblies are assembled, except for the profile cam (part name: *profile.prt*). The profile cam will be assembled to the tire using a cam-follower connection. A servo motor will be added to drive the cam at a constant angular velocity of 360 degrees/sec, therefore pushing and pulling the tire along the vertical direction, mimicking the situation where the racecar goes over humps and ditches.

Note that the example files you downloaded from the publisher's website should consist of 51 files: 38 parts, 12 assemblies, and 1 result, as listed in Table 1. The quarter suspension *quarter_suspension.asm* is completely assembled except for the road profile (*profile.prt*). We will start with this assembly and bring in the profile cam, which will be assembled to the tire using a cam-follower connection. In addition, a completely assembled motion model, *motion_quarter_suspension.asm*, is included for your reference. A simulation result file, *AnalysisDefinition1.pbk*, is also included. You may want to open this motion model and bring up this result file to see the motion animation of the quarter suspension system.

Table 10-1 List of Files in Lesson 10 Folder

Assembly	Part/Subassemblies				Remarks
quarter_suspension.asm					Assembly to start the lesson
	hardpoints.prt				Datum features
	fr_rocker.asm				Rocker
		susp_front_bellcrank.prt			
		susp_rocker_bearing_61903_2RS1.prt (2)			
	shock_upper.prt				Shocks
	shock_lower.prt				
	lcm.asm				Lower Control Arm
		susp_front_rh_lower_a_am.prt			
		susp_025_hab_4t_special_race.prt (2)			
		susp_a_arm_flare.prt (2)			
		susp_3125_pwb_5tg_circ_race.prt			
	prod.asm				Push Rod
		susp_front_push_rod.prt			
		susp_025_pr_com_4_race.prt			
		bolt_03125_allthread_rod_link.prt			
		susp_025_fem_rod_end_asw_4t.prt			
		susp_pushrod_flare.prt			
	fr_upright.asm				Upright
		susp_front_rh_upright.prt			
		susp_front_camber_shim.asm			
			susp_front_camber_shim_8.prt (2)		
			susp_front_camber_shim_8.prt (4)		
		susp_front_rh_steer_arm.asm			
			susp_front_rh_steer_arm.prt		
			susp_front_steer_ackerman_plate.prt		
	lcm.asm				Lower Control Arm
		susp_front_rh_upper_a_am.prt			
		susp_025_hab_4t_special_race.prt (2)			
		susp_a_arm_flare.prt (4)			
		susp_025_hab_4t_special_race2.prt (2)			
	wheel.asm				Wheel
		susp_front_hub.prt			
		susp_wheel_drive_pin.prt (4)			
		susp_front_hub_spacer.prt			
		susp_front_wheelbear_61908_2RS1.prt (2)			
		brake_rotor_hat.prt			
		susp_wheel_assembly.asm			
			susp_wheel_inner_rim.prt		
			susp_wheel_outer_rim.prt		
			susp_wheel_center.prt		
			susp_tire_13inch_20_x_6.prt		
	trod.asm				Tie Rod Assembly
		susp_steering_front_tie_rod.prt			
		susp_025_fem_rod_end_asw_4t.prt			
		Bolt_3125_allthread_rod_link.prt			
		susp_025_hab_4t_special_race.prt			
		susp_front_tie_rod_flare.prt			
	profile.prt				To be assembled
motion_quarter_suspension.asm					Complete Motion Model
AnalysisDefinition1.pbk					Result Data File

Note that the in-lb$_f$-sec unit system has been employed for all parts and assemblies. You may want to choose (from the pull-down menu) *File > Properties* to reassure the choice of the proper unit system.

Simulation Model

There are nine bodies in this motion model, including the ground body. All the key datum features, including datum coordinate systems, datum axes, and datum points, required for assembly are collected in the part called *hardpoints.prt*, as shown in Figure 10-6a. The *hardpoint.prt* was assembled to the overall assembly *quarter_suspension.asm* by aligning coordinate systems *GCS* (*hardpoints.prt*) and *ASM_DEF_CSYS* (*quarter_suspension.asm*). Therefore, *hardpoints.prt* belongs to the ground body, and the coordinate system, *GCS* or *ASM_DEF_CSYS*, becomes the *WCS* (World Coordinate System). Note that the *X*-direction is the forward direction, as shown in Figure 10-6a, and the ground is about 1.4 in. above *WCS* along the *Z*-direction (that is the distance between the lowest point in the tire and the coordinate system *GCS*).

There are two rigid (no symbol), three pin, eight ball, and one cylinder joints, as shown in Figure 10-6b and Table 10-2. Note that axis *A_1* in *hardpoints.prt* is for assembling the profile cam later. A kinematic analysis will be created with a servo motor that rotates the profile cam for 2 seconds. Three measures will be defined to monitor the characteristics of the suspension, including vertical wheel travel, shock travel, and camber angle.

(a) Hardpoints (View B)   (b) Connections (View B)

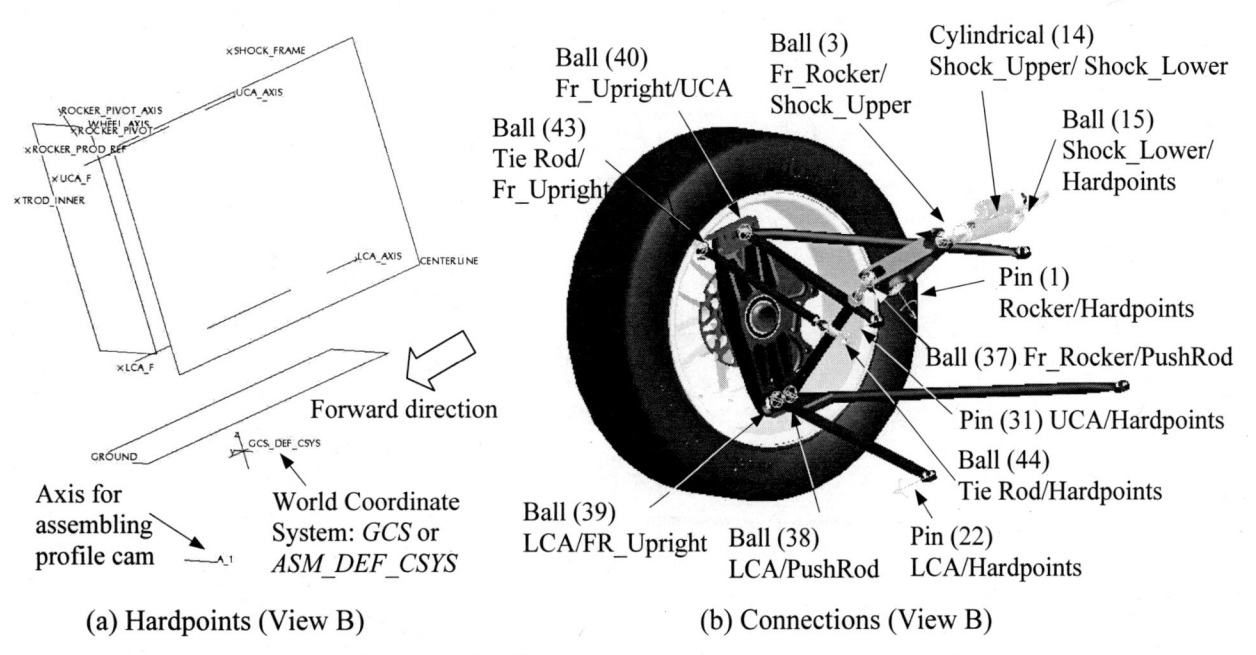

Figure 10-6 Joints Defined for the Quarter Suspension Assembly

10.3 Using *Mechanism Design*

Assembling the Profile Cam

Start *Pro/ENGINEER*, change the working directory, and open *quarter_suspension.asm*. You should see *quarter_suspension.asm* appear in the *Graphics* window with default view *View B* (see Figure 10-3). Note that the *quarter_suspension.asm* consists of ten components, listed in the *Model Tree* window; i.e., HARDPOINTS.PRT, FR_ROCKER.ASM, SHOCK_UPPER.PRT, SHOCK_LOWER.PRT, LCA.ASM,

PROD.ASM, FR_UPRIGHT.ASM, UCA.ASM, WHEEL.ASM, and *TROD.ASM*. You can also see the definitions of bodies and connections in the motion model. You may choose *Applications > Mechanism* to enter *Mechanism Design*. The joint symbols appear, similar to those of Figure 10-6b. The *Model Tree* is split into two sections. You can find the body and connection definitions by expanding these entities, as shown in Figure 10-7. Note that the rigid connections are not listed in *Model Tree*.

Table 10-2 Connections and Placement Constraints

Body	Part or Assembly	Connections	Assembled to	Placement Constraints
Ground Body	*hardpoints.prt*	Rigid	quarter_ suspension.asm	Coordinate Systems Alignment: *GCS* to *ASM_DEF_CSYS*
Body1	*ft_rocker.asm*	Pin (1)	*hardpoints.prt*	Axis Alignment: *ROCKER_PIVOT_AXIS* to *ROCKER_PIVOT_AXIS* Translation: *ROCKER_PIVOT_CENTER* to *ROCKER_PIVOT*
Body2	*shock_upper.prt*	Ball (3)	*hardpoints.prt*	Point Alignment: *SHOCK_UPPER* to *FR_ROCKER*
Body3	*shock_lower.prt*	Ball (15)	*hardpoints.prt*	Point Alignment: *SHOCK_LOWER* to *SHOCK_FRAME*
		Cylinder (14)	*shock_upper.prt*	Axis Alignment: *A_3* to *A_1*
Body4	*lca.asm*	Pin (22)	*hardpoints.prt*	Axis Alignment: *LCA_AXIS* to *LCA_AXIS* Translation: *LCA_FR* to *LCA_F*
Body5	*prod.asm*	Ball (37)	*lca.asm*	Point Alignment: *PROD_INNER* to *ROCKER_PROD*
		Ball (38)	*fr_rocker.asm*	Point Alignment: *PROD_OUTER* to *LCA_PROD*
Body6	*uca.asm*	Pin (31)	*hardpoints.prt*	Axis Alignment: *UCA_AXIS* to *UCA_AXIS* Translation: *UCA_FR* to *UCA_F*
		Ball (40)	*upright.prt*	Point Alignment: *UCA_OUTER* to *UPRIGHT_UCA*
Body7	*fr_upright.asm*	Ball (39)	*lca.asm*	Point Alignment: *UPRIGHT_LCA* to *LCA_OUTER*
	wheel.asm	Rigid (42)	*fr_upright.asm*	Axis Alignment: *A_1* to *A_1* Surface Mate: *F2* to *F9*
Body8	*trod.asm*	Ball (43)	*fr_upright.asm*	Point Alignment: *TIEROD_OUTER* to *TROD_UPRIGHT*
		Ball (44)	*hardpoints.prt*	Point Alignment: *TIEROD_INNER* to *TROD_INNER*

Next, we will bring in the only component, *profile.prt*, to the assembly. Click the *Add component* shortcut button and choose *profile.prt*. The profile cam will be brought in with a default position and orientation similar to those of Figure 10-8. Note that you may need to zoom out to see the profile cam. Move the part closer to the quarter suspension. We will define a pin joint to assemble the cam (*profile.prt*) to the ground body (*hardpoints.prt*). This pin joint will be defined by aligning axis *A_1* in *profile.prt* to *A_1* in *hardpoints.prt* and aligning datum plane *FRONT* in *profile.prt* to *ASM_TOP* in the quarter suspension assembly.

Turn on the datum axis display. You should see a number of axes appear, including the two axes we need. In the *Component Placement* dashboard from the *User Defined* list, choose the *Pin* joint. Turn on

Lesson 10: Kinematic Analysis for Racecar Suspension   10-7

datum axis display and pick *A_1* (*profile.prt*) and *A_1* (*hardpoints.prt*). After picking the axes, turn off the datum axis display and turn on datum plane display. Pick *FRONT* datum plane in *profile.prt* to *ASM_TOP* in *hardpoints.prt*. Turn on datum plane display. Pick *FRONT* and *ASM_TOP*. Note that you may need to zoom out to see datum plane *ASM_TOP*. The profile cam is not properly positioned since the two datum planes are not aligned. We will position *profile.prt* by entering an offset of *24.5* using the *Placement* window, as shown in Figure 10-9.

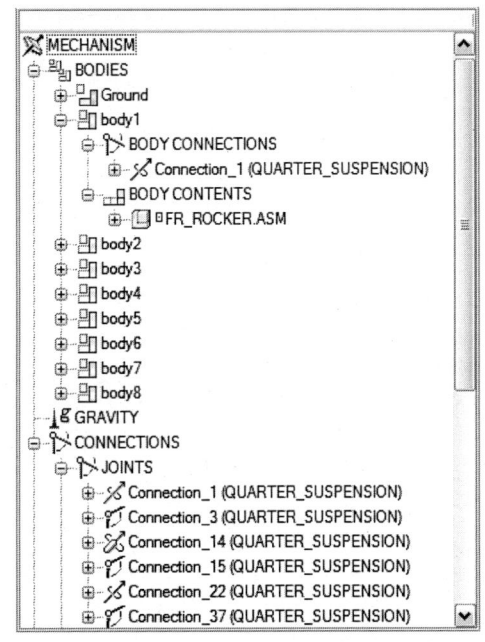

Figure 10-7 Bodies and Joints Listed in the *Model Tree* Window

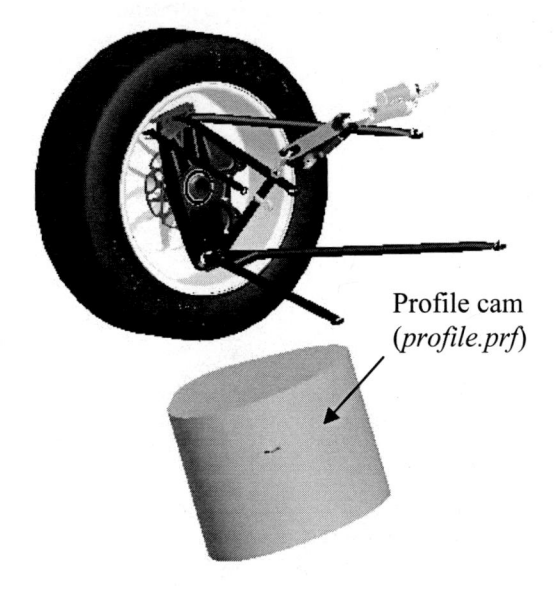

Figure 10-8 *profile.prt* Brought in for Assembly

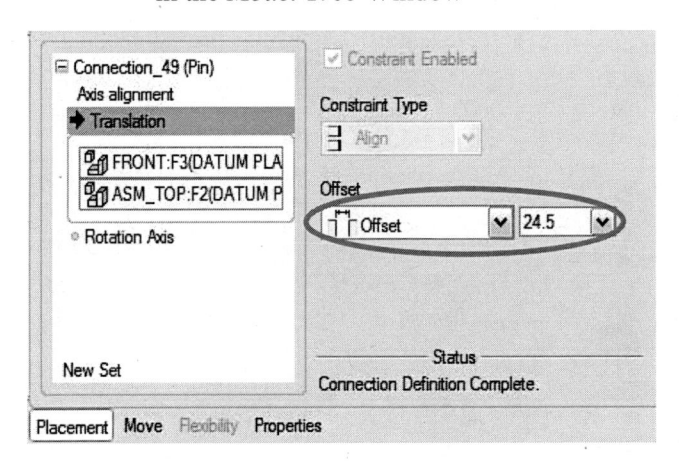

Figure 10-9 Entering Offset for Plane Alignment

Figure 10-10 Defining a Pin Joint for the Profile Cam (*profile.prt*)

The pin joint is now fully defined, as indicated by the status message in the *Placement* dashboard. However, the part may not be properly oriented, as shown in Figure 10-10. We want to have the hump of the profile cam on top; i.e., the suspension being pushed up. We will use the *Drag Packed Components* button later to create a snapshot of the desired configuration for initial condition. For now, accept the definition by clicking the button.

Creating a Simulation Model

From the pull-down menu, choose

Applications > Mechanism.

All connection symbols appear similar to those of Figure 10-6b. We will choose the cylindrical surfaces of the profile cam and the tire to define the cam-follower.

From the shortcut buttons on the right, click *Define Cam-Follower connections* (2nd from the top), or choose from the pull-down menu

Insert > Cams.

The *Cam-Follower Connection Definition* dialog box appears (Figure 10-11). Use the default name (*CamFollower1*), choose *Autoselect* (to select all surfaces surrounding the cam and follower), and click (the *Select* button). Pick the cylindrical surface of the profile cam; all the surrounding surfaces will be selected (see Figure 10-12). Click the *OK* button in the *Select* dialog box (right underneath the *Cam-Follower Connection Definition* dialog box). The surface selected will appear in the *Surfaces/Curves* text area. An arrow will also appear on the surfaces showing the surface normal.

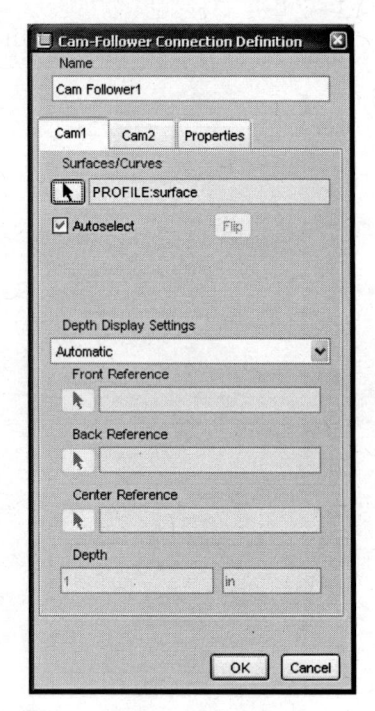

Figure 10-11

Click the *Cam2* tab, and repeat the same process by selecting the outer cylindrical surface of the tire, as shown in Figure 10-12. Click *OK* in the *Cam-Follower Connection Definition* dialog box, a cam-follower symbol will appear between the two surfaces selected, and the profile and the tire will be oriented so that their outer surfaces are in contact.

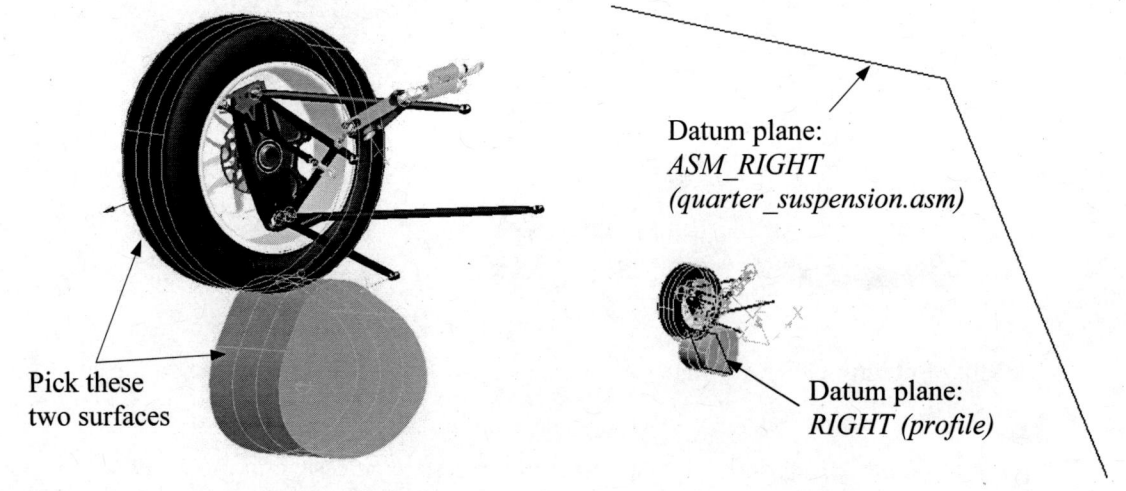

Figure 10-12 Creating Cam-Follower Connection

Figure 10-13 Align Two Datum Planes

Lesson 10: Kinematic Analysis for Racecar Suspension 10-9

Click the *Drag Packed Components* button at the top of the *Graphics* window, click the profile cam, and rotate it by moving the mouse. You should see that the tire is being pushed up and pulled down, and all the suspension components are moving accordingly. Rotate the profile cam as close to the upward position as you can. Create a snapshot by orienting two datum planes, e.g., *RIGHT* of *profile.prt* and *ASM_RIGHT* of *quarter_suspension.asm*, as shown in Figure 10-13 (you may want to zoom out the view to see *ASM_RIGHT*). Save the snapshot. Now the assembly is completed.

Next, we will create a servo motor at the pin joint between the profile cam and the ground body. The servo motor will rotate the profile cam with a constant angular velocity of 360 degrees/sec, therefore, pushing and pulling the tire, mimicking humps and ditches.

From the shortcut buttons on the right, click *Define Servo Motors* (4th from the top), or choose from the pull-down menu

Insert > Servo Motors.

The *Servo Motor Definition* dialog box will appear (Figure 10-14). Leave the default name *ServoMotor1*, leave *Motion Axis* (default) for *Driven Entity* (under *Type* tab), then pick the pin joint of the profile cam. After picking the pin joint, a larger arrow appears at the pin joint to confirm your selection. The next step is to specify the profile of the motor. From the *Servo Motor Definition* dialog box, pick the *Profile* tab (Figure 10-15), choose *Velocity* in *Specification*, and leave *Constant* (default) in *Magnitude*. Enter *360* for the constant *A* (360 degrees/sec) and click *OK*. A driver or servo motor symbol should appear at the pin joint in the *Graphics* window (Figure 10-16).

Figure 10-14

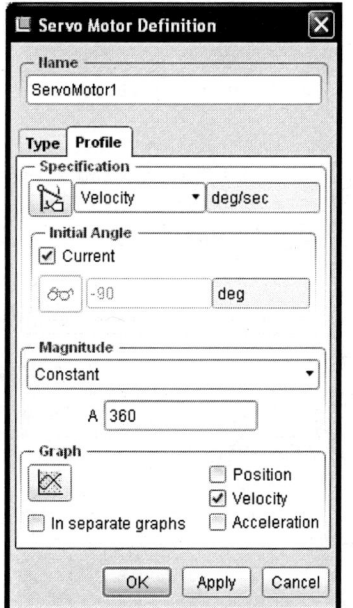

Figure 10-15

Figure 10-16 Driver Added to Pin Joint in Profile Cam

Creating and Running a Kinematic Analysis

From the shortcut button list on the right, click the *Mechanism Analysis* shortcut button to define an analysis. In the *Analysis Definition* dialog box appearing, leave the default name, *AnalysisDefinition1*, and enter the following:

Type: *Kinematic*
Start Time: *0*
End Time: *2*
Frame Rate: *100*
Minimum Interval: *0.01*
Initial Configuration: *Current*

Run the analysis. In the *Graphics* window, the profile cam should start turning, pushing and pulling the tire vertically, causing the suspension components to move. The profile cam should make two complete turns.

Saving and Reviewing Results

Click the *Playbacks* button on the right to bring up the *Playbacks* dialog box and repeat the motion animation. On the *Playbacks* dialog box, click on the *Save* button to save the results as a *.pbk* file.

As mentioned earlier, we will create three measures to monitor the characteristics of the suspension. Note that these three measures provide initial understanding of the suspension design. They do not tell all the details regarding the pros and cons of the design. These measures are the vertical wheel travel, shock travel, and camber angle. Note that the camber angle will be defined as the rotation of the upright along the *X*-axis of *WCS*.

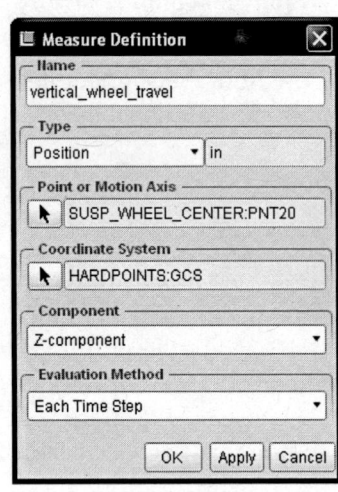

Figure 10-17

Click the *Generate Measure Results of Analyses* button. In the *Measure Results* dialog box appearing, click the *Create New Measure* button. In the *Measure Definition* dialog box, enter *Vertical_Wheel_Travel* for *Name* (Figure 10-17). Under *Type*, select *Position*. Pick datum point *PNT20* in *susp_wheel_center.prt* for *Point or Motion Axis* (see Figure 10-18) and *GCS* of *hardpoints.prt* (for *Coordinate System*). Choose *Z-component* for *Component*. Under *Evaluation Method*, leave *Each Time Step*. Click *OK* to accept the definition.

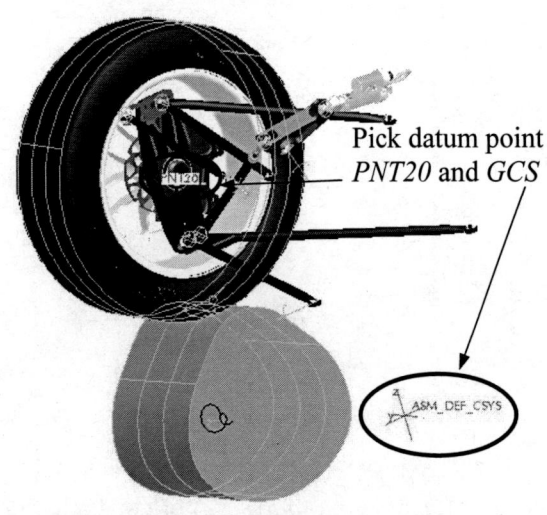

Figure 10-18 Defining Measure: *Vertical_Wheel_Travel*

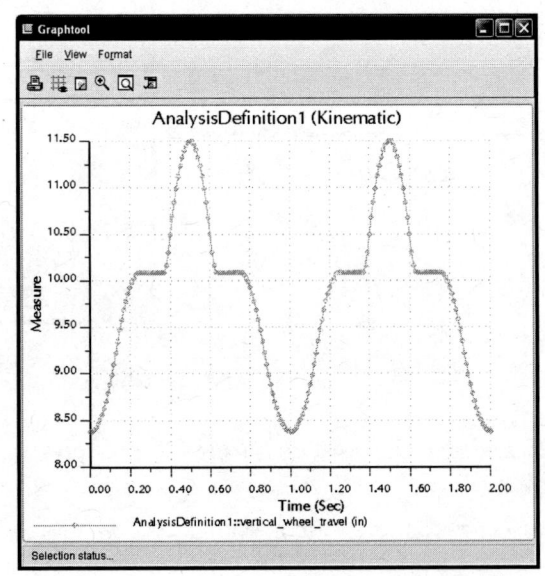

Figure 10-19 Graph of *Vertical_Wheel_Travel*

Lesson 10: Kinematic Analysis for Racecar Suspension

In the *Measure Results* dialog box, choose *AnalysisDefinition1* in the *Result Set* and click the *Graph* button at the top left corner to graph the measure. The graph should be similar to that of Figure 10-19, which shows that the vertical position of the center point of the wheel center. This measure reflects the road profile that the wheel travels. Note that the data do not exactly depict the road profile due to the tire camber angle. The center of the wheel travels vertically between about 11.5 in. and 8.4 in. The flat portion (10.1 in.) reassembles the flat road profile. The distance between the peak and the flat portion is about 1.4 in. due to the 1.35 in. hump. Similarly, the distance between the flat portion and the crest is about 1.7 in. due to the 1.65 in. ditch.

The second measure is the shock travel distance. In the *Measure Definition* dialog box, enter *Shock_Travel* for *Name*. Under *Type*, select *Separation* (see Figure 10-20). Pick two datum points: *SHOCK_FRAME* of *hardpoints.prt* and *ROCKER_SHOCK* of *fr_rocker.asm* (see Figure 10-21) in the *Graphics* window. You may click the right mouse button to bring out *ROCKER_SHOCK* from the overlapped datum points. Choose *Distance* for *Separation Type*. Under *Evaluation Method*, leave *Each Time Step*. Click *OK* to accept the definition.

Follow the same steps to display the graph. The graph should be similar to that of Figure 10-22, which shows that the shock travels between about 6 in. and about 8.5 in. The overall travel distance is about 2.5 in., which is probably too large for such a small hump or ditch. In fact, in the simulation, it appears that the shock is compressed too much, in which the piston penetrates into its reserve cylinder. In reality, this will not happen. However, the simulation raises a flag indicating that there could be severe contact within the shock, leading to potential part failure.

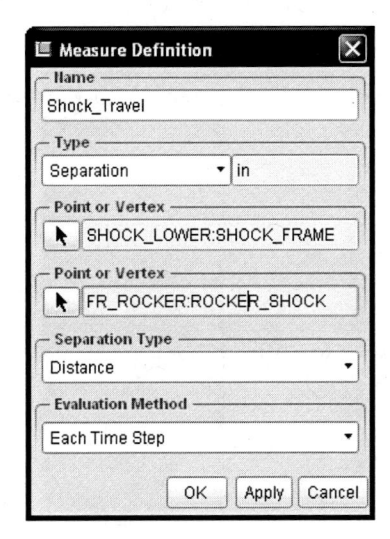

Figure 10-20

Figure 10-21 Defining Measure: *Shock_Travel*

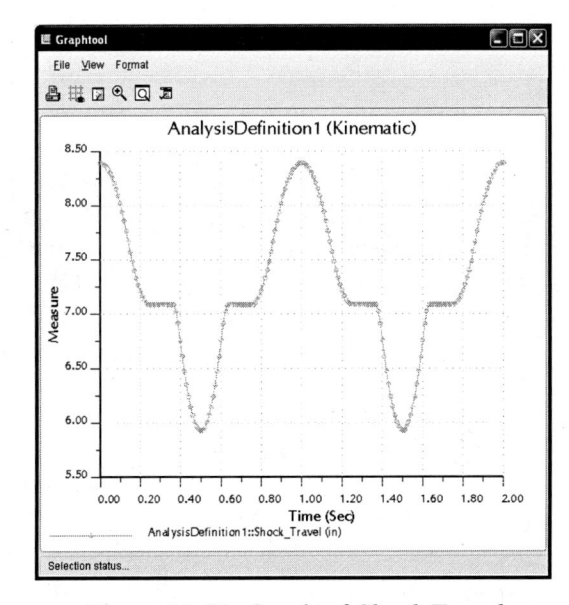

Figure 10-22 Graph of *Shock Travel*

The third measure is the camber angle. The camber angle is the angle made by the wheel of an automobile; specifically, it is the angle between the vertical axis of the wheel and the vertical axis of the vehicle when viewed from the front or rear. It is used in the design of steering and suspension. If the top of the wheel is further out than the bottom (that is, away from the axle), it is called positive camber; if the bottom of the wheel is further out than the top, it is called negative camber. In this model, the camber angle will be defined as the rotation angle of the upright along the *X*-axis of *GCS*. For this measure, enter *Camber_Angle* for *Name* (see Figure 10-23). Under *Type*, select *Body*, and pick *fr_upright.asm* in the *Graphics* window. Choose *Orientation* for *Property*, and click *1* for *Euler Component*, which means the rotation measure is defined along *X*-axis (of the *WCS* as default). Leave *WCS* as the *Coordinate System* (default), which is *GCS* or *ASM_CSYS_DEF*. Under *Evaluation Method*, leave *Each Time Step*. Click *OK* to accept the definition.

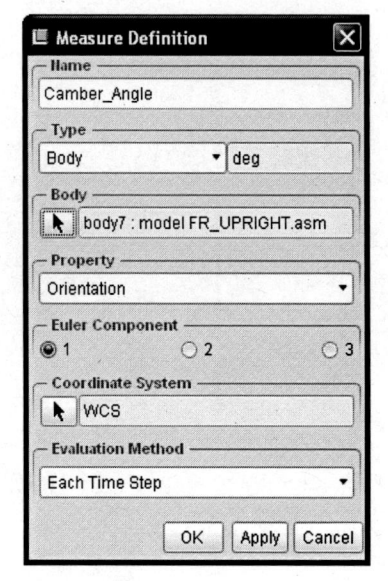

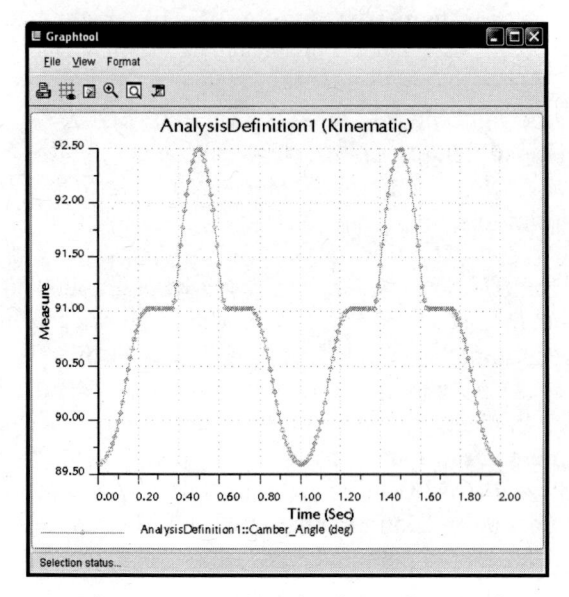

Figure 10-23

Figure 10-24 Graph of *Camber Angle*

As shown in Figure 10-24, the camber angle was set to about 91 degrees on the flat terrain. The camber angle varies to 92.5 and 89.5 degrees, respectively, when the tire goes over the hump and the ditch. In general, camber angle alters the handling qualities of a particular suspension design; in particular, negative camber improves grip when cornering. This is because it places the tire at a more optimal angle to the road, transmitting the forces through the vertical plane of the tire, rather than through a shear force across it. However, excessive negative camber change in hump can cause early lockup under breaking or wheel spin under acceleration. There is only limited information that can be obtained by conducting kinematic analysis of the quarter suspension. Ultimately, a full-vehicle dynamic simulation must be carried out to fully understand the suspension design and hopefully, develop a strategy for design improvement.

A final note: a full-vehicle dynamic simulation model was created in *ADAMS/Car*, using the model templates provided, as shown in Figure 10-25a. With *ADAMS/Car*, users can simply enter vehicle model data into the templates, and *ADAMS/Car* will automatically construct subsystem models, such as engine, shock absorbers, tires, as well as the full vehicle assemblies. Once users create these templates, they can be made available to novice users, enabling them to perform standardized vehicle maneuvers. The vehicle model was then simulated for various test scenarios, including a skid pad racing, which is a constant radius cornering simulation, as shown in Figure 10-25b.

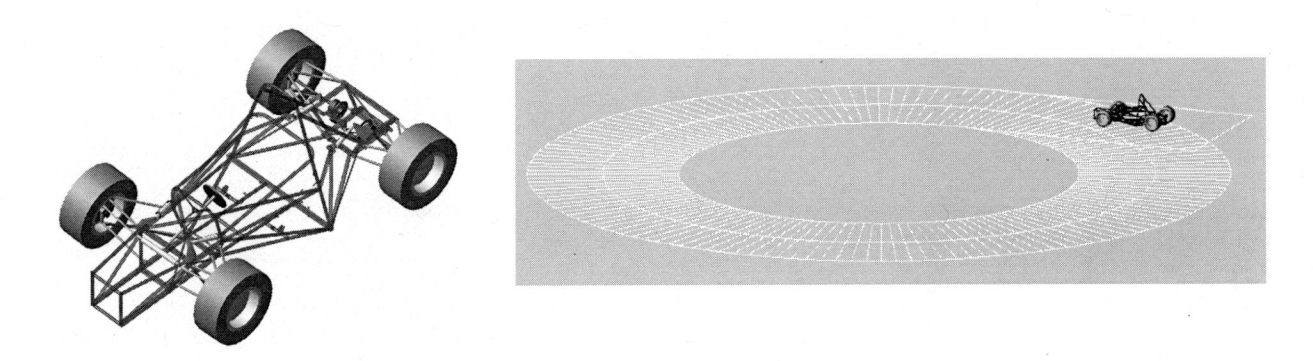

Lesson 10: Kinematic Analysis for Racecar Suspension

(a) 15 dof's *ADAMS/Car* Model (b) Skid Pad Racing

Figure 10-25 Vehicle Dynamic Simulation of Formula SAE Racecar

Notes:

APPENDIX A: DEFINING JOINTS

Degrees of Freedom

Understanding degrees of freedom is critical in selecting the appropriate connections or joints for your mechanism. In mechanical systems, the number of degrees of freedom (dof's) represents the number of independent parameters required to specify the position, velocity, and acceleration of each body in the system. A completely unconstrained body has six degrees of freedom, three translational and three rotational. If you apply a pin connection (or joint) to the body, you restrict its movement to rotation about an axis, and the degrees of freedom for the body are reduced from six to one.

In most mechanical systems, you can determine the degrees of freedom using the following formula:

$$D = 6M - N \tag{A.1}$$

where D is the degrees of freedom of the mechanism, M is number of bodies not including the ground body, and N is the number of degrees of freedom restrained by all connections.

The number of bodies can be found from the model summary window. You may bring up this window by choosing from the pull-down menu:

Info > Mechanism > Summary.

The model summary will appear in the *Graphics* window, as shown in Figure A-1. Note that you may need to scroll down the window to see more model information.

You may apply Eq. A-1 to a door model that is supported by two hinges using pin joints. Note that a pin joint imposes 5 dof's. Insert the number of bodies and dof's into this equation:

$D = (6 \times 1) - (2 \times 5) = -4.$

The calculated degrees of freedom result is –4, which is unrealistic.

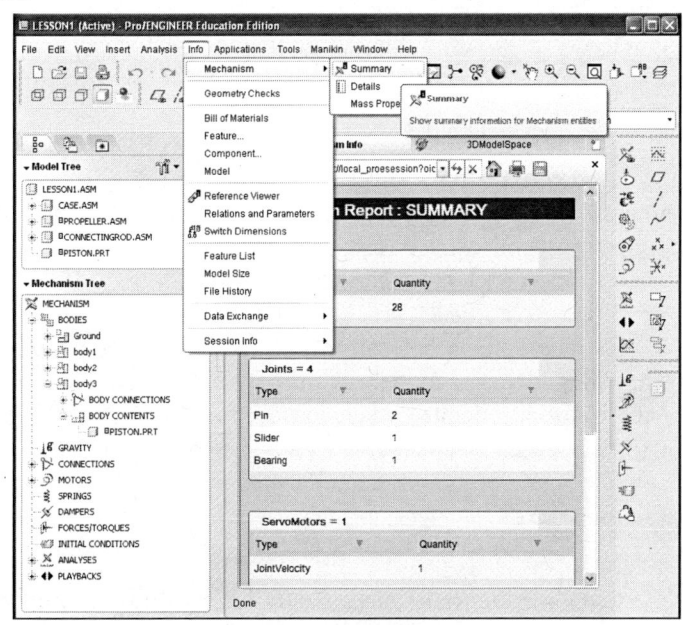

Figure A-1 The *Model Summary* Window

Mechanisms should not have negative degrees of freedom. For most cases, we would like to have the number of dof's equals 1. The challenge is to choose the joints that will give you one dof and still allow the intended motion.

The equations above do not account for the influence of the drivers (servo motors) in your mechanism. Servo motors are defined to drive joint displacements (or rotation), velocities, or accelerations. Drivers will eliminate additional degrees of freedom.

Redundancy

Redundancies are excessive dof's. When a joint constrains the model in exactly the same way as another joint (like the door hinge example), the model contains excessive dof's, also known as redundancies. A joint becomes excessive when it does not introduce any further restriction on a body's motion.

It is important that you eliminate redundancies from your model while carrying out dynamic analyses. If you do not remove redundancies, you may not get accurate values when you measure connection reactions or load reactions.

For example, if you model a door using two pin joints for the hinges, the second pin joint does not contribute to constraining the door's motion. The software detects the redundancies and ignores one of the pin joints in its analysis. The outcome may contain incorrect reaction results, yet the motion is correct. For complete and accurate reaction forces, it is critical that you eliminate redundancies from your mechanism.

For strictly kinematic problems where you are interested in displacement, velocity, and acceleration, redundancies in your model do not alter the design and performance of the mechanism.

You can control the redundancies in your model by your choice of connections. These joints must be able to restrict the same dof's, but not duplicate each other. After you decide which connections you want to use, you can use Eq. A.1 to calculate the dof's and check redundancies.

By default, the software calculates the dof's and redundancies for the model each time you analyze its motion. To check if your model has redundancies, first run a dynamic, static, or force balance analysis. Use the *Measure Results* dialog box to calculate the dof's and redundancies in your mechanism, as described next.

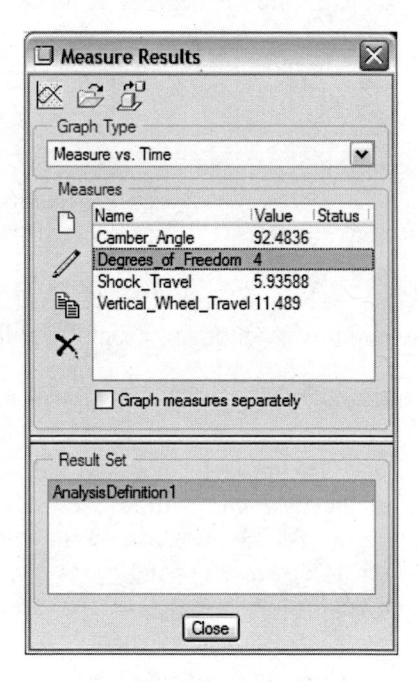

Figure A-2 The *Measure Results* Dialog Box

Click the *Generate Measure Results of Analyses* button (from the button list on the right of the *Graphics* window). In the *Measure Results* dialog box (Figure A-2), click the *Create New Measure* button. In the *Measure Definition* dialog box (Figure A-3), enter *Degrees_of_Freedom* for *Name* (or any other name you prefer). Under *Type*, select *System*. Choose *Degrees of Freedom* for *Property*. Click *OK* to accept the definition. Note that if you have already run an analysis you should see the degrees of freedom displayed in the window (Figure A-2).

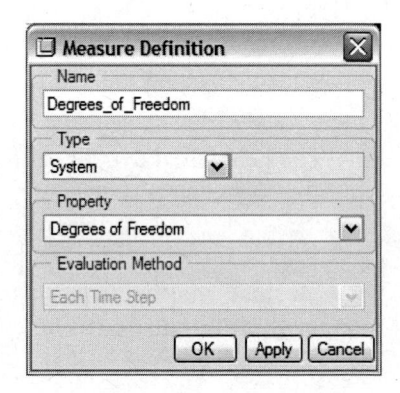

Figure A-3 The *Measure Definition* Dialog Box

Appendix A: Defining Joints

Joint Types in *Mechanism Design*

Before you select a predefined joint to apply to your model, you should know what movement you want to restrain for the body and what movement you want to allow. The following table describes the common joint types you can choose to create motioni models and their corresponding free degrees of freedom.

Joint Type	Number of Constraints			Remarks
	Rotation	Translation	Total	
Rigid	0	0	0	Glues two parts together while changing the underlying body definition. Parts constrained by a rigid connection constitute a single body.
Slider	0	1	1	Translates along an axis Plane-plane align/mate
Pin	1	0	1	Rotates about an axis
Cylinder	1	1	2	Translates along and rotates about a specific axis Point on line Plane–plane orient
Ball	3	0	3	Rotates in any direction Point–point align
Planar	1	2	3	Bodies connected by a planar joint move in a plane with respect to each other. Rotation is about an axis perpendicular to the plane. Plane–plane align/mate
Bearing	3	1	4	Combines a ball joint and a slider joint Point on line

Notes:

APPENDIX B: DEFINING MEASURES

Types of Measure

When you click ▢ on the *Measure Results* dialog box (Figure B-1), the *Measure Definition* dialog box opens (Figure B-2). You can create measures for specific model entities or for the entire mechanism. You can also include measures in your own expressions for user-defined measures.

You can create any of these measures if you have a *Mechanism Dynamics Option* license. If you do not, you can only create Position, Velocity, Acceleration, Separation, Cam measures, and any System and Body measures that do not require mass.

- Position—Measure the location of a point, vertex, or motion axis during the analysis.
- Velocity—Measure the velocity of a point, vertex, or motion axis during the analysis.
- Acceleration—Measure the acceleration of a point, vertex, or motion axis during the analysis.
- Connection Reaction—Measure the reaction forces and moments at joint, gear-pair, cam-follower, or slot-follower connections.
- Net Load—Measure the magnitude of a force load on a spring, damper, servo motor, force, torque, or motion axis. You can also confirm the force load on a force motor.
- Loadcell Reaction—Measure the load on a loadcell lock during a force balance analysis.
- Impact—Determine whether impact occurred during an analysis at a joint limit, slot end, or between two cams.
- Impulse—Measure the change in momentum resulting from an impact event. You can measure impulses for joints with limits, for cam-follower connections with liftoff, or for slot-follower connections.
- System—Measure several quantities that describe the behavior of the entire system.
- Body—Measure several quantities that describe the behavior of a selected body.
- Separation—Measure the separation distance, separation speed, and change in separation speed between two selected points.
- Cam—Measure the curvature, pressure angle, and slip velocity for either of the cams in a cam-follower connection.
- User Defined—Define a measure as a mathematical expression that includes measures, constants, arithmetical operators, *Pro/ENGINEER* parameters and algebraic functions.

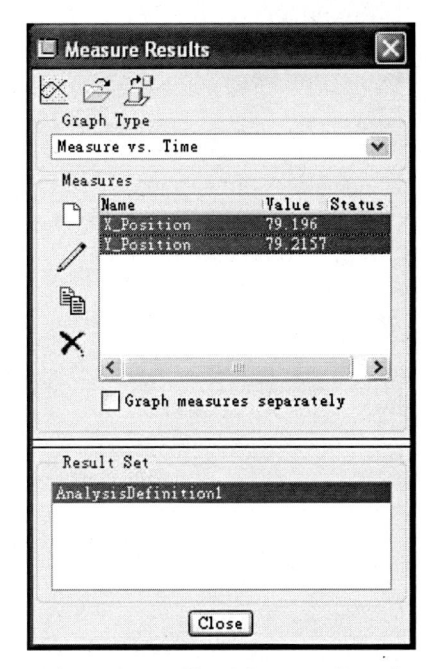

Figure B-1 The *Measure Results* Dialog Box

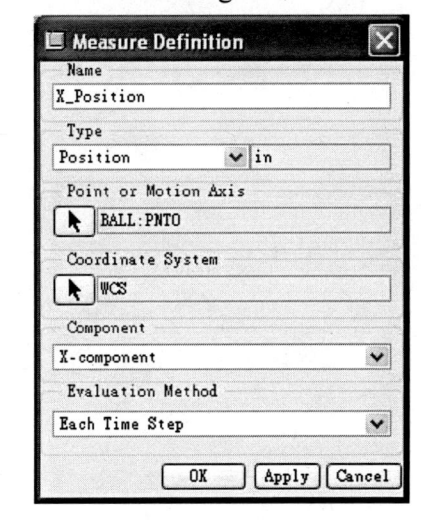

Figure B-2 The *Measure Definition* Dialog Box

About Measures Associated with Model Entities

This table organizes *Mechanism Design* measures according to the type of model entity that you select to define the measure.

Entity	Measure
Point	Position, Velocity, Acceleration, Separation—distance, speed, change in speed
Motion axis	Position, Velocity, Acceleration, Net load
Joint connection	Connection reaction, Impact, Impulse
Cam-follower connection	Cam—curvature, pressure angle, slip velocity, Connection reaction, Impact, Impulse
Slot-follower connection	Connection reaction, Impact, Impulse
Gear-pair connection	Connection reaction
Spring, damper, force, torque, servo motor, force motor	Net load

Appendix B: Defining Measures

About Measure Results

Measures can help you understand and analyze the results of moving a mechanism and provide information to improve the mechanism's design.

Before you can calculate and view measure results, you must have run or saved and restored results from one or more analyses for your mechanism.

You can create these types of measures:

- Position, distance separation, velocity, acceleration, or cam measures using the *Measure Results* dialog box. You can also create system and body measures that do not require a mass definition.
- Several additional types of dynamics measures using the *Measure Results* dialog box if you have a *Mechanism Dynamics* option license.
- Analysis measure features using the *Analysis > Measure* command. Distance and angle analysis measures are the most useful types of datum analyses for graphing measure results.

The following table tells you which measures give the most useful information for each analysis type:

Analysis	Measures
Kinematic	Position, Velocity, Acceleration, Separation, *Pro/ENGINEER* features, Degrees of Freedom, Redundancies, Time, Body orientation, Body angular velocity, Body angular acceleration
Dynamic	All except loadcell
Static	Position, Connection reaction, Net load, All system measures, All body measures, *Pro/ENGINEER* features
Force Balance	Position, Connection reaction, Net load, Loadcell, All system measures, All body measures, *Pro/ENGINEER* features
Position	Position, Separation (distance), Degrees of Freedom, Redundancies, Time, Body angular acceleration, *Pro/ENGINEER* features

You can graph the results of a measure for one or more analyses. You can retrieve a saved results file, save the measure results to a table file, or print them.

It is normally more efficient to create measures before you run an analysis. Measures that you create after running an analysis require that the software compute the evaluations before it creates the graph. These measures will take more time to graph when compared with measures that you create before running an analysis. Some measures may not be computed after the initial analysis run. In this case, run the analysis a second time.

Use graphing to plot a measure over time or a measure against another measure. You can create a graph of multiple measure curves for one set of analysis results, or you can see how a single measure varies with different result sets. You can also graph multiple measures with multiple analyses.

About Evaluation Methods

When you define dynamics measures, you can choose from several evaluation methods. The graph of the measure and the quantity displayed under *Value* on the *Measure Results* dialog box are different for different evaluation methods. These options are not available for loadcell reactions or for the cam reaction measure slip component.

Evaluation Method	Value	Graph
Each Time Step	Value of the measure at the last time step	The value of the measure, calculated at each time interval of the analysis
Maximum	Maximum value over analysis	The maximum value attained so far in the analysis
Minimum	Minimum value over analysis	The minimum value attained so far in the analysis
Integral	The integrated value of the measure at the last time step	The integration of the function up to a given point in time
Average	The value of the average at the last time step	The average value of the measure up to each time step of the analysis
Root Mean Square	The root mean square value at the last time step	The root mean square of the measure up to that point at a given time step
At Time	The value of the measure at a specified time	The value of the measure represented as a bar at the specified time

For *Each Time Step*, you can define your measure after you run the analysis. For the other methods, you must define the measure before running an analysis. If you define a measure with *Maximum*, *Minimum*, *Integral*, *Average*, *Root Mean Square* or *At Time* evaluation methods after you run an analysis, the *Status* column on the *Measure Results* dialog box reports *Not computed* when you select the analysis.

The values found are reported at each interval at which calculations are performed. These are not necessarily equivalent intervals. Intervals on a measure results graph are not the time intervals that are used to calculate results. The software adjusts its calculations to ensure accurate results. Consequently, your specified intervals may not be used for a dynamic analysis.

For analyses in which the quantities measured are changing quickly, the sampling rate is greater. For example, to accurately calculate an impact event, the software uses a greater sampling rate close to the time that the impact occurs. The intervals you specify when you define a dynamic analysis are used as the maximum time interval step size. The actual interval may be smaller, depending upon the demands of the calculation.

The assembly tolerance settings are used to determine the time intervals it uses for analysis calculations. The lower the tolerance, the more precise the calculations.

To verify the accuracy of a minimum or maximum value, rerun the analysis at a lower (more precise) tolerance and repeat until the reported minimum or maximum values do not change significantly from run to run.

APPENDIX C: THE DEFAULT UNIT SYSTEM

The *in-lb$_m$-sec* Unit System

The default unit system employed by *Pro/ENGINEER*, therefore the *Mechanism Design*, is *in-lb$_m$-sec* (inch-pound mass-second). This unit system is not quite common to many engineers. The basic physical quantities involved in determining a unit system are length, time, mass, and force. These four basic quantities are related through Newton's second law,

$$F = ma \tag{C.1}$$

where F, m, and a are force, mass, and acceleration (length per second square), respectively.

In the default unit system, *in-lb$_m$-sec*, the force unit will be determined by length (in.), mass (lb$_m$), and second (sec) through Eq. C.1; i.e.,

$$1\ lb_m\ in/sec^2\ (force) = 1\ lb_m\ (mass) \times 1\ in/sec^2\ (acceleration) \tag{C.2}$$

where the force unit, lb$_m$ in/sec^2, is a derived unit.

From Eq. C.2, a 1 lb$_m$ in/sec^2 force will generate a 1 in/sec^2 acceleration when applied to a 1 lb$_m$ mass block, as shown in Figure C-1a. The same block will weight 1 lb$_f$ on earth (see Figure C-1b), where the gravitational acceleration is assumed 386 in/sec^2; i.e.

$$1\ lb_f\ (force) = 1\ lb_m\ (mass) \times 386\ in/sec^2\ (acceleration) \tag{C.3}$$

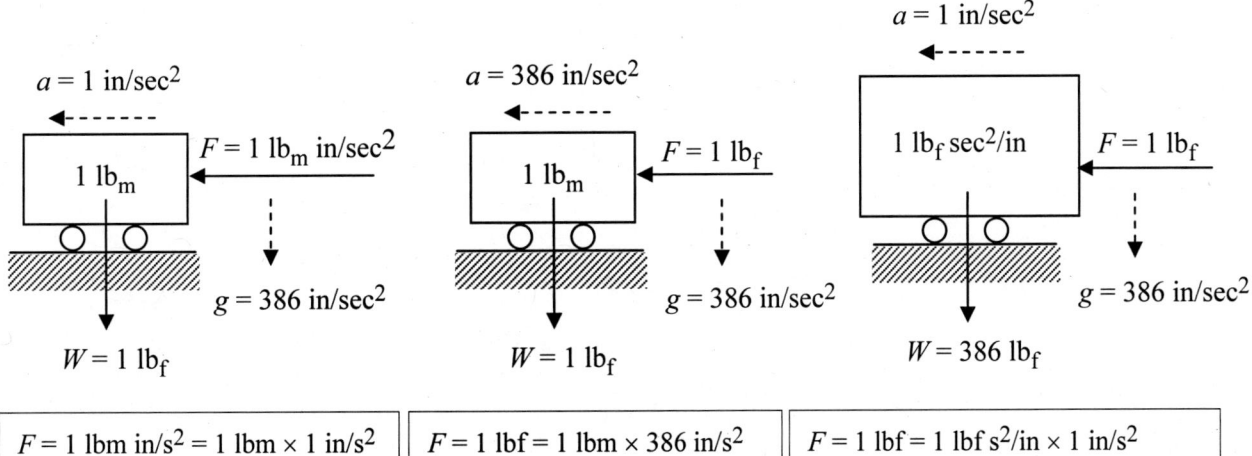

(a) A 1 lb$_m$ in/sec^2 Force Applied to a 1 lb$_m$ Mass Block

(b) A 1 lb$_f$ Force Applied to a 1 lb$_m$ Mass Block

(c) A 1 lb$_f$ Force Applied to a 1 lb$_f$ sec^2/in Mass Block

Figure C-1 Forces Applied on Blocks of Different Masses

Therefore, from Eqs. C.2 and C.3, we have 1 lb_f = 386 lb_m in/sec^2. That is, the force quantity entered into *Mechanism Design* is in the lb_m in/sec^2 unit by default, which is 386 times smaller than 1 lb_f that we are more used to. When you apply a 1 lb_f force to the same mass block, it will accelerate 386 in/sec^2, as shown in Figure C-1c. Therefore, you must be very careful in entering numerical figures while defining your analysis models. For example, if you apply a 1,000 unit force to a mechanical component in the default unit system, it is indeed just a 1,000/386 = 2.59 lb_f, a very small force.

On the other hand, we have the mass unit, 1 lb_m = 1/386 lb_f sec^2/in. It means that a 1 lb_m mass block is 386 times smaller than that of a 1 lb_f sec^2/in block. Therefore, a 1 lb_f sec^2/in block will weight 386 lb_f on earth. When applying a 1 lb_f force to the mass block, it will accelerate at a 1 in/sec^2 rate, as illustrated in Figure C-1c.

APPENDIX D: THE MAGNITUDE SETTINGS

Depending on the type of motion you want to impose on your mechanism, you can define the magnitude of your servo motors or force motors in many ways. The following table lists different types of functions that are used to generate the magnitude. You need to enter the values of the coefficients for the functions. The value of x in the function expressions is supplied by the simulation time or, for force motors, by either the simulation time or a measure you select.

Function Type	Description	Required Settings
Constant	Use if you want a constant profile.	$q = A$, where A = Constant
Ramp	Use if you want a profile that changes linearly over time.	$q = A + B*x$, where A = Constant B = Slope
Cosine	Use if you want to assign a cosine wave value to the motor profile.	$q = A*\cos(360*x/T + B) + C$, where A = Amplitude B = Phase C = Offset T = Period
Sine-Constant-Cosine-Acceleration (SCCA)	Use to simulate a cam profile output. SCCA can only be used when Acceleration is chosen. This profile is not applicable for force motors.	
Cycloidal	Use to simulate a cam profile output.	$q = L*x/T - L*\sin(2*Pi*x/T)/2*Pi$, where L = Total rise T = Period
Parabolic	Can be used to simulate a trajectory for a motor.	$q = A*x + 1/2\ B(x^2)$, where A = Linear coefficient B = Quadratic coefficient
Polynomial	Use for generic motor profiles.	$q = A + B*x + C*x^2 + D*x^3$, where A = Constant term coefficient B = Linear term coefficient C = Quadratic term coefficient D = Cubic term coefficient
Table	Use to generate the magnitude with values from a two-column table. If you have output measure results to a table, you can use that table here.	
User Defined	Use to specify any kind of complex profile defined by multiple expression segments.	
Custom Load	This option is only available for the force motor definition. Use it to apply a complex, externally-defined set of loads to your model.	